MAKE IT NEW

MAKE IT NEW

The History of Silicon Valley Design

Barry M. Katz

The MIT Press
Cambridge, Massachusetts
London, England

MIT Press books may be purchased at special quantity discounts for business or sales promotional use. For information, please email special_sales@mitpress.mit.

This book was set in Gentium and Futura by Toppan Best-set Premedia Limited. Printed and bound in the United States of America.

Katz, Barry, 1950-

 Make it new : the history of Silicon Valley design / Barry M. Katz.

  pages cm

 Includes bibliographical references and index.

 ISBN 978-0-262-02963-6 (hardcover : alk. paper) 1. Industrial design–California–Santa Clara Valley (Santa Clara County)–History. 2. Industrial design–Social aspects–California–Santa Clara Valley (Santa Clara County)–History. I. Title.

 TS171.4.K38 2015

 745.209794'73--dc23

                          2015009382

10   9   8   7   6   5   4   3   2   1

This book is respectfully dedicated to the design community of Silicon Valley, past, present, and future, which has given me far more than clean lines and intuitive interfaces.

CONTENTS

FOREWORD

At a recent MIT event, I had the opportunity to listen to a variety of stories as told by Professor Nicholas Negroponte on how the MIT Media Lab came to be. He shared many great ones—ranging from his chance dinner encounter with Buckminster Fuller on a cruise ship, to how he came to know William J. Mitchell just when he had arrived in the United States, to his chauffeur-driven adventures with his mentor, MIT president Jerome Wiesner, in launching the Media Lab in the early 1980s.

But frankly it was difficult for me to concentrate too closely on what Nicholas was saying, as he had arranged to shorten his presentation so that I might share a few words on the stage with him about my adventures in Silicon Valley. I've never ceased to be a little nervous around my mentors—especially when asked to present with them. Then in one of Nicholas's stories he shared a name that had recently become familiar to me: Bob Noyce.

So I started to pay full attention, as it sounded similar to a name I had recently encountered in my efforts to improve my understanding of the history of Silicon Valley: Robert Noyce.

You see, for most of my professional life, I knew the world of technology only through the MIT lens. I am a product of MIT's undergraduate and graduate education programs in electrical engineering and computer science. Silicon Valley was way, way, far away for me. The closest I came to Silicon Valley was in my sophomore year when I landed the #2 spot for a summer co-op position at Rolm (I had to Google that name as I realized that I don't hear it anymore). But I ended up at Texas Instruments instead, and went to Dallas every summer thereafter to co-op. My next stop in life was to leave the United States and go to Japan to study design, and I came back to MIT after that.

I got to Silicon Valley to visit a few of the Media Lab's sponsors there, but I spent most of my time active in the design communities in Europe, Asia, and New York. Now at the age of almost 50, I feel a profound regret that I didn't spend more of my time in California—in a way, I am trying to make up for it as much as possible by focusing the majority of my energies there.

I've been taught that if you don't know something, you go and learn it. I've read countless web pages, viewed countless hours of documentary videos, and met countless numbers of people within the Silicon Valley ecosystem. But I know now that if I had read Barry Katz's book *Make It New* I could have saved myself a ton of time getting to the realization I now have: *Design isn't only now getting big in Silicon Valley; it has always been big, but its role had never been well understood.*

Reading Barry's book renewed my love for Hewlett-Packard, which folks today might think of as just a PC or printer company; back in the day, we MIT nerds knew it as the company that made the best oscilloscopes and calculators. The HP calculators were absolutely worshipped in the eighties— not just for their functionality, but for their design. Back then, I didn't know the word *design*. But hearing Barry recount the story of the HP-35, and imagining how liberating it must have felt to free oneself from carrying around a slide rule, it might have well been the iPhone of the day for the geek community.

This is what every story in Barry's book comes back to: how each little design-driven innovation by a high-tech company, combined with each birth of a new design agency or consultancy in Silicon Valley, combined with each shift in how a nearby academic institution, like San Jose State (and not just Stanford), contributed one or two key graduates to the ecosystem of innovation there. With each new encounter with an anthropologist, or game designer, or financier, or bold young Brit named Bill Moggridge chancing to open an office far away from his home country just because of an inkling that this "computer thing" might get really big, what has mattered and endured is the larger picture of the essentiality of each individual person played out over multiple decades.

The design ecosystem in Silicon Valley, which has been fostered by a true melting pot of creative disciplines in concert with amazing technologists, is what led to the possibility that Steve Jobs would have been able to give us more than one instance of his "one more thing"—not just to the cheers of computer-loving scientists and professors, but to hobbyist geeks, to college students, to graphic designers and architects, to businesses of all size, and to grandmoms and granddads and all kinds of people all over the world. The diversity of the ecosystem of Silicon Valley becomes evident through studying its evolution as firsthand journeys by Barry. A visual scan of all the folks he has interviewed, some of them no longer with us, to create this history lays testament to the real importance of this work.

Circling back to Robert Noyce, I came across his name in studying the genesis of the venture capital firm where I am currently a partner, Kleiner Perkins Caufield & Byers. It sits on the mythical "Sand Hill Road" that Barry refers to in one of his chapters, and it is the venture capital firm to which the younger Larry and Sergey turned to when launching their search engine company now known as Google. In studying the history of KPCB, I came upon the story of the founding of Fairchild Semiconductor and the "Traitorous Eight"—with Eugene Kleiner among them. I learned by studying its history that the leader of the pack, in *Ocean's Eleven* George Clooney-style, was a charismatic and brilliant technologist named Robert Noyce, who later went on to cofound Intel.

Nicholas was sharing his earliest memories of building special graphics technology in the predecessor to the Media Lab, and how they were always starved of memory because it was so expensive and hard to obtain. Luckily, Nicholas had a special "angel" in the semiconductor industry who was a friend of MIT and who would drop by from time to time, "Bob Noyce would come by MIT once a in a while, and unceremoniously hand me a crinkled brown lunch bag filled with memory chips. Much like your uncle might hand you a bag of candy." And it was in that moment, that I felt that sort of "zap!" of electricity that you feel inside you when multiple worlds collide and connect. I immediately felt my MIT worlds and Silicon Valley connect at the core. Me to Nicholas. Nicholas to Robert Noyce. Robert Noyce to Eugene Kleiner. And Eugene Kleiner, via KPCB, back to me in Silicon Valley.

And it was during that same "zap!" moment that I finally understood Barry's excitement from many months prior when I first arrived to be resident in Silicon Valley. Barry, whom I hadn't met until that evening, had arranged for us to dine at the Stanford Faculty Club to celebrate my joining KPCB as a "design partner"—the significance of which was totally lost on me. We spent most of our time sharing stories about our beloved friend in common, the late Bill Moggridge, but Barry would often turn the conversation back to the fact that I had joined a very special venture capital firm in Silicon Valley. I hadn't the slightest idea about the reason for his enthusiasm, but now his wide-eyed excitement makes sense. Barry foresaw a time when design leaders would be invited into all aspects of the Silicon Valley ecosystem of innovation. He knew that the venture capital space was the last domain in which that hadn't occurred, and he was having his own "zap!" moment that evening.

If you have been resident in Silicon Valley during its many heydays, you will love the many stories that Barry tells in this book and feel more than a few "zaps"; if you were like me, where you were always more than an arms length away from it, you might find your own "zap!" moment as you see worlds connect inside you as well—directly connected to people you may recall, or companies you've touched, or even companies you may currently be partnering with.

It's obvious that design plays a role in how technology is consumed today, and yet it's much less obvious that it has always played such a role. This book has the capability to extend the "ecosystem of innovation" well beyond the borders of Mountain View, Palo Alto, Menlo Park, Santa Clara, San Jose, and San Francisco. I wish you the same enjoyment that I feel fortunate to have received by studying this rare work of scholarship and friendship. I'm truly proud to be associated with this extraordinary book.

John Maeda, Design Partner
Kleiner Perkins Caufield & Byers
Menlo Park, California

ACKNOWLEDGMENTS

I cannot even begin to acknowledge all those who made this book possible: the design community of Silicon Valley, as I have tried to show, is a complex ecosystem within an ecosystem. It includes designers from a dozen disciplines, the engineers and artists who work alongside them, the offices that employ them, the clients who hire them and the people who use, inhabit, and otherwise experience the products they help to create.

Although I have verified the accuracy of any quotes attributed to them, in order to avoid conflicts of interest (and sometimes just plain awkwardness) I have resisted the temptation to ask any of the designers discussed in this book to read it in advance of publication. Doing so would doubtless have saved me from errors of fact and judgment, but at the risk of unbalancing the narrative or yielding to a particular point of view. At certain critical junctures, however, I have turned to independent experts to ensure that I have not mangled some technical issue that is beyond my reach (I had a bad experience with FORTRAN when I was fifteen and never looked back): My very deep thanks go to Charles House, John Leslie, Larry Miller, and Charles Irby. The comments and criticisms of these highly accomplished engineers were generously offered and gratefully received, and of course they bear no responsibility for any errors or misjudgments that remain.

If I were to multiply the number of designers I have interviewed by the amount of time they have spent with me times their average hourly billing rate, I would have to conclude that the Silicon Valley design community has invested well over $100,000 in this book. I doubt that any of them will ever see a measureable return on their investment, but my greater hope is that they will see themselves accurately reflected in its pages and will gain an appreciation of the historical dimensions of their practice. It is a privilege to thank the following individuals, starting with those who will not have opportunity to evaluate my work:

Carl Clement (d. 2011)
Douglas Engelbart (d. 2013)
Steve Jobs (d. 2011)
Matt Kahn (d. 2013)
Bill Moggridge (d. 2012)

I have interviewed the following individuals, mostly in person but in a few cases I have had to resort to telephone, Skype, or e-mail. They are listed here in the approximate order in which their principal affiliations are represented in the book:

Allen Inhelder (Hewlett-Packard)
Charles House (Hewlett-Packard)
John Leslie (Ampex)
Jay McKnight (Ampex)
Larry Miller IBM, (Ampex)
Peter Hammar (Ampex)
Roger Wilder (Ampex)
Darrell Staley (Ampex, IDSA)
Douglas Tinney (Ampex)
Chas Grossman (Ampex, Atari)
Jay Wilson (Ampex, GVO)
Donald Moore (IBM)
Edward Lucey (IBM)
Budd Steinhilber (Tepper Steinhilber)
Frank Guyre (Lockheed)
Dan De Bra (Lockheed; Stanford)
Bill English (SRI; Xerox PARC)
Philip Green (SRI International)
Charles Irby (SRI; Xerox PARC)
Jack Kelley (SRI/Herman Miller)
Donald Nielson (SRI International)
Jeanette Blomberg (Xerox PARC)
Stuart Card (Xerox PARC, Stanford)
John Ellenby (Xerox PARC; GRiD Systems)

Austin Henderson (Xerox PARC)

David Liddle (Xerox SDD; Interval Research)

Tim Mott (Xerox PARC)

Severo Ornstein (Xerox PARC)

Jeff Rulifson (Xerox)

Abbey Silverstone (Xerox SDD)

Robert Taylor (Xerox PARC)

Larry Tesler (Xerox PARC; Apple; Amazon)

Arnold Wasserman (Xerox; I.D Two)

Lucy Suchman (Xerox PARC)

Dave Rossetti (Convergent Technology)

Karen Toland (Convergent Technology)

Nolan Bushnell (Atari)

Warren Robinett (Atari)

Robert Stein (Atari)

Kristina Hooper Woolsey (Atari Research Labs; Apple)

Brenda Laurel (Atari Research Labs; Interval Research; CCA)

Michael Naimark (Atari Research Labs; Interval Research)

Eric Hulteen (Atari Research Labs; Interval Research)

Peter Lowe (Ferris-Lowe, Interform, Palo Alto Center for Design)

James Ferris (Ferris-Lowe, Apple)

Marnie Jones (Stanford; Palo Alto Center for Design; IDSA)

Peter Mueller (Interform)

John Gard (Steinhilber-Deutsch-Gard; Inova; GVO; IDSA)

Steve Albert (GVO)

Mike Wise (GVO)

Robert Hall (GVO)

Michael Barry (GVO)

Gary Waymire (GVO)

Philip Bourgeois (Studio Red)

Regis McKenna (Regis McKenna)

Rob Gemmell (Apple)

Tom Hughes (Apple)

Jony Ive (Apple—interviewed 1998)

Susan Kare (Apple)

Jerry Manock (Apple)

Clement Mok (Apple)

Terry Oyama (Apple)

Tom Suiter (Apple)

Bill Dresselhaus (Apple, Stanford)

Hugh Dubberly (Apple; Dubberly Design Office)

S. Joy Mountford (Apple; Interval Research)

Donald Norman (Apple)

Aaron Marcus (AM+A)

Abbe Don (Apple; IDEO)

Michael Gough (Adobe Design Center)

Gary Guthart (Intuitive Surgical)

Sal Brogna (Intuitive Surgical)

Stacey Chang (Intuitive Surgical; IDEO)

Ricardo Salinas (Intuitive Surgical)

James Adams (Stanford University)

David Beach (Stanford University)

Bill Burnett (D2M; Apple; Stanford University)

Larry Leifer (Stanford University)

Robert McKim (Stanford University)

Bernard Roth (Stanford University)

Sheri Sheppard (Stanford University)

Terry Winograd (Stanford University)

Del Coates (San Jose State University)

Kathleen Cohen (San Jose State University)

Brian Kimura (San Jose State University)

John McCluskey (San Jose State University)

Robert Milnes (San Jose State University)

Pete Ronzani (San Jose State University)

Ralf Schubert (San Jose State University)

Leslie Speer (California College of the Arts; San Jose State University)

Leslie Becker (California College of the Arts)

Sue Ciriclio (California College of the Arts)

David Meckel (California College of the Arts)

Michael Vanderbyl (California College of the Arts; Vanderbyl Design)

Colin Burns (Interval Research Corporation; IDEO)

Gilliam Crampton-Smith (Interval Research Corporation)

Sally Rosenthal (Interval Research Corporation)

Doug Solomon (Interval Research Corporation; IDEO)

Ellen Tauber Siminoff (Inteval Research Corporation)

Rob Tow (Interval Research Corporation)

William Verplank (Xerox; Interval Research Corporation; Stanford)

Meg Withgott (Interval Research Corporation)

David Kelley (Hovey-Kelley; David Kelley Design; IDEO; Stanford)

Mike Nuttall (ID Two; Matrix Design; IDEO)

Dean Hovey (Hovey-Kelley Design)

Tim Brown (ID Two; IDEO)

Dennis Boyle (IDEO)

Rickson Sun (IDEO)

Jim Yurchenco (IDEO)

Peter Spreenberg (ID Two; IDEO)

Jane Fulton-Suri (ID Two; IDEO)

Scott Underwood (IDEO)

Paul Bradley (IDEO; frogdesign)

Aleksey Novicov (Softbook)

Hartmut Esslinger (frogdesign)

Herbert Pfeiffer (frogdesign; Montgomery-Pfeiffer))

Steve Peart (frogdesign; Vent)

Jock Hokanson (frogdesign)

Peter Weiss (frogdesign)

Jeanette Schwarz (frogdesign)

Doreen Lorenzo (frogdesign)

Mark Rolston (frogdesign)

David Hodge (frogdesign)

Dan Harden (frogdesign; Whipsaw)

Gadi Amit (frogdesign; New Deal Design)

Robert Brunner (GVO; Interform; Lunar; Pentagram: Ammunition)

Brett Lovelady (frogdesign; Astro Studios)

Yves Béhar (frogdesign; fuseproject)

Branko Lukić (frogdesign; IDEO; Studio NONOBJECT)

Jeff Smith (GVO; Interform; Lunar)

Gerard Furbershaw (GVO; Interform; Lunar)

Jeff Salazar (Lunar)

Ken Wood (Lunar)

John Edson (Lunar)

Sam Lucente, IBM, Hewlett-Packard

John Guenther (Design Four; Hewlett-Packard)
Astro Teller (Google)
Jon Wiley (Google)
Isabelle Olsson (Google)
Mike Simonian (Google, Mike & Maaike)
Bill Wurz (IDEO, Jump!; Google)
Kate Aronowitz (Facebook)
Paul Adams (Facebook)
Soleio Cuervo (Facebook; Dropbox)
Aaron Sittig (Facebook)
Maria Giudice Hot Studio; Facebook)
Christopher Ireland (Cheskin Research; Mix and Stir)
Davis Masten (Cheskin Research)
Dan Adams (Tesla Motors)
Franz von Holzhausen (Tesla Motors)
Gregg Zehr (Amazon Lab 126)
Fred Bould (Bould Design)
Eliot (Seung-Min) Park (Samsung Design America)
Jim Newton (Tech Shop)
Mark Hatch (Tech Shop)
Krista Donaldson (D-Rev)
Heather Fleming (Catapult Design)
Jocelyn Wyatt (IDEO.org)
Valerie Casey (Designers Accord)

Additional thanks are due to:

Leslie Berlin (Stanford)
Kristin Burns (Stanford)
Chris Bliss (CCA)
Kate Brinks (Nest)
Cathy Cook (Facebook)
Raschin Fatemi
Rebecca Feind (San José State University)
Davina Inslee (Vulcan Investments)
Kathy Jarvis (Xerox PARC)
Chirstopher Katsaros (Google)
Bert Keely

Leslie Letts (Amazon)

Sarah Lott (Computer History Museum)

Henry Lowood (Stanford)

Anna Mancini (Hewlett-Packard)

Karin Moggridge

Anna Richardson White (Google)

Kinley Pearsall (Amazon)

Elizabeth Sanders

Dag Spicer (Computer History Museum)

Josilin Torrano (Facebook)

Richard Saul Wurman (TED)

Brandon Warren (IDSA)

As noted at several points in the text, I have multiple professional affiliations including some with organizations discussed in this book: California College of the Arts, Stanford University, and IDEO, Inc. Readers will have to judge for themselves whether I have succeeded in my conscientious effort to maintain a balanced and independent point of view. Although I have tried to conduct all of my interviews in a professional manner, it should be noted that I also have innumerable friends, colleagues, and acquaintances at these institutions and throughout the Silicon Valley design community (or I did prior to publication!) and have benefited in profound but un-documentable ways from many years of informal conversation. I offer my thanks to the literally hundreds of additional people who I may have been unable to name, and I extend my apologies to any I may have unwittingly overlooked.

INTRODUCTION

"Make it new."

—Ezra Pound (1934)

Rarely does a month go by in which I do not host a delegation of visitors who hope to build a Silicon Valley in Ireland or Poland or Chile or Taiwan. My answer is usually some variant of "You can't, and you shouldn't." Silicon Valley is the product of a unique confluence of circumstances that cannot be replicated in time or in space. That is the bad news. The good news is that every region has its own unique set of cultural assets, and the challenge of innovators is to identify them, organize them, and light the fuse.

Silicon Valley evolved as a dense network of interconnected parts. Although the famous technology companies may occupy center stage, they operate within a web of interdependencies that also includes venture capital funds that launch them, law offices that protect their intellectual property, trade publications that promote them, and universities that supply their workforces; all of these have received their fair share of attention.[1] Surprisingly, one critical component of the Silicon Valley ecosystem has been overlooked: apart from a few picture books, some celebrity profiles, and ephemeral reviews of the latest gizmos and gadgets, almost no attention has been paid to the role of design. This is an egregious oversight, for designers have played a significant role in transforming the region from a whistle-stop for the San Francisco gentry into the economic engine of the United States. The first objective of this book, then, is to show how design is the missing link in the Silicon Valley ecosystem of innovation.

The migration of the computer from the backroom to the desktop was the prime mover, but the Silicon Valley design community was decades in formation, and a second task of this book is to trace it back to its origins and describe the arc of its growth. This returns us to the immediate post–World War II era, when a small number of electronics firms could be found scattered among the orchards and vineyards that covered the "Valley of Heart's Delight." The larger ones—Hewlett-Packard, Ampex, IBM—employed a handful of designers who labored to package specialized electronic equipment in suitable enclosures. Only in the late 1970s, when companies such as Commodore, Radio Shack, and the fledgling Apple Computer began to direct their attention toward the consumer market, were designers called upon to address the nontechnical user. Most people do not buy printed circuit boards or lithium-ion battery packs or LED panels; they buy tablet computers and automobiles and televisions and a host of other products that have been rendered more-or-less useful and enjoyable—by design. This began a profound shift in the very character of the profession that continues unabated: The design teams at Palantir Technologies who are working to make Big Data accessible to intelligence community, or at Coursera to enhance the educational experience of massive open online courses (MOOCs), are working on problems that did not exist a decade ago. As the director of Google[x] explains it, "Design unlocks the space and reframes the question."

When they first arrived in what would become Silicon Valley, designers waged an ongoing guerilla campaign to gain a hearing from their engineering overlords. Sixty years later the designers at Google and Facebook plead with management to leave them alone so they can get some work done. A third theme, then, concerns their dramatic rise in acceptance: "I used to have to persuade clients of the value of design," recalled the CEO of one of the valley's most prominent consultancies, but "the battle has been won. It is recognized at the C-level that a design strategy is at the same level of importance to a company's survival as a business plan." It is emblematic of the changed fortunes of design that its leaders are less likely to be seen speaking to the local student chapter of the IDSA than addressing Fortune 100 CEOs at the TED Conference, mingling with heads of state at the World Economic Forum in Davos, or chatting with the First Lady at the White House. Indeed, some observers have dared to speak of the "rise of the DEO."[2]

The integration of designers into the Silicon Valley ecosystem was anything but a deliberate process—to the contrary, as one of my interlocutors noted, "I could never get over how *ad hoc* everything was."[3] If an informed observer had been asked, in the early 1980s, to identify the leading centers of design there would have been an easy consensus: Milan, London, New York, and perhaps Tokyo. Mention of the San Francisco Bay Area would have been met with blank stares. Today there are arguably more design professionals working in Silicon Valley and its Bay Area environs than anywhere else in the world: large consultancies such as IDEO and frog, and one-person studios with names like Monkey Wrench and Shibuleru (Swiss German for "calipers"); world famous corporate design offices (Apple, Amazon, Adobe); and academic programs to train the next generation of their employees. Whole new fields of design have their origins in Silicon Valley as the profession has responded to the challenges of electronic games, personal computers, interactive multimedia, and hybrid products that may be portable, wearable, or implantable. Making them work has been the historic task of engineering; making them useful is the job of design.

It may be helpful to provide a few explanations and qualifications. Although it might be expected that such an endeavor would start with definitions, I have preferred to let both the geography of "Silicon Valley" and the concept of "design" emerge from the narrative itself. This decision arises partly from the evolving character of the profession: Over the course of their sixty-year history, designers have been asked to place a VHF signal generator in a sheet metal enclosure and the Like button on the Facebook homepage. They have been strategists and implementers, contractors and consultants, employees and entrepreneurs. Further complicating the picture is the complexity and heterogeneity of the design process itself, which involves a continuum of practices that may operate independently, sequentially, or simultaneously. Its practitioners may have been trained as engineers, in PhD programs in the social sciences, in art schools, or not at all. They may work in corporate laboratories, independent consultancies, boutique studios, or at home, virtually. The attention of the UX (user experience) designer of a Bluetooth headset may be trained on the aspirational lifestyle of the "end user," whereas the industrial designer may have an unhealthy fixation on the intertragic notch in the lower concha of her ear. They may despise MBAs, or be MBAs, or both. Some see the professional societies as their advocates, others as their enemies, and for many they are simply sponsors of no-host bars at annual conventions. A definition that embraces them all is unlikely to be of much help.

By the same token, "Silicon Valley" is no longer a meaningful geographic designation, in part because the activities it connotes now extend from Santa Cruz in the south to Skywalker Ranch an hour's drive north of the Golden Gate Bridge. Furthermore—as more than a few of my interlocutors have reminded me—the history of Silicon Valley does not begin in, nor is it confined to the Bay Area of Northern California: There would be no Xerox PARC without Bolt, Beranek, and Newman in Cambridge, Massachusetts; no Augmentation Research Center without the Washington-based largesse of ARPA's J. C. R. Licklider; no Shockley Semiconductor without Bell Labs in New Jersey; no Atari Research Labs without MIT's Architecture Machine Group; we would not be teaching interaction design to graduate students at the California College of the Arts, for that matter, had it not been for the westward migration of the English Arts and Crafts Movement one hundred years ago. At the other end of the historical spectrum, I hope it is obvious that my decision to write about the exceptional story of Silicon Valley does not imply that there are not innovative designers, influential consultancies, successful web-based startups, important technology incubators, and excellent design schools in other regions of the country and the world. There is no ecosystem—including Silicon Valley's ecosystem of innovation—that does not exist within a larger one.

Finally, it should be noted that although objects surely play a part in this story, readers should not expect a "design" book featuring professionally photographed, museum-ready products. I am at least as concerned with people and practices, ideas and institutions, and I endeavor to trace products upstream to the research laboratories where they may have had their origins and follow them downstream to the clients who will sell them and the customers who will use them. Along the way I do my best to avoid buzzwords like "upstream" and "downstream."

Every work of history is as much about what is excluded as what is included, and *Make It New* is clearly no exception. A history of the Civil War cannot recount every battle, every strategy, every weapon, and every soldier's tale, and the art and craft of the historian is measured by a willingness to make judicious selections, to allow one thing to stand for many things, and to capture broad themes with enough detail to give them substance and, conversely, to give singular facts sufficient context to make them meaningful.[4] That has not always been easy, and no one is more aware than I am of all of the talented people, creative companies, and innovative products that do not receive focused attention here. Behind every firm I have discussed stand dozens of others; behind every product, hundreds. Since my focus has tended toward what uniquely characterizes the Silicon Valley region, whole disciplines—architecture, for one—will have to wait for more individualized treatment.[5] I can only hope that stepping back, most readers will find the overall picture to be fair and accurate.

Many of my decisions derive from my effort to base this account as fully as possible on original, previously unpublished, primary sources: these include university archives, company records, business and personal correspondence, drawings, prototypes, computer files, and scores of interviews with design leaders from every industry and epoch. Where I have discussed familiar episodes—the development of desktop computing at SRI and Xerox PARC, for instance—I have done so from the unusual perspective of design. Conversely, products such as the "insanely great" i-flowers that perennially bloom in the enchanted garden of Apple receive comparatively little attention here because they, and their creator, have been so thoroughly covered by the business, the technical, and the popular press. Since I have been privileged with access to a vast array of restricted sources, I have left it to readers interested in the more accessible ones to prowl the Web at will.

It is my hope that this book will fill a void that has been strangely neglected, but also serve as a provocation both to historians of Silicon Valley (by demonstrating that design is as important as any of the other factors that have defined the region) and to historians of design (by demonstrating that design today is about much more than form-giving and object-creation). Even more, I hope that it will prove informative and perhaps even inspiring to the community of design professionals whose story it is, and to whom it is respectfully dedicated.

1   THE VALLEY OF HEART'S DELIGHT

In summer 1951, a few weeks after graduating from the University of Washington, Carl Clement found himself in Sacramento, completing a two-week stint in the Army reserves. A friend had just taken an engineering job at Hewlett-Packard, a 250-person instrument company in Santa Clara County, so Clement climbed back into his 1938 Chevrolet and made the three-hour drive to Palo Alto. On a whim, he arranged an interview with Ralph Lee, head of HP's production engineering group. Clement explained that he had just completed a degree in "industrial design," to which Lee replied, "Why—couldn't cut it as an engineer?" He nonetheless offered him a job as a draftsman and arranged for him to be outfitted with a four-legged stool, a drafting table, and a box of pencils. On August 1, 1951, Carl Clement became the first designer to work in what visitors' guides still called the "Valley of Heart's Delight."

Every detail of this charming anecdote carries historical weight: Lee, who had spent the war years at MIT's secret Radiation Lab before moving west, shared the prevailing view of industrial design as an artsy form of technical drawing and a refuge for those who "couldn't cut it" in the test-and-measure world of electrical engineering. Clement, whose studies had been interrupted by three years of wartime service as a radar technician in the Army Signal Corps, envisioned a more challenging future than simply bringing the form and function of consumer products into harmonious alignment. And Santa Clara County, although home to a growing electronics industry and despite the tireless efforts of Frederick Terman, Stanford University's famously entrepreneurial engineering dean, was still far better known for its apricot orchards, walnut groves, and verdant fields of lima beans.

Hewlett-Packard, in the first postwar decade, supplied instrumentation to the radio and television industries, and Clement set out to prove to his new employer that industrial design could profitably be applied to technical devices and not only to kitchen gadgets and office furniture. It took nearly three years of menial drafting work, but he finally received a bona fide design assignment when he was asked to recommend improvements to the size, color, and graphics on HP's cardboard shipping cartons. It was an important, if inauspicious, start.

Clement's real interest, however, was the electronic products themselves and not simply the cardboard boxes in which they were shipped. The company's catalog at that time listed an array of test oscillators, waveform analyzers, and vacuum-tube voltmeters, some in wooden cases, most consisting of off-the-shelf components housed in riveted sheet-metal enclosures. Although promotional literature assured customers of "the traditional -hp- 'family characteristics,'" this referred to technical considerations such as "generous overload protection" and "trouble-free performance" rather than any sort of coherent design language. As he learned to streamline his routine drafting tasks, Clement began to spend extra hours in the machine shop tinkering with the housings. These experiments led him to propose a set of concepts intended to improve access to controls and bring some consistency to the HP line.

Before long Hewlett-Packard's one-man industrial design department had created cabinets and accessories for a dozen of the company's flagship products. In comparison with the utilitarian boxes of the older models, the redesigned instruments are readily identifiable by their rounded aluminum cases, compact vertical configuration (to minimize their footprint on an engineer's workbench), and, to emphasize their light weight and portability, a carrying handle.[1] It was a first and conspicuously preliminary effort, but it was well received and Clement was becoming known internally as "HP's Raymond Loewy"—a tag he did not particularly appreciate on account of the wide gulf that separated the streamlining of Coca Cola dispensers from the design of signal generators and klystron power supply units.

The watershed moment came in 1956, when the company agreed to send him to MIT for a two-week summer course on "Creative Engineering and Product Design" taught by John Arnold, a lapsed psychologist who had taken a second degree in mechanical engineering. The iconoclastic Arnold had been rattling the conservative MIT engineering establishment with his insistence that what students needed was not more analytical training but a comprehensive approach that would help them overcome blocks to their latent creativity; the same, he argued, could be said for the working professionals who attended his workshops.[2]

For many of the 250 industry professionals in the audience that summer—engineers and managers from such stolid companies such as General Motors, IBM, DuPont, and GE—lectures from the likes of cartoonist Al Capp, "comprehensivist" Buckminster Fuller, and humanistic psychologist Abraham Maslow would have been a hard sell.[3] It probably did not help that they were seated within walking distance of the sites of MIT's wartime Rad Lab and Terman's Radio Research Laboratory at Harvard, which had applied a rigorously analytical approach to the development of microwave radar and electronic countermeasures with devastating success. To Carl Clement, however, the insight that engineers are trained to define problems in such a way as to imprison their thinking within self-imposed parameters came as an epiphany and he resolved to enlighten his colleagues at Hewlett-Packard. "For example," he wrote upon his return to California, "suppose we are given the problem of 'designing a new toaster.'" The typical starting point is to define the problem so narrowly that the "new toaster" will likely be little more than the old one with a few cosmetic adjustments.

> Now on the other hand, suppose we state the problem this way: We are trying to find a way to heat, dehydrate, and brown the surface of bread. This restatement of the problem in basic generic terms opens up all kinds of possibilities. We may well begin by considering the various types of energy which we could use—electrical, mechanical, chemical; perhaps we can add some substance to the bread itself which will produce an exothermic reaction when the bread is sliced, and the newly-exposed surfaces will be self-toasted by exposure to air.[4]

Clement concluded his report with an invitation for people to contact him if they might be interested in a course on creative engineering at HP, but there were apparently no takers.

This is not to say that his efforts went unappreciated. To the contrary, the industrial design functions at Hewlett-Packard expanded steadily and the staff tripled, first with the hiring of classmate Tom Lauhan from the

University of Washington and then Allen Inhelder, the first of a new generation of talent from the Art Center School in Los Angeles. In time, the company's products began to win recognition within the industry for their "visual clarity of function," "ease and safety of operation," and "appropriateness of appearance."[5] Aesthetics remained a more-or-less fortuitous byproduct of technical considerations, of course, and Clement readily conceded that in contrast to the products of the automotive or consumer appliance industries, "The morality and economics of planned obsolescence, for reasons either of appearance or performance, is one problem we've never had to consider." No less an eminence than the mercurial William Hewlett acknowledged the growing importance of design, even in the black-boxed domain of electronic test equipment: "In many instances it is becoming just as important as the circuitry within the instrument itself."[6]

In less than a decade, Clement had advanced from being the lone designer in a sea of engineers to supervising an industrial design section of nine young men who showed up at work every morning in white shirts and very skinny black ties.[7] It was, however, a section in name only. The designers did not sit together but were arrayed throughout a large R&D room crammed with electronics workbenches and drafting tables. But within this restrictive domain, Clement was able, finally, to apply the "creative engineering" strategies he had learned in his summer course at MIT on a larger scale.

HP's product line, by 1959, had grown to 373 devices, packed into some sixty-five different shapes and sizes of enclosures, most manufactured both as a nineteen-inch rack-mounted unit and in a narrower bench-top version. At the end of that year, as a cost-saving measure, management instructed the industrial design group to develop a more efficient system for the packaging of its instruments. Many of these devices had been conceived and developed independently, which made it difficult to use them as an ensemble; customers complained that the enclosures impeded access for service and maintenance; the relentless advance of miniaturization had shortened their life spans and rendered many of them obsolete; and the duplication of manufacturing resources required by the rack-mounted and bench-top program made no economic sense.

The traditional approach would have been to address the specific points at which an existing apparatus might be improved; indeed, this was precisely the strategy of HP's production engineers, who proposed trimming the bezels and installing hinged trapdoors for easier access.[8] Instead, inspired by John Arnold's philosophy of creative engineering, Clement encouraged his group to back up and define the problem in the most general possible way: Rather than, "Redesign the oscilloscope," the problem was restated as, "Find the simplest and most compact structure that will satisfy the requirements of the instrument, the environment it occupies, and the people who use it." From this generic starting point he instructed his designers to attack the problem using the full range of Arnold's problem-solving methodologies: brainstorming, attribute listing, user observations (as clumsy and intrusive as they must have been). The outcome of the ensuing eighteen-month program was not an improved enclosure, but a fully integrated modular system built around a single pair of interchangeable die-cast aluminum frames. The savings in manufacturing time, warehouse space, shipping costs, and functionality repaid the company's $250,000 investment many times over, and there was also the intangible benefit of a cohesive corporate identity.[9]

The integrated "System I" cabinet concept, rackable, stackable, and eminently portable, was introduced in March 1961 at the annual meeting of the Institute of Radio Engineers where, in the unbiased opinion of HP's president, David Packard, it was immediately recognized as "the most impressive contribution to the packaging of electronic instrumentation that has ever been made."[10] In fact, both the electronics industry and the industrial design profession shared this favorable assessment. At the Western Electronics Show that summer it received an Award of Excellence for Outstanding Industrial Design; Alcoa selected it in 1962 for its annual Industrial Design Award "for outstanding design in aluminum," and the "Clement Cabinets" were featured at the end of that year in a special four-page supplement in *Fortune Magazine*.

Despite the attention lavished upon them, the population of designers at HP remained small and individual careers loomed disproportionately large. Incidents that may at the time have played out as personal rivalries or office politics can in retrospect be seen as skirmishes in a simmering intergenerational tension. Clement, with a university-based industrial design degree and a strong engineering bent, never learned to draw, whereas his early hires came from arts institutions whose entire curriculum was built around the visual execution of ideas. At Art Center, for instance, they had taken semester-long courses in sketching, drawing, two-point perspective, three-point perspective, rendering, color, surface development, product illustration, layout and presentation, typography, and model construction even before going on to their respective majors in product design, packaging and display, or "transpo," and the last six months were spent developing a portfolio.[11] They were typically recent vets with young families to support, were serious about themselves and their work, and carried with them the art school ethos of remaining at the bench all day and all night to finish what they had started. If the tools they needed were not quite right, they simply wandered over to the machine shop and either modified them or fabricated them from scratch. They were also car nuts, aficionados of "modern" furniture, and they believed that it was necessary not just to *do* design but also to *live* design, even on their $450 per month salaries.

Clement's attention remained focused on gaining acceptance from above, even as his authority was being challenged by a gathering insurgency from below; ultimately, he would be outflanked from both directions. In 1957 Hewlett-Packard, which had been growing steadily and in fact doubled in size in that year alone, reorganized its research and development department into four new product divisions: oscilloscopes, electronic counters, microwave and signal generators, and audio and video equipment. Notably absent was anything remotely approaching an "industrial design division," and it had become increasingly clear that design would never be more than an auxiliary service. Clement soldiered on, but with no prospects of a company-wide leadership position, and a loosening grip on the upstart generation he had sired, he announced his resignation effective January 1, 1964. David Packard commended him for work that displayed "imagination and innovation" while remaining "practical and effective," thanked him for his services, and bid him farewell.[12]

Carl Clement's role in the formation of Silicon Valley design was destined to take one more dramatic turn, but the immediate effect of his departure from Hewlett-Packard was the transition to a management style that more accurately reflected the demands of the products themselves. Believing that the only way to understand an instrument was to embed with the engineers responsible for it, some of HP's younger designers had already defected from a regime they perceived as overly autarkic and autocratic: Andi Aré moved to the oscilloscope division; Jerry Priestly decamped to the computer group; Allen Inhelder lobbied hard to be transferred to the new microwave division, despite a blunt warning from V.P. Bruce Wholey that "If you irritate my engineers, you're outta here."[13]

In order to gain credibility among the engineers, the designers had to demonstrate that their work had the potential to add measurable value not just to the appearance of a product, but also to its performance. Allen Inhelder, newly embedded in HP's largest and most profitable division, endeavored to do so with the utmost care. Before moving back to California, Inhelder had spent two years working on automotive interiors at Ford, where he added a deep immersion in human factors to the formal skills he had been taught at Art Center: from the automaker's engineers he learned that a protruding ignition key can result in a debilitating knee injury in even a minor collision, and from their bible, Woodson and Conover's standard *Human Engineering Guide,* that the designer must shun "style idiosyncrasies" and not be led astray by "'arty' concepts which destroy good human engineering practices."[14]

The mechanical engineers in the microwave division were favorably disposed to this new, "human-centered" approach, which promised to go beyond surface styling and ground their physical products in rigorous ergonomic data. The electrical engineers, however, who always formed the elite core of the Hewlett-Packard organization, saw no conceivable relevance of psychology and physiology to their work and were completely uninterested. Inhelder's strategic initiative was calculated to win them over by demonstrating that good product design meant more than simply protecting their precious electronics from dust and damage.

To support his argument, Inhelder selected the Model 608 VHF signal generator, a product that owed its success to its technical reliability rather than its ease of operation. Through a clever sequence of transparencies overlaid on a rendering of Model 608's control panel, he explained to a gathering of microwave engineers how nearly every aspect of the 1954 interface was arbitrary, inconsistent, and illogical. Because the designers had been summoned after the basic layout had been established, they were able to do little more than simply package the apparatus in a sheet-metal box with holes poked into it to accommodate the already-positioned controls. Had they been part of the product development team from the outset, the process would have begun with a "related function analysis" to clarify the relation among the instrument's constituent assemblies. They would have then clustered the frequency, modulation, and attenuation controls in formally distinct and logically sequenced partitions, each with its own clearly demarcated centerline, and then gone on to specify such details as labeling, color, placement of displays, and selection of knob types. The result would be an instrument whose faceplate was, in effect, a visual schematic of the electronics inside.[15] The e-e's were delighted, and by the end of his presentation the microwave division was ready to welcome its first industrial designer.

Inhelder's role in the Microwave Division ended abruptly one day in November 1964, when Ralph Lee marched into his office, instructed him to gather up his belongings, and sent him upstairs with the title of manager of corporate industrial design. In his new leadership position, Inhelder oversaw a central industrial design department of nine people and another six who remained attached to specific divisions. It was a mark of the status design had achieved within the company that his new office was walking distance from that of the crusty David Packard, who only a few years earlier had glanced at the airbrushed renderings in his Art Center portfolio and remarked, "It's very nice, but we don't need that here."[16]

"Corporate" handled about fifty design projects per year during Inhelder's twenty-eight-year tenure, with the overall mission of preserving a coherent design language across all of HP's divisions and product categories. Central to their work was the idea that they were not designing individual products so much as components of an integrated, open-ended, and scalable system. Sometimes this meant narrowing their focus to the functional compatibility of a plotter, a desktop calculator, and the extruded aluminum desk on which they sat. At the opposite end of the scale it fell to the design group to salvage an ill-conceived corporate identity program that had been contracted to Walter Landor Associates, a prominent San Francisco branding firm with little experience in the high-technology realities of Silicon Valley.[17]

The staff of the industrial design group approached their work with precision, rigor, and depth, and no detail was too small. Removing an unnecessary screw from a cabinet assembly became a badge of professional honor, if not a moral imperative. Early in 1964 Inhelder launched a two-year knob study, which he justified by explaining that this seemingly insignificant detail is actually the point of physical contact between a complex electronic device and its human operator. A chance remark from William Hewlett upon returning from an IEEE convention—"Why is it so hard for us

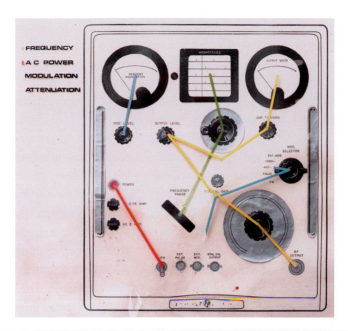

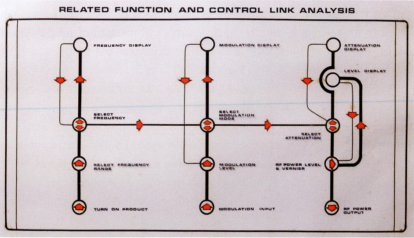

Figure 1.1
Before/after: Related function and control link analysis. Source: collection of Allen Inhelder.

to match up two shades of gray?"—sent them off into a months-long research program that included color science, color technology, and highly paid color consultants. As a spectrophotometer replaced paint chips and ultrasonic welding replaced glue, they worked as if they were inventing the field of instrument design in the high-technology hothouse the region had become. Indeed, this was not far from the truth.

The dominant characteristic of Silicon Valley was—and remains—the exceedingly fast pace and dynamic instability of the product development cycle within a rapidly changing technology environment. More densely packed circuits required improved accessibility; radiated electrical interference had to be mitigated as the frequency of digital signals approached the nanosecond range; and the miniaturization of electronic components, in scrupulous adherence to Moore's Law, continued unrelenting. Design was—by design—kept in the background at Hewlett-Packard, and there was never any doubt that technology remained the company's fundamental driver, but this came to be seen more as a challenge than an impediment: "The basic approach," wrote Inhelder in describing System II, the successor to the so-called Clement Cabinets of 1961, "was to be 'inside-out,' in which all the servicing, manufacturing, electrical, mechanical, and thermal needs would be met first, after which the esthetics of the design would be considered."[18]

There was one small exception to this technology-driven, "inside-out" role of industrial design—small enough, in fact, to fit into the shirt pocket of an HP engineer—but it would mark a shift of the most far-reaching importance. In 1970, overruling dismissive market forecasts, formidable technical challenges, and strenuous internal opposition, CEO Bill Hewlett personally authorized a $1 million crash program to develop a miniature, hand-held successor to the successful 9100 series desktop scientific calculator launched four years earlier. By that time, the HP catalog listed some 1,600 products, none of which sold more than ten units per day. Within six months of its launch in January 1972, the new HP-35 was selling 1,000 per day, and a year later accounted for a staggering 41 percent of the company's total profits. Graduate students bought them at college bookstores; accountants bought them at Macy's; and Hewlett-Packard had, in spite of itself, ventured to the edge of the uncharted territory that separated the engineering of technical instruments from the design of consumer goods.[19]

For all of its runaway, game-changing popularity, the thirty-five-key HP-35 scientific calculator was still an assertively technical device and remained so in its three subsequent models. William Hewlett expressly conceived of it as designed for "the engineer at the next bench," and at $395 it was seen as a replacement for the ubiquitous slide rule rather than a convenient household gadget (much less a lifestyle accessory). It was, nonetheless, the first regional technology product to point beyond the engineering community toward a wider public. The unprecedented success of the HP-35 would have major implications not just for Hewlett-Packard, but also for Silicon Valley and ultimately for the design profession at large.

In order to meet the terms of the Hewlett's brief, the designers of the HP-35 had to depart from the company's "inside-out" orthodoxy. The a priori requirement of size meant that in a fundamental reversal of HP's corporate practice, form rather than function was the primary driver in the development of a new product. Edward J. Liljenwall, the Art Center graduate who was given responsibility for the overall design of the calculator, put it this way:

> The industrial design of the HP-35 was unusual not only for Hewlett-Packard, but for the electronics industry in general. Usually, the mechanical and electrical components of a product are determined before the exterior is designed. The HP-35 took the opposite approach.[20]

The design brief, in other words, was framed not by the technical criteria of allowing the user to execute transcendental functions using a pseudomultiplication algorithm displayed in Reverse Polish Notation; it was, rather, defined by the physical criteria of building "a shirt-pocket-sized scientific calculator with four-hour operation from rechargeable batteries at a cost any laboratory and many individuals could easily justify."[21] For the first time, the designer was not brought in after the fact to package an assemblage of electronic components; it was the engineers, rather, who were given the humbling assignment of creating a product that could be accommodated by a 9-ounce, 5.8-inch by 3.2-inch chassis. It would be too much to claim that with the HP-35 the designer was placed in the driver's seat, but neither was he a third-class passenger relegated to the back of the bus.

The design team responsible for the HP-35 had to surmount obstacles both factional and functional. Liljenwall had fashioned three low-resolution prototypes out of cardboard and auto body putty that, when tarted up with a spiffy paint job, were enough to sell Hewlett on the feasibility of a shirt-pocket device. There were highly placed skeptics, however, who insisted upon standard 3/4-inch key spacing that only a book-sized device could accommodate (the pod vs. the pad, as it were, *avant la lettre*). The designers responded with a methodical human factors analysis in which they stained the pudgy fingertips of machinists, manicured receptionists, and nail-biting executives and observed them as they pressed various key combinations. Once they had tabulated their data and defended their case, Liljenwall was able to concentrate on building a dozen fully detailed plaster appearance models.

The wedge-shaped base of the calculator cants inward to allow it to be slipped into the shirt pocket of an (obviously male) engineer—Hewlett's overriding directive. When sitting on a desktop, this tapered form factor kept the base in shadow, creating the illusion that the device is even smaller and thinner than it already is. To accommodate 35 keys on a top panel that measured barely 2 1/2 inches by 4 1/2 inches, Liljenwall departed from conventional keypad design and developed a new approach based on placement, color, and nomenclature. The research that went into printing symbols and numerals on three surfaces, not to say materials, spacing, and color, was probably unprecedented in electronics design and represented a new standard in the professionalization of the field. And since a handheld product will be viewed from all sides, the designer allowed no exposed screws or visible fasteners and based his selection of the texture of the case as much on look and feel as the need to create a secure nonslip surface. Remarkably, given the time and the place, many of these problems in "human engineering" were addressed even before the parameters of the electronic design had been established.

If the inversion of the classical form-follows-function dogma was the first major contribution to creating a regional design culture, the second was the success of the HP-35 in the market. Chung C. Tung, a member of the original development team, imagined the calculator being carried into the field by "a pilot making an in-flight course correction, a surveyor running a traverse in the field, a businessman estimating returns-on-investment during a conference, a physician evaluating patient data."[22] While these are still specialized professional applications, they represent a significant expansion of HP's established user base and it was inevitable that

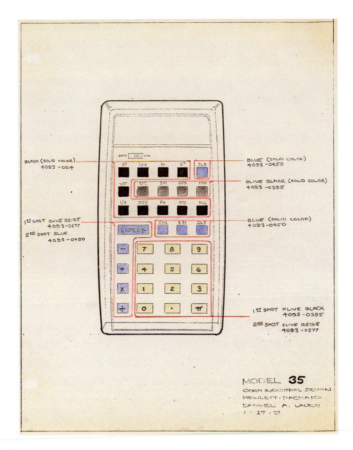

Figure 1.2
Darrell A. Lauer, corporate industrial design: Color study of the Model 35 scientific calculator (1.27.73) Source: Hewlett-Packard Corporate Archives.

subsequent generations of pocket calculators would be used by shoppers waiting in grocery-store checkout lanes and sports fans comparing the stats on their favorite teams. The HP-35 represents the first major instance of a regional technology beginning to migrate out of the R&D laboratory and toward the wider market.[23]

In general, however, the research-oriented technology companies avoided what the valley's resident journalist, Michael S. Malone, called "the siren call of the consumer business." Intel's foray into digital wrist-watches proved to be an unmitigated disaster, as the founding partners readily admitted: "We went into the watch business because we saw it as a technical problem and we felt we knew how to solve technical problems," stated Robert Noyce. "But, in a sense, we solved them so well that they stopped being a factor of importance. It turned into a jewelry business and we didn't know anything about jewelry." Gordon Moore continued to wear his Microma—which he referred to as his "$15 million watch"—as a reminder of the abyss that separated the equation-driven world of technical engineering from the vagaries of consumer-oriented design. Hewlett-Packard fared no better with the HP-01 watch-calculator, a truly hideous marvel of miniaturization whose twenty-eight tiny buttons had to be pressed by a stylus built into the strap.[24] Even selling chips that went into consumer products (like televisions) was distasteful to those, like AMD's Jerry Sanders, who wanted to be at the forefront of technology, and the recession of 1974–75 served only to confirm the folly of this brief misadventure.

A year before the HP-35 made its dramatic appearance, a series of articles in a weekly trade newspaper, *Electronics News*, had begun referring to the strip of Santa Clara County bounded by Highway 101 and the newly constructed Highway 280 as "Silicon Valley, USA" in reference to the material substrate of the region's burgeoning semiconductor industry.[25] The growth of Fairchild Semiconductor and its successor companies—Intel, National Semiconductor, and ultimately scores of others—engendered a web of suppliers, contractors, fabricators, patent attorneys, venture capitalists, and entrepreneurial professors that would turn the peninsula into the equivalent of industrial Manchester 150 years earlier and a formidable rival to the technology corridor along Route 128 in Massachusetts.[26] The characteristic products of Silicon Valley, however—audio oscillators, gas analyzers, disk drives—were remote from most people's lived experience, and in the popular imagination "California Design" still evoked the art furniture movement personified by Sam Maloof or the lingering midcentury modernism of Charles and Ray Eames.[27] The professional community certainly shared this perception. In a special issue dedicated to "Design on the West Coast," *Industrial Design* magazine unwisely predicted that "despite the pleasant environment and the proximity of centers of scientific investigation . . . [the San Francisco Bay region] may never challenge Los Angeles for industrial primacy on the West Coast."[28] These words were written in 1957, and the editors may be forgiven for failing to notice the opening in that year of the

Shockley Semiconductor Laboratory in a storefront on the nondescript border of Palo Alto and Mountain View.

An incipient professional practice was nevertheless emerging, and was beginning to play a discernible role in the densely networked, horizontally integrated infrastructure of specialists that defined the region's emerging industrial ecosystem. Almost without exception, the first generation of designers worked on the products of the manufacturing companies that employed them, and these were few and far between: Paul Cook, president and CEO of Raychem Corporation in Menlo Park, retained his friend Dan Deffenbacher of the nearby California College of Arts and Crafts as a part-time design consultant. Henry H. Bluhm served as the founder, director, and sole member of the industrial design department of Magna Power Tools in Palo Alto, Fred Robinett headed up design at FMC, and Beckman Instruments had a "design director" in the person of David J. Malk. The so-called "design group" at Memorex—still confined to the computer tape and disk drive business and not yet a presence in consumer media—was managed by Ron Plescia. Across the Bay Elmer Stolz led a team of five staff designers who worked on electromechanical calculators for the Friden Calculating Machine Company in San Leandro, which promoted its four-function automatic calculator as "the thinking machine of American business." Some of the early settlers—Clement from HP, Frank Walsh from Ampex, IBM's Jack Stringer, Ed Jacobson of the Hiller Helicopter Company in Menlo Park, Robert McKim, who had not yet found his place at Stanford— took to meeting regularly at the home of one or another of what McKim described as "a designers' support group."[29]

The defense contractors, who played an enormous but largely unacknowledged role in the growth of Silicon Valley, contributed not just to the security of the nation but to that of a handful of designers as well. The president of the Watkins-Johnson Co., a manufacturer of microwave tubes, retained the firm of Tepper-Steinhilber to ensure that every product that left its plant in the Stanford Industrial Park carried a consistent corporate look. The nature of their products, however—traveling-wave tubes, wafer deposition ovens, rack instrumentation—did not allow the designers much leeway, and once the visual guidelines were met, "we were still pretty much limited to machined castings, extrusions, and folded sheet metal."[30] Frank Guyre, who had studied sculpture at San Jose State with a minor in industrial design, began his career at Lockheed's new campus in Sunnyvale

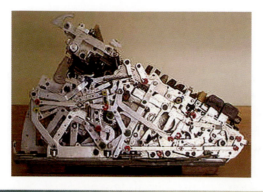

Figure 1.3
The Friden Model ST-W electro-mechanical calculator, naked and "skinned." Courtesy of the Old Calculator Museum. http://www.oldcalculatormuseum.com/fridenstw.html

where, in the precise terminology of aerospace engineering, he helped figure out "how you stuff six pounds of shit into a two-pound box."[31] As a rule, most companies allowed the nature of the technology they were developing to determine the character of their products: "Of course, these electronic devices/products needed some mechanical structure and housing for their enclosures," recalled one early toiler in the valley's former vineyards, "but this was considered only a necessary evil most of the time—the real product was the electronics and function, and the mechanical and aesthetic parts were, at best, considered secondary."[32]

The singular case of IBM is suggestive of the situation that prevailed in a region in which orchards had not yet given way to technology parks. In an outpost in pastoral San Jose, a diverse team had been deployed to work on the revolutionary random-access memory machine, the 305 RAMAC, the first to use a magnetic hard disk for data storage. "To develop this idea into a working computer," intones the narrator of a 1956 newsreel, "required the skills of accountants and artists, chemists and clerks, engineers and electricians, stenographers and salesmen." Apparently the scriptwriter could find no suitable alliteration for "industrial designer," despite the presence there of an embryonic ID staff led by Jack Stringer.[33]

In February of that year, fired by the revelation on the part of chairman Thomas L. Watson, Jr., that "good design is good business," IBM had launched its global corporate design program under the direction of Eliot Noyes, who stipulated that every touchpoint—from the machine to the room it occupied to the building in which it was deployed to the campus in which it was located—should be part of a single, seamless interface. Within two years the San Jose team was working out of a 190-acre garden campus on Cottle Road designed by the California modernist John Savage Bolles.[34]

In 1960, Donald Moore succeeded Stringer as manager, and during his fourteen-year tenure the IBM Design Center grew from four or five to about a dozen while the underlying technology shifted from magnetic disks to microchips. Moore had graduated from Art Center with honors in transportation design and was working as a senior stylist for the Ford Motor Company in Dearborn when the Michigan winter finally drove him back to his native California, where the departure of Stringer freed up one of the only industrial design positions to be had in this decidedly nonindustrial region. Watson had famously "bet the company" on the integrated System 360 family of compatible computers, and the industrial designers worked first on the floor-to-ceiling cabinets of the System 360, and then the seating, controls, and display of the "sit-down" 1130 console system that was released in the following year. Their avowed mission was to preserve the visual design language decreed by Noyes without compromising the internal functions of the machines of which they understood, in Moore's modest estimation, "absolutely nothing."[35]

The designers in San Jose, like those at each of IBM's regional design centers, were subject to the dictates issued by Noyes from his base in New Canaan and the guidelines issued by the Advanced System Development Division in Poughkeepsie, which exercised control over data processing products and whose manager, Walter Kraus, was very clear that "we can't

Figure 1.4

IBM general products division, Cottle Road, San Jose (1958). John Savage Bolles, architect; Douglas Baylis, landscape. "Think" Advertisement, 1962; photographer unknown.

have a West Coast style."[36] Finding common ground between corporate design standards and the requirements of local engineering teams resulted in negotiations that were not always cordial: "It was more like establishing battle lines within a war zone," Moore recalled, "but if you had a good relationship with engineering and marketing you could get a lot done." Still, there was little danger that the San Jose group would venture far from the mother ship.

Although it was an auspicious beginning, in comparison with the phenomenal growth of the semiconductor industry during the 1960s and 1970s this smattering of design professionals was a footnote to a footnote in Silicon Valley history. The acknowledged centers of design in the United States were tied to the manufacturing centers around New York, Chicago, and Ohio, and as Budd Steinhilber discovered, having made the impulsive decision to relocate to the Bay Area in 1964, "any sensible person could have told you that, geographically, this was a really dumb place to establish an industrial design practice."[37] To say that opportunities were limited would be an understatement, and most people would have agreed with the assessment of one early job seeker that in the Bay Area, "Hewlett-Packard and Ampex were pretty much the only game in town."[38]

From modest beginnings as a supplier of precision electric motors to the U.S. Navy, Ampex Electric and Manufacturing Company had built a global reputation on the basis of two Telefunken "Magnetophon" machines and fifty reels of BASF tape liberated from a defeated Germany in 1946 and modified, in the best Silicon Valley tradition, in a garage workshop in San Carlos. Two years later, in April 1948, Ampex delivered to the American Broadcasting Company seven Model 200A magnetic tape recorders. The broadcast and recording industries accepted the new standard almost immediately, and within a decade, in a textbook case of what a later generation would call "disruptive innovation," Ampex completely dominated the market for professional high-fidelity audio and video recording equipment.[39]

The driving force behind these early product development efforts was Harold Lindsay, employee no. 8 at Ampex and one of the acknowledged pioneers of modern audio recording. Lindsay, revered by his coworkers as the model of an engineer's engineer, brought to his work a seemingly encyclopedic knowledge of fasteners, extrusions, materials, and manufacturing techniques, as well as a refined aesthetic sensibility and an almost moralistic sense of the engineer's obligations to the people who would use his creations. He could be less solicitous of his colleagues who had to build them: "Harold drove us mad at times," recalled Myron Stolaroff, who outranked Lindsay as employee no. 0. "He was an absolute perfectionist. Nothing could go that didn't look beautiful, wasn't beautifully arranged, that did not have a marvelous appearance and superb workmanship."[40]

The founders of Ampex believed that they were opening up an entirely new industry. "There was nothing available in the technical literature to tell you how magnetic tape recorders worked," Harold Lindsay told a room full of new recruits. "We had no references to go to."[41] No clear distinction was made between engineering and design, and the absence of precedent can hardly be overemphasized. Robbie Smits, who joined the original Ampex team in 1948, recalls being told, "Here's a head, here's an amplifier, here's a top plate; make a tape recorder out of it."[42]

Within this uncharted domain, it was Lindsay's aesthetic values, combined with his previous on-the-job exposure to drafting, machining, and industrial design that governed the formal qualities of the first Ampex machines. There were, to be sure, external constraints. The Model 200A was developed with the support of Jack Mullin, the former army major who had discovered the original German Magnetophone machines in a castle outside of Frankfurt, dismantled them, packed them up, and shipped them back to the United States as "souvenirs" in nineteen mail sacks. Mullin generously made them available to the Ampex engineers so that they could test the playback heads Lindsay had built, but this required that they be engineered to the same specifications as the German machines. On a larger scale, the overall dimensions, and even the finish and color scheme, were fixed by the requirement that they slide into the studio rack space previously occupied by the industry-standard Scully disk-cutting lathes they sought to replace.[43]

Guided by his credo of "rugged and reliable," Lindsay created an intuitive design language that would govern the first generation of Ampex professional machines. Having no formal design training, he naturally allowed his decisions to be driven by engineering considerations and by the professional uses to which the machines would be put. The elegance of the first magnetic recorders, however—especially considering their defining role in an industry and the almost complete absence of any precedent—is striking, and attests to Lindsay's fastidious attention to detail. Two round openings in the cabinet of the Model 200A serve as convenient and attractive door pulls that allow access to the electronics and for mechanical adjustments; a myth soon began to circulate that their dimensions corresponded to his very precise calculations of the venting requirements of the motors inside.

During its first decade, Ampex shipped a new product almost every year, and an "Ampex look" began to emerge—although in the words of engineer Larry Miller, "A certain family resemblance will almost certainly evolve if you keep trying to put a pair of massive, 2″ tape reels into a machine."[44] The $4,000 Model 200A came first, followed by its compact successor, the Model 300, the less successful Model 400, the militarized 500, and the portable 600 encased in outrageously expensive matched speaker cabinets of rare African hardwood. In April 1956, Ampex released the world's first video recorder, which revolutionized the television industry. The VR-1000 was developed by a team of engineers led by recording pioneer Charles Ginsburg, who had joined Ampex in 1952. The heroic years may have reached their apex with the MR-70 mastering audio recorder in 1964, designed to dub Beatles masters for Capitol Records in the United States. With its die-cast aluminum frame, its "mil-spec" (military specification) tolerances, and its precision alignments, the MR-70 is widely recognized as a masterpiece not only of audio engineering but also of industrial design. By this time Ampex machines could be found in nearly every major radio, television, and professional recording studio in the country, as well as in a growing number of laboratories, universities, military proving grounds, and corporate data centers.

As Ampex matured and its product line diversified to include consumer as well as professional equipment, even the gifts of Harold Lindsay were insufficient to service the industry it had created. In 1958, in a pattern that would become emblematic of the whole of Silicon Valley design, the "engineer with taste" was succeeded by the trained designer. With Lindsay's blessing, Roger Wilder, one more in a long line of Art Center graduates to migrate to northern California, became the first industrial designer to join the company, and shortly thereafter Frank T. Walsh was hired to assemble a professional design staff. By the time Walsh stepped down a decade later, Ampex had relocated its labs, shops, and eight-person industrial design studio to a sprawling forty-acre campus in Redwood City, a few miles closer to the nerve center of Silicon Valley. This was a fitting move, symbolically, at least, as it was only logical that a company that had learned how to capture sound and then image on magnetic tape had extended its reach into instrumentation for the recording of data of every sort.

Walsh's successor was Arden Farey, who became incapacitated by multiple sclerosis and emerged as a leading figure in the IDSA's design-for-disability movement. It therefore fell to Darrell Staley to preside over the phase change from magnetic tape to "digital storage for the visual information age."[45] Staley had drifted through a series of one-year jobs after graduating from Art Center in 1959: designing surface elements for refrigerators at the Frigidaire division of General Motors in Detroit, ground support equipment for the Apollo Mission at North American Rockwell in Los Angeles, and mobile farming equipment for the FMC Corporation, which brought him to San Jose. From the day he entered the ground-floor studio at Ampex, opening onto an interior courtyard that kept the work of the

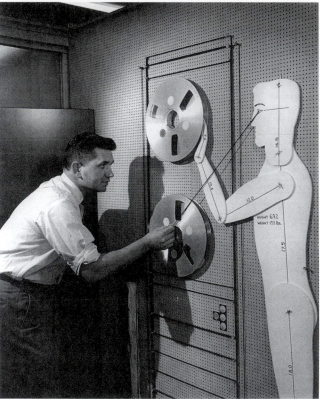

Figure 1.5

From engineer with taste to industrial designer. Top: Harold Lindsay with Ampex Model 200A; bottom: Frank Walsh, manager of the Ampex industrial design department, with "Elmer Average," an articulated anthropometric figure. Source: Department of Special Collections, Stanford University Libraries: Ampex collection, M1230, Box 53, folder 7439.

designers sheltered from the eyes of curious visitors, he knew that his wanderings were over.

During a thirty-year tenure as manager of corporate industrial design, Staley oversaw the evolution from the early analog machines, which pulled reels of two-inch tape across three heads, to the breakthrough helical scan recorders, which wrapped tape around a revolving drum. Each shift changed the scale of the product and confronted the designers with new challenges and opportunities, but nothing prepared them for the day, sometime in the late 1980s, that one of the engineers walked into the design studio and announced, "We're not going to use tape anymore." The physical requirements of accommodating reels of magnetic tape had framed their entire design practice from the outset, in much the way that vacuum tubes and CRTs had predetermined the form of most televisions. With the adoption of digital technology the industrial designer's traditional chore— to wrap a skin around an assembly of physical components—changed almost overnight.

As the products of the recording industry entered the digital age, so also did the tools the designers had at their disposal. Nowhere was this more evident than among Ampex's graphic designers, who were responsible for all of the company's internal and external printed materials. This group was formed around 1977, when Douglas Tinney, who had studied at the California College of Arts and Crafts with such industry legends as Joseph Sinel, joined a team of three "graphic artists."[46] At its peak Tinney managed a team of forty-four professionals who produced marketing materials, annual reports, user manuals, and technical documentation. Over the course of his twenty-two-year career at Ampex, Tinney, along with a crew of designers, photographers, illustrators, and printers, navigated the sea change from X-Acto knives and rubber cement and galleys shipped by Greyhound bus to the first Macintosh Classic computers. By the end, when the design staff had withered to almost nothing, he was downloading PDFs and returning the corrections to subcontractors by email without even going in to work.

This progression of tools was not, of course, unique to Silicon Valley. What was specific to the region's fast-moving technology sector was the nature of the products they were being asked to explain, illustrate, and market. Graphic designers trained in art school environments had to learn enough about the functioning of complex technical instruments to be able to express visually their relation to other pieces of apparatus, whether or not manufactured by Ampex. They had to prepare promotional materials far in advance of the launch of an actual product, often having only plywood mockups to work with.

Despite this proliferation of trained professionals, Ampex failed to build design into the overall product development process, and even in the best of times the studios were seen as links in a strictly hierarchical chain rather than partners sitting at the same table. When turf wars erupted the designers would usually lose, as Jay Wilson quickly discovered while working on the VPR-6 professional video series: "At one time I got so frustrated fighting over what I considered small design issues that I sent a memo to engineering saying, in effect, that if they wanted to design the product to let me know in writing and ID will bow out."[47] Like Hewlett-Packard, Ampex was at its core a research-based, engineering-driven company with a weak understanding of the vast chasm that stretches between professional products and the consumer market. The chain of command began high above in the advanced technology division and passed through the engineering department before reaching the first-floor studio where the designers were instructed to make it cheaper, add some features, and put it in a box. A few Ampex engineers—most notably Harold Lindsay—appreciated designers; some tolerated them, most saw them as superfluous. The prevailing attitude seemed to be one of engineering hubris: "This thing is gonna change the world; nobody will care what it looks like."[48]

Only in the late 1970s, when Ampex began to experience serious competition for the first time in its history, did management begin to appreciate the value of design as part of corporate strategy, but by that time it was too late. The Sony exhibits at the annual trade show of the National Association of Broadcasters grew bigger and more impressive, morale plummeted, and the company suffered the centrifugal effects of the "five little Ampexes" that had been spun out a decade earlier.[49] A series of catastrophic managerial decisions further eroded its technological edge, and today there is almost nothing left of the once-invincible company except a landmark blue and white sign, silently saluting motorists heading southbound along Highway 101 to the campuses of Yahoo!, Google, and Facebook.

Design came to Silicon Valley on the heels of engineering, and there were no reliable guides or even a clear sense of what it meant to "design" a variable attenuator or a helical-scan video recorder—much less of their relevance to the consumer market. Steinhilber reflected that "When I started out in the design field in New York most of our work was for the "white goods" industry (major appliances). When I moved to Ohio I had to learn the language of the machine-tool industry. But here was an infant field whose vocabulary was still in gestation. They were making it up as they went along."[50] The first generation of practitioners approached this terra incognita on the basis of creativity, intuition, instinct, and taste, and they sought out inspiration from wherever they could find it: HP's Carl Clement traveled to MIT to experience "creative engineering"; Myron Stolaroff retreated to a cabin in the Sierra Nevada where he administered LSD to eight fellow Ampex engineers in an effort to unlock their latent creativity. At the Stanford Research Institute, computer pioneer Douglas Engelbart dabbled in the human potential movement and enrolled his unwilling staff in est seminars.[51] With every new technological lurch the need for a more specialized set of professional skills became apparent, but also, paradoxically, for a wider vision. "We are creating products that have never existed before," Allen Inhelder regularly reminded his colleagues at HP, "and we need to design them so that our customers know how to use them." From his seat at Ampex Darrell Staley observed that "the California designer has had to be a mini-Renaissance man for years, and has not even thought twice about it. It comes with the territory."[52]

It was, however, an uphill fight for designers to gain credibility among highly trained, highly placed, and highly paid engineers, for whom even a simple enclosure was at best a necessary evil. More than a few were worn down by the constant battle to be invited into development teams at the outset of a project, and not simply handed a bundle of components to be packaged at the end. For those whose spirits sagged under the weight of corporate bureaucracy or whose egos bristled at their status as "exotic menials," or "short-order cooks,"[53] the alternatives were few and far between. Some managed to climb the corporate ladder into positions of management, often leaving their design skills (or lack thereof) behind; a few others headed "back east" to the established consultancies of Chicago or New York. Only two dared to explore a third way.

Dale Gruyé and Noland Vogt had been friends since their student days at the Art Center School in Los Angeles, then as colleagues at General Electric in Utica, New York. In March 1966, having left their positions in the corporate design offices at Hewlett-Packard (Gruyé) and Ampex (Vogt), they joined with George Opperman, rented a nondescript storefront on the southern edge of Palo Alto, and began hunting for clients. The three young designers were optimistic and ambitious, and dreamed of building a business that would escape the provincialism of the midpeninsula and acquire a national clientele. Although their office on San Antonio Road was only a few blocks up from the site of the former Shockley Semiconductor Laboratories where the new technology was born, they had no idea that with the launch of the GVO partnership they were writing the first lines of an entirely new chapter in the history of Silicon Valley, the "Valley of Heart's Delight."[54]

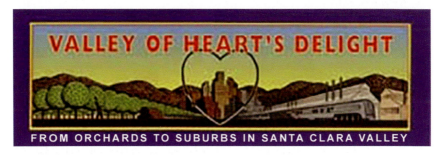

Figure 1.6

2   RESEARCH AND DEVELOPMENT

The mid-1960s saw an explosion of research into "ergonomics," literally, the design of work environments. In Michigan the Herman Miller company spun off a research division whose mission was "to find problems outside of the furniture industry, and to conceive solutions for them." From its Connecticut headquarters the Xerox Corporation, flush with cash from its near-monopoly over the copier industry, announced plans to open a state-of-the-art research facility in Palo Alto with the mandate of inventing "the office of the future." And at the Stanford Research Institute in Menlo Park, Douglas Engelbart was setting up the Augmented Human Intellect Research Center to explore collaborative tools that could "raise the collective IQ" of knowledge workers distributed across time and space. Inevitably, these programs became intertwined within the volatile, research-driven culture of Silicon Valley in which the computer was fast becoming both the object and the tool of design.

Throughout the midpeninsula a proliferation of corporate research labs, private think tanks, and academic institutes had begun to generate a steady stream of technical breakthroughs that, when translated into products, would change the manner and even the definition of work. Engelbart's lab is the iconic case in point. In 1968, supported by an $80,000 grant from NASA and a blossoming friendship with Herman Miller research director Robert Propst, Engelbart set out in search of inspirational design concepts that might guide him in equipping his lab and its centerpiece, a networked installation he called the oN-LineSystem (NLS). When Associate Director Bill English left SRI for the Xerox Corporation's Palo Alto Research Center (PARC), he brought with him key elements of NLS where they contributed to the evolution of the prototype Alto and its commercial successor, the Star workstation. As the idea of a personal and even portable computer began to spill out of the laboratory and into the volatile arena of venture-funded startups, a few Xerox veterans began to seek out designers to help them transform innovative technologies into marketable products. Design surely played a role in the shaping of the computer, but far more important was the role the computer played in the shaping of design.

As computing moved from the back room to the front office and prepared to enter the home, it generated product opportunities that could not be realized by scientists and engineers alone. Designers could provide the missing link between research and development, but in northern California they were few and far between: in 1974 exactly nine offices were represented in the San Francisco Bay chapter of the IDSA, and none of them, for obvious reasons, had ever worked on, worked with, or in most cases even seen a computer. Among them was the GVO partnership, stepchild of the corporate design studios of Hewlett-Packard and Ampex, and the first of the independent consultancies that would eventually play a defining role in Silicon Valley's ecosystem of innovation.

GVO's first five years were spent chasing clients and trying to keep a month ahead of the rent. Initially, the partners had hoped to create a business based on the natural affinity between design and advertising that had proven itself in other parts of the country.[1] In the Santa Clara Valley, however, where companies were typically pushed by new technology rather than pulled by consumer demand, each of these functions tended to act as a drag on the other, and in 1971 George Opperman allowed himself to be bought out. The remaining partners reformatted themselves as the Gruyé-Vogt Organization, moved their office to Tasso Street in downtown Palo Alto, and focused their attention on the decidedly more prosaic fields of industrial and tradeshow exhibit design.

Although their clients came mainly from traditional industries, Noland Vogt and Dale Gruyé moved the design community into new and uncharted territory. The recession of 1970–71 very nearly derailed them—most of the fifteen-person staff had to be let go and Vogt mortgaged his house to keep the company afloat—but by mid-decade they had begun to rebuild a core team: John Gard, who had been working on consumer product design for the Mel Boldt consultancy in Chicago, made an initial cold call that began, "You don't know me but we do the same thing," to which Gruyé replied,

"What's that—lose money?" He nonetheless accepted GVO's $14,000 salary offer and moved to California in April 1974. Gard was followed in 1975 by industrial designers Elliot Blank and Steve Albert, and Mike Wise joined in 1976 as a model maker—although in those early days everybody did a bit of everything. From time to time a recent design school graduate would knock on the door in search of an entry-level job, and Vogt or Gruyé would emerge from the shop, covered in sawdust, and conduct an impromptu interview.

More important than mere growth, the original business model itself evolved to meet the demands of Silicon Valley industries in which technical factors dominated and human factors were at best secondary. Gruyé owned the building on Tasso Street and rented office space to a consulting mechanical engineer who patiently answered a multitude of technical questions from the designers. Vogt, who had studied engineering before taking up industrial design, always had a technical bent, and when their tenant moved to larger quarters they conceived the idea of adding an in-house engineering capability.

It was uncommon, at that time, to find designers and engineers cohabiting under a single roof, but the nature of their work demanded it. The first opportunity came in the context of a project for the Cordis Corporation, which retained GVO in 1976 to handle the industrial design of an advanced hemodialysis apparatus in a joint venture with Dow Chemical. Over the course of the two-year program, the engineers on the Cordis-Dow team gradually came to respect the designers' insistence upon combining usability for the clinical technician who would be operating the device with a nonthreatening appearance for the patient who would be experiencing it. The designers at GVO in turn came to appreciate that a product of this sort could not be approached as a problem of concealing complex technology within a sleek enclosure. At the conclusion of the project Vogt invited the lead engineer on the Cordis-Dow side, Robert Hall, to move over to GVO to build an engineering base. Initially Hall's role was not so much to *do* engineering as to be able to *talk* engineering, both with GVO's designers and with their clients, but in time this evolved into a formal division, complete with a prototyping laboratory equipped with an Auto-Trol CAD system and even a newfangled fax machine. In other respects, however, the partners adapted slowly and cautiously to new trends: when the first generation of younger hires from San Jose State began to arrive a decade later, Vogt gazed with the deepest misgivings upon their flat, modernist-inspired slabs: "The trouble with you guys," he scolded, "is that you never learned to work in clay."[2]

GVO's strategic idea was to bring projects in at an early stage and integrate engineering and design from the outset. At the time, this represented a bold innovation, given the difficulty of persuading clients in highly constrained technology industries that properly positioned controls, practical enclosures, and a coherent, unifying narrative amounted to an investment worth making. In building an in-house engineering capability, GVO was hoping to advance its capacity to make this case, and the results seemed to bear out the wisdom of this considerable risk. Within a few years, the firm had acquired a distinctively regional character and boasted a client list that included such marquee technology companies as Syntex, Memorex, NCR, National Semiconductor, Intel, and Varian. There was even a foray into an emerging industry that had been almost completely untouched by design but would decisively shape its future: computers.

The Osborne Computer Company, now an almost-forgotten footnote in the annals of Silicon Valley, was for a brief moment poised to dominate the field of personal computing. Born of an unlikely collaboration between Adam Osborne, a colorful and highly ambitious entrepreneur, and Lee Felsenstein, a founder of the famous Homebrew Computing Club and champion of Ivan Illich's populist quest for "tools of conviviality," Osborne was the first to offer a cheap, portable microcomputer that a business traveler could carry through an airport and fit under his airplane seat. Prototypes were displayed with great fanfare at the West Coast Computer Faire in April 1981, but the metal case proved both heavy and prohibitively expensive, so—in a manner typical of the subordinate role of the designer in those days—it was handed over to GVO for further development. Mike Wise conducted initial experiments with vacuum-forming and pressure-forming (crudely put, sucking from below and pushing from above), which resulted in what Adam Osborne, in an internal memo, described as "an ugly duckling." For the next iteration, Philip Bourgeois created an ingenious injection-molded housing that could be snapped together in under two minutes. By September, the twenty-six-pound Osborne 1A—with its bundled software, five-inch screen, folding keyboard, and a carrying handle that qualified it as the world's first portable personal computer—was selling an unprecedented 10,000 units per month.[3]

The demise of the Osborne Computer Corporation—a victim of stiffening competition from IBM and Commodore and a catastrophic marketing blunder on the part of Adam Osborne himself—left the GVO partners wary of the enticements of the untested computer industry and its equally untested champions. When the next pair of "refugees from the human race" showed up at Vogt's office, clad in jeans, T-shirts, and sporting a proposal to swap $1,700 worth of design services for stock in a company founded on April Fool's Day and named after a piece of fruit, Vogt demurred. "The problem," he ruefully recalled, "was that companies like Apple came and went very fast in those days . . . . So we decided to pass."[4]

There was, in any case, plenty of work in more established industries, but even that was beginning to take on a new and regionally specific character. In the overheated, innovation-driven climate of the early 1980s, many of the companies GVO was courting expressed the desire for evidence-based validation before embarking upon expensive new product initiatives. The designers, for their part, were becoming increasingly disillusioned with their role as technical contractors, "executing bad ideas really well."[5] To address the frustrations both of their clients and themselves, GVO found itself evolving—gradually and intuitively—from a practice-based to a research-based organization. Three projects, spread over a five or six year period, reveal the expanding role that research came to play in the region's emerging model of professional practice.

The first of these was undertaken for Syntex, the Palo Alto–based pharmaceutical giant, which had entered the animal health field during the previous decade with a hugely successful portfolio of natural cattle hormones and antiparasitics. The science was cutting edge, but the usual delivery system was primitive—force-feeding the animal orally, which neither cows nor cowhands particularly enjoy. Syntex's scientists wished to explore the feasibility of injecting the proprietary formula directly into the animal's rumen, where the target parasites reside, but had absolutely no idea how to do this. In 1982 they turned to GVO for assistance.

There is more than a little irony in the fact that the rumen injector—a project that left several of GVO's industrial designers wishing they were working on attention-getting consumer goods for Loewy, Dreyfuss, or Teague—would be honored by the IDSA as one of the "Designs of the Decade."[6] This recognition was due in part to the unprecedented research phase that preceded and accompanied the actual design work. Noland Vogt

himself led a team that headed out literally into the field to interview vet-
erinarians, ranchers, and field hands. Their research took them to feed lots
in California, Australia, and Colorado, where the locals introduced them to
regional delicacies such as Rocky Mountain "oysters." They resigned themselves to the fact that whereas their counterparts in the consumer goods
industries had become experts in human factors, they were mastering
bovine factors. But ultimately they developed a heavily automated injector
device that achieved 100 percent accuracy and zero waste, while requiring
only ten minutes of training, and that earned praise from the client and
widespread recognition from the professional design community.

A few years later, GVO was approached by Johnson Controls International, a global manufacturer of industrial building controls. Squeezed by a
larger competitor, JCI asked for help in reducing the cost of a $1,000 sheet
metal cabinet containing the switches and circuits that manage a building's environment, energy use, lighting, fire safety, and security systems.
GVO responded with a $30,000 cabinet. The story, needless to say, is more
complicated than it appears.

In the early years of the Gruyé-Vogt partnership, this type of project—
the stock in trade of any industrial design shop in the country—would have
been treated as a straightforward problem of form and fabrication. From a
research-based perspective, however, the physical dimensions of the box
proved to be merely the visible expression of a larger problem that needed
to be understood systemically. Accordingly, GVO assembled a core team
that included not just its own industrial designers, but executives, software
engineers, technicians, and sales staff from JCI and took them out into the
field to perform what might today be called a comprehensive life-cycle
assessment. Together they conducted on-site observations of tooling and
manufacturing facilities; they rode around in trucks with the guys who
delivered, installed, and serviced the units; they gathered qualitative data,
photographic evidence, and anecdotes, and they immersed the JCI members of the team—often for the first time—in their customers' world. GVO's
lead design engineer resigned midway through the project because he was
unable to cope with the open-ended methodology, and the client needed to
be coaxed along as well: to guard the initiative against the antibodies that
organizations develop to kill off new ideas, they set up what was in effect a
shell company within JCI, operating under the corporate radar. The team
logged thousands of miles of air travel, in the days before email, hauling

computers back and forth between California and JCI's headquarters in Milwaukee.

The key insight derived from this early exercise in protoethnography was that the end product—the cabinet—was a minor component in a much larger system that was rife with inefficiencies. In particular, the labor costs involved in installation and maintenance of the control box, and the coordination of the numerous skilled tradesmen necessary to service it, overwhelmed the cost of the product itself. The solution was a family of modular, scalable snap-in panels, designed back in GVO's Palo Alto studios and manufactured under its auspices.[7] It proved wildly successful in the market, and JCI's initial investment was returned in savings of hundreds of thousands of dollars over the lifetime of the installation.

A third project, this one for Canon, rounds out the arc of the story. Having observed that the high sales rate of its color printers contrasted with inexplicably low levels of domestic use, in 1992 the Japanese electronics manufacturer hired GVO to find out why there was such resistance to home printing. A conventional industrial design process might have begun by analyzing the existing product, evaluating it against competitors, and exploring alternative materials, finishes, and methods of fabrication; the final deliverable would likely have been an improved model, restyled, rebranded, and tricked out with a few new features to "make it new." GVO's final deliverable, in sharp contrast to the prevailing norms in a technology industry, was not an artifact but a document. An ethnographic study of thirty selected families had revealed that whereas office workers hit "print" at the end of a job, at home people are more likely to need printed materials at the onset of a family project—photo albums, kids' artwork, the planning of vacations, and so on. In a report entitled "A Study of Printed Matter in the Home," GVO recommended that Canon stop thinking of the home printer as an office printer under a different roof, but rather as a domestic appliance in its own right, with a unique set of software capabilities. What the client needed, in other words, was not a better answer but a better question.

The challenges put to them by clients such as Syntex, Johnson Controls, and Canon pushed GVO from the familiar landscape of industrial design into the uncharted realm of ethnographic research, anthropological fieldwork, and sociological analysis. Their first steps were tentative and largely intuitive—"It was just designers and engineers getting out in front of the process and asking stupid questions"[8]—but the hiring of a new wave of trained professionals added formal rigor to acquired experience, and design research steadily evolved into a distinct service offering. In 1992, Gary Waymire migrated to GVO from the Herman Miller Research Corporation in Ann Arbor; he was joined, in the following year, by sociologist Tom Williams, and by anthropologist Susan Squires in 1997. Michael Barry, who had been hired as a product designer after stints at Ampex and Atari, took to sneaking into cultural studies classes at Stanford, and GVO's bookshelves soon began to bulge with titles such as Roland Barthes's *Mythologies*, Clifford Geertz's *The Interpretation of Cultures*, and Erving Goffman's *Frame Analysis: An Essay on the Organization of Experience*.[9] As their own frame of analysis shifted from materials and manufacturing to rituals of human behavior, even the most pedestrian problems came to look richer, harder, and more interesting.

Although it was becoming increasingly clear that the human sciences had a decisive role to play in the Silicon Valley innovation engine, their integration was not always smooth or easy. Cultural strains began to emerge between the GVO's engineering, design, and research divisions; clients were wary of untested methodologies; academic scholars trained in the disinterested pursuit of knowledge often resisted the reorientation required by applied research; and the designers themselves often felt that they were bootstrapping themselves into a domain that they themselves were still struggling to explain. Although already a veteran researcher, Gary Waymire recalls his hands shaking as he set up the overhead slides for his first pitch on ethnography as a method of design. The conceptual realignment that was taking place at GVO anticipated one of the most vital elements in the future course of Silicon Valley design, but the timing could not have been worse: The implosion of the Internet economy was imminent, and GVO did not survive the bursting of the dotcom bubble. The pioneering consultancy, already shaken by internal fault lines, spiraled into bankruptcy and closed its doors in September 2001.[10]

The designers at GVO were certainly not the first to have ventured into the field to understand a client's problem at its roots before hunkering down in the studio to develop forms. As a strategic shift in the core business model of a major consultancy, however, the ethnographic turn represented a new and largely unprecedented development.[11] At a time when fewer than one out of every five American anthropologists was employed in industry—and almost none in the design industry—the arrival of social scientists such as Lucy Suchman at Xerox PARC, Bonnie Nardi at Hewlett-Packard, Brenda Laurel at Atari Labs, Bonnie Johnson at Interval, and Susan Squires at GVO, marked the faint beginnings of a shift not only in the gender balance of the design community but in its center of methodological gravity as well: from studio practice to field research, from the exploitation of desire to the analysis of needs, and from the self-contained technical artifact to what Suchman famously called the "situated experience" of its real and intended users.[12] Some, such as industrial designer Jay Wilson, felt that this redirection could serve only to undermine the fragile credibility that designers had struggled to achieve, and decided that it was time to move on—a parting of the ways that anticipated the animated controversies that are roiling the design community today. Others, such as Michael Barry, Robert Hall, and Gary Waymire, welcomed the opportunity to refine a set of tools with which to look beyond the object. A third cohort—Peter Lowe, Robert Brunner, Jeff Smith, and Gerard Furbershaw—left GVO to found Interform, a consultancy that formed an important bridge between the first and the second generation of Silicon Valley design firms.

For a full decade, GVO was almost alone in the field, a situation that would change only gradually. The first hint of competition came a year after Gruyé, Vogt, and Opperman founded the practice, and was occasioned more by circumstance than by any indication that the demand for design services was heating up. Following his somewhat inglorious departure from Hewlett-Packard, Carl Clement landed a position with Spectra Physics, a new company that supplied precision optical equipment to the microelectronics and semiconductor industries. The "compact and functional design" of the helium-neon induction ion laser he executed for Spectra earned him the prestigious Pacesetter award at the Western Electronics Show and Convention in 1965, and a long-coveted executive position within the company.[13] Emboldened by his success—and propelled by a generous severance package—Clement left Spectra in 1967 to found DesignLabs, so named to emphasize the continental divide that separated the atelier of the creative artist from the laboratory of the research scientist.

Within a few years, DesignLabs had grown from a drafting table in Clement's home to an office with a dozen employees, and had completed sixteen projects for high-technology clients in the data processing, medical, industrial, and scientific industries: a storage device for silicon wafer cassettes for Monsanto; an electrostatic printer for Versatec; an automatic histology stainer for SmithKline. It was always a challenge to maintain an active pipeline, and Clement filled in his down time by helping to launch the San Francisco chapter of the IDSA and teaching industrial design at San Jose State University and in the product design program at Stanford, lately founded by his old mentor from MIT's creative engineering seminar, John Arnold.

In June 1972, while the California economy was still clawing its way out of recession, Clement received a very welcome letter from William English informing him that DesignLabs was one of three firms identified by a lab of a very different sort. PARC, the Palo Alto Research Center, had been established two years earlier as a western outpost of the Xerox Corporation, which hoped to tap into the academic communities of Stanford and Berkeley and the seemingly bottomless reservoir of technical expertise in Silicon Valley. The request for proposals from PARC's Systems Science Lab specified five elements of an "intellectual augmentation system."[14]

The design brief could not have been more straightforward—in stark contrast to the system it described, which was utterly revolutionary. In language that bordered on the banal it called for an apparatus that would serve as "a replacement for the pad and pencil," consisting of a vertical CRT screen and a horizontal surface capable of supporting a conventional keyboard, a small binary keypad, and a curious "writing-pointing device." The implications were nevertheless abundantly clear to Clement, who responded with alacrity: "We share your feeling that a completely new concept is necessary, which will not only dramatize the essence of the System but which will relate it to the user—or should we say, participant— almost as an extension of himself."[15] He estimated that two finished and fully documented prototypes could be delivered in twenty-six weeks at a cost to Xerox PARC of $12,980, time, and materials.

Carl Clement claimed, with justifiable pride, to have "designed" the first personal computer and he bristled that the mantle for this achievement seemed to have fallen upon Apple Computer, but the reality is more complex. In fact, all the components of the system had been publicly revealed in December 1968 at the semiannual meeting of the Joint Computer Conference in San Francisco. With English serving as the wizard behind the curtain, Douglas Engelbart had demonstrated to a spellbound gathering of

computer scientists accustomed to punched cards and coils of paper tape
how the computer might be used as an interactive medium of communication and collaboration. Relaxing in front of a custom-designed console,
talking nonstop through a headset to his team thirty miles to the south in
Menlo Park, and—with a binary keypad in his left hand and a mouse in his
right, "dealing lightning with both hands"—Engelbart had given the world
its first glimpse of the computer not as a disembodied electronic brain but
as a physical, interactive, designed experience.[16]

Although it is still mischaracterized today—as it was by his SRI managers in the 1960s—in technological terms, Engelbart always insisted that his
oNLineSystem (NLS) was not a machine but a program to "enhance," "supplement," or "augment" the human intellect and facilitate the real-time
sharing of knowledge among geographically dispersed "intellectual workers." The first embodiment of the NLS concept, however, was undeniably
physical: a $100,000, desk-sized CDC 160A computer workstation fitted out
with a porthole-like cathode ray tube display, a keyboard cannibalized
from an IBM Selectric, and an assortment of experimental pointing
devices—at various times head-mounted, knee-mounted, and handheld—
that enabled the operator to select and manipulate "objects" on the screen.
Engelbart expected that as new tools were introduced, "a co-evolution will
occur between the tools and the people who use them." Intrinsic to this
hypothesis was the idea that the hardware and software tools should
demand *increased* levels of cognitive involvement on the part of the human
operator; our present-day notion of "user-friendliness," had it existed at
the time, would have been anathema to him, but a relaxed, ergonomic
work environment was not.[17]

To the contrary: in conceptualizing and outfitting his lab, Engelbart had
given equal weight to physical, social, and psychological factors.[18] In this
regard his vision ran parallel to that of Robert Propst, visionary president
of the Herman Miller Research Corporation, who, like Engelbart, drew
heavily upon the work of behavioral psychologists, anthropologists, and
mathematicians. This was more than a superficial coincidence of the sort
that playwrights and historians love to indulge, for the two had in fact
developed a close personal bond during their most productive years. Only
a few months before Engelbart's famous demonstration at the Fall Joint
Computer Conference, Propst—who preferred to describe himself not as a
furniture designer but as "a researcher studying large problems in a

changing world"[19]—had upended his own conservative industry with his study of *The Office: A Facility Based on Change,* in which he argued that a flexible, modular "work station" was the only way to cope with an information-saturated world.[20] The publication was timed to coincide with the release of the Herman Miller Action Office II, whose impact upon the American work environment, it could be argued, has been second only to that of the networked computer workstation.[21] Indeed, borrowing one of Engelbart's core concepts, the personal computer and the personal workstation may be said to have "coevolved."

The mutual attraction of the scientist and the designer is not hard to fathom: like Engelbart, Propst was not interested in hardware per se, but in the problem of optimizing human performance in an era characterized by an "information deluge." In the course of his research he aggressively sought out what he called "the exceptionally able performer," people who handled large quantities of information in unusually creative ways. While Engelbart immersed himself in the writings of Christopher Alexander, which privileged the manner in which people use spaces over the ways in which architects define them, Propst studied the actual practices that were evolving the office from a workplace to "a thinking place."[22] Believing that "the real office consumer is the mind," Propst was among the first to argue for the relevance of the computer both as the centerpiece of the modern, modular office and as a tool for the design of it. His description of a facilities designer sitting before a graphical CRT interface, wielding a light pen and flanked by a drum plotter for hard copy readout, could have been lifted almost verbatim from Engelbart's conjectural description of an "augmented architect at work" in his 1962 report to his sponsor, the Air Force Office of Scientific Research.[23] It could be said, with only modest poetic license, that Engelbart was inventing interaction design while Propst was inventing design for interaction. Clearly, each of their programs implied the success of the other's.

In order to advance their complementary missions, Propst sent his principal research deputy, Jack Kelley, to Menlo Park to study the functional relationship of the components of Engelbart's NLS system, evaluate the "work vectors" around it, and design a set of solutions. The resultant prototype specified adjustable sixty-two-inch vertical panels and horizontal work surfaces, display tack boards, and mobile easel pads. Everything was on wheels—desks, tables, storage units—to encourage flexible interaction among the scientists and allow for the continuous adaptations that both Engelbart and Propst had envisioned. Inspired by Propst's rallying cry— "We must come to terms with modularity!"—the Augmentation Research Center (ARC) at SRI may well have been the first professional work space in the world to deploy the Action Office II.

As the date of Engelbart's demonstration approached, Kelley returned to SRI to work with the ARC team on the design of an experimental "all-in-one" console that could be mounted on a swivel-tilt Eames armchair to support a variety of work styles: seated, standing, "perched," or— Engelbart's own preferred position—leaning back with one's feet up on a desk. The console supported an embedded typewriter keyboard in the center; set into a tray on the left was the five-key "chordset" and on the right the three-button mouse whose two perpendicular flywheels allowed it to control an on-screen cursor as the operator moved it about on a small pad. The system, which had been refined and simplified to support groups of simultaneous users, thus blended two radical but fully complementary explorations of the future of work. Jack Kelley correctly describes it as "the very first modular panel and console workstation designed specifically for interacting with the computer."[24]

Within weeks of the 1968 demonstration, the trade magazine *Electronics* reviewed Engelbart's accomplishment, which included not just the visible on-stage "arena" but a microwave relay linked through the San Francisco International Airport and forty miles of coaxial cable routed along Skyline Boulevard to the SRI computer in Menlo Park. The editors praised the system "that permits a user to add, delete, or change information [on a CRT screen] almost as fast as he can think"; they were forgiving of the jerkiness of the cursor and the flicker of the screen; but they called for "more human engineering on the mouse."[25] The personal computer joined to the personal workstation represented a dramatic, revolutionary innovation, but there was more design work to be done.

William English brought the major elements of Engelbart's oNLineSystem with him when he migrated from the Augmentation Research Center at SRI to the Systems Science Lab at Xerox PARC in 1971. Often described as a mutiny, the transition was in fact very smooth, on personal, legal, and technical grounds, and English maintained a close working relationship with SRI as he built a program around its successor, the PARC On-line Office

Figure 2.1
Top: Douglas Engelbart (r.) and Robert Propst; bottom: Douglas Engelbart (l.) and Jack Kelley. "We expect that as tools are introduced and used, a co-evolution will occur between the tools and the people using them." Courtesy of Jack Kelley.

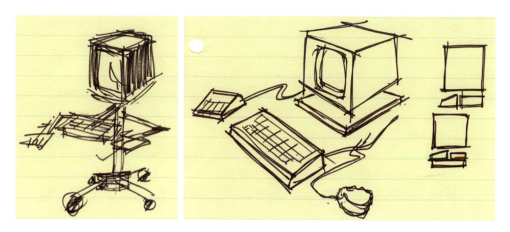

Figure 2.2
Concept development (DesignLabs #72-17 Job Book). Courtesy of Carl Clement.

System (POLOS). He even arranged for Carl Clement to visit SRI so that his team could be briefed on the operation of the original NLS. On the basis of his meetings with Engelbart, Clement generated a series of concept drawings, a foam-core mockup, and finally a hard model, and in due course he was informed that DesignLabs had won the competition and was awarded a contract to proceed.

The elements of the system DesignLabs was asked to improve were derived expressly from NLS: a bitmapped display in vertical, "portrait" mode intended to mimic a sheet of 8 1/2 × 11-inch paper and capable of displaying a pictorial interface; Engelbart's rolling, three-button "x-y position indicator," redesigned by a local mechanical engineer, Jack Hawley, to use a 360-degree roller ball rather than the original perpendicular fly-wheels; the ill-fated chordset with which an operator could, by pressing any of the five keys singly or in combination, generate thirty-one unique alphanumeric characters. The only familiar element was the modified QWERTY keyboard, but in contrast to the all-in-one panel designed by Jack Kelley four years earlier, it was conceived as a detached unit, "garageable" in the base of the display when not in use.[26] Clement and his team translated their concepts into reams of notes and drawings, negotiated with vendors over subminiature switches, power supplies, and antireflective glass coatings, and moved the project sequentially from analysis and research to conceptual mockups, appearance design, and fabrication and assembly.

The POLOS project was operated out of PARC's Systems Science Lab and was expressly seen as an exercise in "bootstrapping"—Engelbart's signature concept of building tools whose use would enable the building of the next generation of tools.[27] POLOS envisioned a future in which "dumb" photocopy machines would merge with "smart" computers in a single, integrated office environment. Physically, it was conceived as a distributed time-sharing system in which individuals at separate interactive terminals would feed off of a larger bank of Nova minicomputers. For three years it ran parallel to a program under development in PARC's neighboring Computer Science Lab. The CSL project, by contrast, envisioned a world of highly accessible, single-user "personal computers" that were networked together but not tethered to a larger computer. Lab director Robert Taylor dubbed it the Alto.

As a protégé, then colleague, and finally successor to J. C. R. ("Lick") Licklider at the Advanced Research Projects Administration (ARPA), Taylor was a tenacious advocate of the computer as a personal, intuitive, generally accessible tool of communication, and in that sense POLOS and Alto represented competing paradigms.[28] The best way to determine which of the two approaches held greatest promise, suggested Butler Lampson, one of CSL's key researchers, was to build ten to thirty Altos and use them: "If our theories about the utility of cheap, powerful personal computers are correct, we should be able to demonstrate them convincingly on Alto. If they are wrong, we can find out why."[29]

From the standpoint of computer architecture, POLOS and Alto represented rival philosophies, but at the user end they were physically compatible, so it was easy enough to share Clement's display, pointing device, and binary keyboard housings between them. With the decline of POLOS, DesignLabs was contracted to set up a production line to manufacture a pilot run of eighty units, and by the end of 1973, Altos were sitting on the desks of research scientists, lab directors, and secretaries throughout the PARC facility, linked to one another and to a scanned laser output terminal (SLOT) in a local area network called the Ethernet. By the end of the decade there were 1,000 Altos in existence.[30]

The major innovation of the Alto lay not in its appearance or even its underlying human factors, of course, but in redefining the human–machine interface: in the new paradigm, as Butler Lampson put it, "users *interact* with the system, almost to the exclusion of *programming* it."[31]

Consideration of manufacturability, ergonomics, or end-user aesthetics was at best secondary, industrial design was minimal and strictly functional, and apart from Clement's keyboard and display housings, almost every component was off-the-shelf. Indeed, the most widely admired physical aspect of the second generation Alto II was the chassis that sat under the user's desk and remained largely out of sight. John Ellenby, who organized the integrated design, engineering, and manufacturing team that built the Alto II, made a respectful nod to the ethnicity of Bob Nishimura, the Japanese-American engineer in the special projects group who designed it, calling it "an origami in folded metal."[32]

As a corporate research lab, the mandate of PARC was to prove the viability of the automated office by building functioning machines in sufficient numbers to be used, tested, and studied. This program represented an obvious advance over the conceptual research program of Engelbart's Augmentation Research Center at SRI, but it was nevertheless a transitional stage. Although working models would find their way into university labs at Stanford, MIT, and Carnegie Mellon, into the corporate headquarters of various customers of the Xerox Corporation, and even into the Carter White House, the Alto was fundamentally a research platform. This is clear from the casual voice of the *Alto User's Handbook*, an internal Xerox document created to initiate neophytes into the mysteries of personal computing: If you've gotten this far, "take a rest." If you're stuck, "ask an expert." If it breaks, "get it fixed." And following one particularly thorny set of instructions, "This is best understood by watching someone else do it."[33] PARC had been chartered as a corporate research center, even if the Systems Science and Computer Science Labs did not pursue "research" in the academic sense of uncovering new knowledge. "We were basically building stuff," explained Tim Mott. "It was not, 'Look at this important paper I published,' so much as, 'Look at this cool thing I made'"— even if the "cool thing'" was just a string of code or a wireframe prototype.[34]

The charge of the researchers at PARC was to invent an enabling technology and demonstrate its technical feasibility: in response to a request from Xerox management that he clarify the business case for its modeless graphical user interface text editor, lab director George Pake responded, "PARC does not compare Gypsy with other products on the market because it is not a product prototype but a research prototype."[35] Once the concept of a desktop computer had been made manifest, it would be necessary to

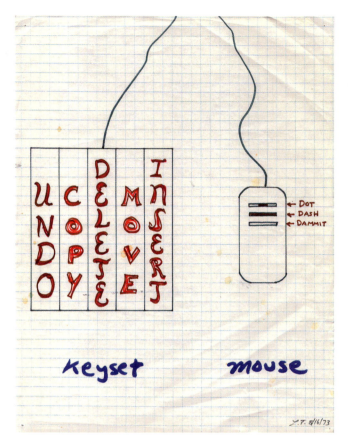

Figure 2.3

Larry Tesler, mouse-keyset label study (1973) exploring two ways to adapt Engelbart's novel input devices to contemplated experiments with a text editor for novice users. Tesler subsequently shifted to language borrowed from the publishing industry: "Cut/Copy-Paste." Courtesy of Larry Tesler.

adapt the ideal of the laboratory to the realities of the market. This responsibility fell to the Systems Development Division (SDD), a unit of Xerox geographically adjacent to PARC but organizationally separate from it. From its origins as a small systems architecture and planning group, SDD had grown steadily, and by 1976, when David Liddle took over as director, it had begun to turn seriously to commercial product development based on Xerox technology: laser printers, electronic copiers, and the famous "Xerox 8010 Information System," known as the Star.[36]

The Star incorporated all of Alto's essential innovations—the bitmapped display, the icon-based graphical user interface with its distinctive simulated "desktop" and popup menus; documents that integrated formatted text, tables, formulas, pictures, charts, and graphics in overlapping "windows"; electronic mail; printing. These were all subsumed under the category of what was variously called "user-interface" or "dialog design," concepts that were at that time very poorly understood and certainly no part of the training of any designer. Indeed, the universal adoption of such terms may obscure just how opaque they were in the mid-1970s: Budd Steinhilber recalled the day that a PARC scientist visited the offices of Tepper-Steinhilber Associates to discuss the "paperless office" of the future:

> He explained that they were developing software programs for computer systems. Since these programs would be used internationally he wanted to substitute what he termed "icons" in place of word legends. I looked over at Gene [Tepper] and silently said, "Does he mean symbols?" These icons would have to be simplified images that the user could "click on," that would act on the represented data. His list of icons included: *Document*, *File*, *Open*, *Delete*, *Print*, and *Copy*. Clicking on a selected icon would be done using something called a "mouse."[37]

Steinhilber went down the list of PARC's proposed icons but was stumped by the "Document" symbol. "A sheet of paper? What the hell can you do with a basic vertical rectangle? We didn't get the job."

In fact, the graphical information display—the choice of borders, buttons, fonts, and icon shapes—was the least important part of the overall design. The visual display certainly mattered, as did uniformity and consistency across different command applications. Of far greater importance, however, was the need to ground the design process in the conceptual model a "casual" user was expected to bring to the machine. This was the key finding of an elite team drawn from PARC and SDD's information technology group that was charged with developing a methodology to guide the design of the Star.[38] What followed were hundreds of hours of user observations, scenarios, and testing as the development team grappled with the fundamentals of user interface design.

This process was essential to the development of the Star, which, in contrast to the Alto, was always intended to be a commercial product. The person tapping on the keyboard of the 8010 or wielding its two-button mouse was no longer assumed to be a laboratory scientist but rather an executive enthroned in a corner office, a receptionist sitting at the front desk, or white-collar professionals who were interested in getting their work done—and not in computers. There was little to guide them, however, and as a result, the design process behind the Star was as innovative as the product itself: "Rather than deciding what the system would do, then figuring out how to produce interfaces, the developers engaged psychologists and designers from the beginning in an extensive set of mockups, prototypes, and user tests to see what would work, and how it could work."[39] Much as Hewlett-Packard's HP-35 calculator marked a shift in the balance between industrial and electronics design, the 8010 marked a fundamental a shift in the balance between hardware and software, one that would only accelerate in succeeding decades. The external cabinetry was refined to present clean lines and a consistent appearance, but there was never any question that the interface was the focal point of the system: "I did not go out and interview a bunch of red-shoelaced designers," Liddle recalled. "We wanted a simple housing, a keyboard without a zillion extra keys, and a mouse."[40]

As the 1970s drew to a close, and Commodore, Tandy, Altair, and Apple began to emerge from the sidelines, PARC director Bert Sutherland asked Larry Tesler to assess what some analysts were already predicting to be the coming era of "hobby and personal computers." "I think that the era of the personal computer *is* here," Tesler countered; "PARC has kept involved in the world of academic computing, but we have largely neglected the world of personal computing which we helped to found."[41]

His warning went largely unheeded. Xerox Corporation's parochial belief that computers need only talk to printers and filing cabinets and not to each other meant that the "office of the future" remained an unfulfilled promise, and in the years between 1978 and 1982 PARC experienced a dispersal of core talent that rivals the flight of Greek scholars during the declining years of Byzantium: Charles Simonyi brought the Alto's Bravo text editing program to Redmond, Washington, where it was rebooted as Microsoft Word; Robert Metcalf used the Ethernet protocol he had invented at PARC to found the networking giant, 3Com; John Warnock and Charles Geschke, tiring of an unresponsive bureaucracy, took their InterPress page description language and founded Adobe Systems; Tesler himself brought

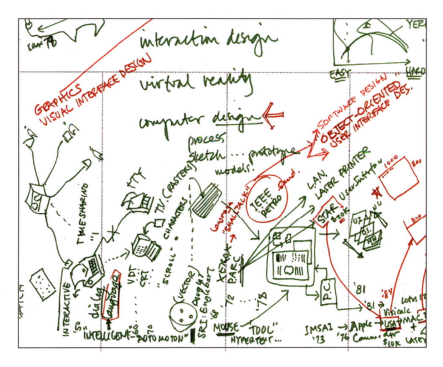

Figure 2.4
Bill Verplank, the Star Ecosystem. Courtesy of Bill Verplank.

the icon-based, object-oriented Smalltalk programming language with him when he joined the Lisa engineering team at Apple, and Tim Mott, his co-developer of the Gypsy desktop interface, became one of the founders of Electronic Arts—five startups that would ultimately pay off the mortgages and student loans of many hundreds of industrial, graphic, and interaction designers, and provide the tools of the trade for untold thousands of others.[42]

Two smaller spinoffs from the Xerox research community would influence the growth of a professional design practice in Silicon Valley even more directly. At the end of 1978, John Ellenby and Tim Mott drafted a detailed "Proposal for a Capability Investment" in which they outlined the case for commercializing the Alto under the codename "Wildflower": the technology had been proven; the market for a low-cost "personal computer" was by this time certain; the design, implementation, and manufacturing capabilities were in place, and—not incidentally—the competition was waiting in the wings. The study analyzed the short-term and midterm advantages of creating an integrated "quick reaction systems group," and identified one additional benefit, less easily quantifiable: "In the longer term we can turn out better designs and, more important, better designers.[43] Ellenby's proposal gained no hearing within the Xerox corporate structure, and one harrowing year later he left and founded GRiD Systems to pursue what his erstwhile colleague, Alan Kay, had envisioned as an "active briefcase":[44] a self-contained, notebook-sized computer that could be carried into a conference room, a combat mission, or even into space.

Ellenby's thinking had been galvanized by the comments of a staff member in the executive office of the White House, which had received one of the original Altos: "My job as a senior member of this establishment," the official had told him, "is to go where the problems are. It's not my job to hang out in the office."[45] Having overseen the development of the Alto II—whose overall dimensions, even without the display and keyboard, were roughly those of a dormitory refrigerator—Ellenby proposed that a powerful computer could be shrunk to a size that could fit comfortably into his own somewhat battered leather briefcase.

The challenges were formidable, and his previous experience at Ferranti in Britain and Xerox in the United States had convinced him that the entire team—project management, engineering, manufacture, marketing, finance, and design—needed to be sitting around the table from the very outset: "It was obvious," he said simply.[46] But when he began to interview local industrial designers he found that none of them wanted to be involved in discussions of the mechanical and electrical issues at the heart of the project. Ellenby turned instead to a fellow Briton, Bill Moggridge, who jumped at the chance to help visualize the machine in its entirety, and not simply as a problem of superficial styling or corporate identity. Although he was in over his head from day one, the industrial designer had found his place at the table and he usually got his way.

In direct contrast to the prevailing American practice, in which the designer was invited in once the overall character of the product had been established, Ellenby determined that the industrial design of the GRiD Compass 1101 must precede the other design phases: "We did this to provide the physical constraints within which the design team would work and to ensure that human factors and mechanical design were appropriate for the unique integrated product design we were undertaking."[47] The process began by fashioning an assortment of foam blocks representing the motherboard, the battery, the display, and the other large physical components, which they proceeded to manipulate in much the way that the young Frank Lloyd Wright had played with his Froebel kindergarten blocks one hundred years earlier. Indeed, the fact that it was a wholly new product category did not make all that much difference: Like any other product, commented Moggridge's partner Mike Nuttall, "You start with a cardboard box full of components."[48] Eventually they settled on a horizontal, "laptop" configuration that served to maximize both keyboard and screen size, but continued to explore many variations including one in which the keyboard slid forward and the screen was hinged at the back. Along the way they produced reams of drawings, which Moggridge dutifully submitted for the group's objective consideration, though it was Ellenby's suspicion that there was always one—executed with a bit more precision or an extra dash of color—that the designer himself favored.

As the project moved forward, Ellenby asked Moggridge's group to produce a three-dimensional appearance model, which he used to raise an initial round of seed money from Silicon Valley grandees Gene Amdahl and Robert Noyce; his engineers, meanwhile, worked to wrestle the circuit board assembly and power supply down to manageable size and weight. They found a vendor who was able to produce a compact keyboard that still met basic ergonomic requirements, and from the Osaka laboratories of Sharp Electronics secured an advanced six-inch, 320×24-pixel electroluminescent screen. On the basis of some rather creative field-testing, Moggridge developed a lightweight magnesium case that could dissipate the considerable heat generated by the machine's Intel 8086 processor, and withstand the abuse of freight handlers at Federal Express. Ultimately they produced five sleek, black working machines, which Ellenby carried with him as he went out in search of venture funding for the world's first laptop computer. The product, to be sure, represented a radical innovation and the first move toward mobile computing. Equally decisive, however, was the precedent that the designer be involved from the very outset and remain active throughout the duration of the project. This represented a turning point in the history of design whose impact would be felt not just in Silicon Valley, but across the United States and ultimately throughout the world.

Figure 2.5

The GRiD Compass 1101. Left: 2-D rendering; right: 3-D model. Courtesy of Bill Moggridge.

The stream of innovations that began at SRI and flowed through PARC and the Systems Development Division produced one other spinoff of enduring relevance to Silicon Valley design. Metaphor Computer Systems was founded in 1982 by David Liddle and his former boss at Xerox, Don Massaro. Their intended clients, like Ellenby's, were Fortune 500 companies whose analysts were beginning to experience the information tsunami of the digital age and required extremely fast, real-time access to corporate databases. This was a target population that used computers only intermittently, however—mostly they hired other people to use them—and who would be offended by the sight of a keyboard and a tangle of wires cluttering the executive suite: "Keyboards belong on typewriters," they were repeatedly told, "and typewriters belong on the desks of secretaries." The design principle, then, was to make the system seem to disappear from the desktop.

The process could not have been more different from that of their former employer, the Xerox Corporation. In the vast, autarchic empire that was Xerox, the attitude prevailed that everything should be done with Xerox's own resources and on Xerox's own timetable. At Metaphor, a six-person startup operating within an eighteen-month window of survival, this was not an option. Decisions that would have taken weeks at Xerox were made in an afternoon—or less—because there was no "installed base" of hardware, software, routinized practices, or consumer expectations.[49] Nothing was developed from scratch that could be purchased off-the-shelf, and everything that could be contracted out, was. Among their contractors was Mike Nuttall, head of the newly formed Matrix Design, who was asked to solve the design problem of the Metaphor workstation, and Jim Yurchenco of David Kelley Design (DKD), whose job was to figure out how to engineer it.

Matrix had just separated from Moggridge's ID Two, and was born of the same European tradition in which the designer is asked to create the basic configuration of a product at the outset, rather than perform an incremental styling job at the end; DKD was a new product development consultancy with its roots in Stanford's product design program and a nativist orientation toward new technologies and emerging industries. Metaphor operated like a soccer team, where every player is given great latitude within a designated position on the field, and the designers forged a tight working relationship.

The design phase, which consumed about five months, began with a set of early explorations that ranged "from the outrageous to the banal" as Nuttall and Yurchenco probed Metaphor's boundaries. Some featured flat screens that hung on walls or folded into desk surfaces; other ideas were deliberately conservative so as to avoid the contrived appearance of a product trying too hard to be different. Gradually an overall concept emerged, which was to suppress the sense of physical presence altogether. Compromises continued to be made—to accommodate Metaphor's own engineering team on the one hand and the formidable demands of manufacturing on the other—but once the strategic direction was established, the tactical design decisions fell into place.

Although it would be photographed in the glossy design annuals as if it were a standalone desktop computer, the Metaphor workstation was actually one component of a large, integrated, and extremely sophisticated system of servers, PCs, and printers, all of which were touched by the design program. As the point of user contact, however, it posed a set of exceptionally complex challenges. The workstation was distinguished by four distinct input devices (a keyboard, a mouse, a numeric keypad, and a four-function keypad) that an operator could use separately or in combination. To address the problem of visual clutter, the team redesigned the

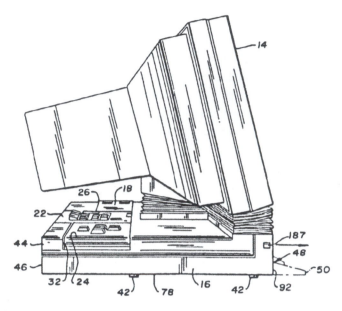

Figure 2.6

U.S. Patent Number 4,689,761 (August 25, 1987). Metaphor Workstation: Multiple Independent Input Peripherals.

components using wireless infrared technology. In the same spirit in which Eero Saarinen had gone to war against the "slum of legs" underneath typical chairs and tables, each of the input devices could now be "docked" in its own recessed recharging station, integral with the horizontal surface of the L-shaped assembly. Rubber bellows hid the vertical tilt mechanism of the CRT, and Nuttall specified a fine mesh fabric that stretched over the screen to flatten out its telltale curvature, neutralize reflection, and render it opaque to a nosy visitor sitting even a few degrees off to the side. Metaphor Computer Systems was derailed by the stock market crash of 1987—it was ultimately bought by IBM for one-third of its planned valuation—but the industrial design profession had already judged the product itself to be a winner: a letter in Yurchenco's files reads, "Faced with more than 300 entries, the jury considered your submission an outstanding example of design achievement and has awarded it the 1985 IDEA [Industrial Design Excellence Award] for office products."[50]

Ironically, all of the renderings for the GRiD Compass and the Metaphor workstation were done by hand, and every view was drawn on a separate sheet of paper—nobody, in the early eighties, was rotating 3-D wireframes with a trackball! The computer, in its inexorable march from the think tank to the corporate research lab to the market, became the force driving Silicon Valley design first as the object of design, and only then as its indispensable tool. Together with the unending stream of digital products that followed, it raised an entirely new set of challenges: What is the relation between hardware and software? Between functionality and usability? Between invention and innovation? Between an instrument to be used by technical professionals and an appliance to be marketed to the consuming public? Precisely because they were newcomers to the conversation, designers were in a position to add a distinctive voice.

The proliferation of market-oriented startups, driven by new technologies, fueled by an exploding venture capital industry, protected by armies of patent lawyers, and motivated by an unshakable certainty that they were about to change the world, permanently altered the landscape of design. It created a natural client base for nimble, independent consultancies that were in a position to leverage ideas from across companies, industries, and core technologies in ways that the corporate design offices could not. Their beginnings were modest at best: when ID Two moved out of Moggridge's Palo Alto garage it was into a former mortuary; the graduate students who formed Hovey-Kelley Design started out in a $90-a-month studio, not much bigger than a Stanford dormitory room, above Kitty O'Hare's Dress Shop in downtown Palo Alto; and the first home of Lunar Design was a month-to-month rental on the second floor of an abandoned helicopter factory in a dicey part of Menlo Park. There was a definite buzz in the air, but little indication of the sea change that was about to transform Silicon Valley into the most important design center in the world.

3 SEA CHANGE

Peter Lowe looked up from his desk at the Center for Design, a grass-roots nonprofit that had just opened its doors in a Palo Alto storefront. It was spring 1979, and the center's visitors that week already included a psychiatric nurse studying the effect of environments in cancer treatment, an elementary school teacher upset with the poor quality of pedestrian signage in downtown Cupertino, a local recycling activist, a lost (and mildly inebriated) architect from San Francisco, and two graphic designers looking for work. A tall, well-spoken Englishman had wandered in and was browsing the center's modest library of books and periodicals, and the two of them struck up an easy conversation.

The visitor had recently arrived from London, where he had left behind a flourishing industrial design practice in hopes of planting his first overseas colony. Having ruled out Italy and Japan for linguistic reasons, he had narrowed the field to the United States and its most dynamic technology centers: the established, vertically integrated corridor around Route 128 in Massachusetts, and the emerging, horizontally networked valley squeezed between Highways 101 and 280 in Silicon Valley. Like generations of prospectors before him he decided to take a chance on California, but before setting sail for the New World he had identified thirteen companies deemed "likely" clients and another twenty that were "possible." Bill Moggridge was now methodically calling upon each of them, portfolio in hand, to offer his services. Things were not going well.

Lowe was intrigued by the first ripple of what would prove to be a wave of immigration from Europe. Silicon Valley was by this time the uncontested epicenter of the new technology, and was halfway through a sustained economic boom that would last into the early eighties. Like other elements of the Silicon Valley ecosystem—venture capital, high-tech

marketing, intellectual property law, technical publishing, model-making—
the design community had grown rapidly as well, with 127 offices in Palo
Alto alone. The numbers are misleading, however: apart from the Gruyé-
Vogt organization, six partners who formed the flamboyant but short-lived
consultancy, Inova, and the Mountain View branch of San Francisco-based
Steinhilber, Deutsch, Gard, the great majority of them were one- or two-
person studios that worked on everything from restaurant interiors to
trade show exhibits to plastic parts.[1] Those who were able to gain a hearing
within the technology-centric semiconductor or disk drive industries spent
an inordinate amount of time explaining themselves to engineers who
believed their instruments already had been "designed."

Ferris & Lowe, begun in 1969 by two innocents who had just graduated
from the industrial design program at San Jose State University, was typical of the small, independent firms that would spring up in the region: "Our
intention was to jump straight in and do product and communications
design without having to 'learn the business from the ground up,'" recalls
James Ferris. "We had some fun, designed some neat stuff, got our feet wet
as entrepreneurs, met interesting people."[2] They understood themselves to
be neophytes, however, and deferred to the icons of "European" design. In
1976–77 the partners went so far as to organize a pilgrimage that brought
a dozen aspiring American designers to the offices of Philips in Eindhoven,
the Porsche Automotive Design Studio in Stuttgart, the Royal College of Art
in London, and Domus Adademy in Milan, ending up with a behind-the-
scenes tour of the Pompidou Center, nearing completion in Paris. The
accepted view was that although the opportunities were greater in the
United States, higher standards prevailed in Europe.

Adding insult to injury, they also felt neglected by the American design
establishment, which seemed to hold a Saul Steinberg-esque view of the
barren hinterland west of the Hudson. From his perch as manager of corporate design at Ampex, Darrell Staley caught the mood of many western-
ers who felt marginalized by the lofty pronouncements emanating from
"the land of Loewy, Bel Geddes, Dreyfuss and Teague." While the heirs of
the great design impresarios of the thirties remained content to cast pearls
before their swinish clients and then withdraw, "The design practice in
California demands that we are proficient in all of our design skills as
well as in the additional skills of mechanical engineering, human factors,
product planning, [and] a multitude of manufacturing techniques that the

eastern designer would probably consider beneath his dignity."[3] Some disaffected practitioners retreated into the engineering cultures of their parent companies—HP, FMC, IBM, Raychem, Lockheed, and NASA—but others chose to throw in their lot with the profession and appeal for recognition by the national organizations.

The Industrial Designers Society of America (IDSA) had been created in 1965, with "Northern California" forming one of ten original regional divisions. During most of its first decade the San Francisco chapter—which actually stretched from central California to the Canadian border—led a fairly obscure existence and attracted little notice from the national office. Only nine offices were represented in the organization in 1974, and the community was small enough that chapter president John Gard could still show up at the front doors of new arrivals as a one-man IDSA welcome wagon. Toward the end of the 1970s, however, its membership had grown restive and the SF chapter emerged, in the words of national president Carroll Gantz, as "the epicenter of IDSA discontent."[4] A new generation of industrial designers, fired by the writings of E. F. Schumacher, Victor Papanek, and the *Whole Earth Catalogue*, was coming to see corporate America as the engine of mindless consumerism and impending environmental calamity rather than the source of lucrative contracts. "Young designers wanted to design cities, not toasters," Gantz recalled, and they saw the IDSA as an inbred old boys' club—"stuffy, traditional, autocratic and bureaucratic." At the climax of the 1968 student protest movement, the old boys were holding their annual meeting at the Playboy Club in Lake Geneva, Wisconsin.

In February 1977, Marnie Jones, secretary to the IDSA-SF and a recent dropout from Stanford's graduate design program, mailed out the first issue of a monthly newsletter to one hundred members of the burgeoning design community. The first few issues were produced on a Smith-Corona portable electric borrowed from her roommate, but the feeling was that there was nowhere to go but up: "The IDSA newsletter ought to portray the personality of the society," she wrote with undue modesty, for it was the first of its kind in the nation and destined to become an active force not just in portraying but in shaping the collective personality of an emerging community: "Do we want to be seen as a bunch of stiff business-types, or a group of people who are principled, on the ball, smart, creative, practical, straightforward and financially essential to corporations?"[5] By the end of its first year the IDSA-SF *NEWS* was being read by five hundred subscribers, less than a third of whom were card-carrying members of the organization. "This is a chapter newsletter," Jones noted," but I see it as serving the local design community—not just our members."[6]

A kind of pre-Internet blog, the *NEWS* rallied people around a range of issues that helped define the perimeter of a regional design culture: environmental challenges; design for disability; design education; cross-disciplinary collaborations; the computer ("a curiosity more than anything else—it's not really useful"). Iconoclastic guest authors excoriated the crass commercialism of Raymond Loewy and ridiculed the idealized anthropometric stereotypes in Henry Dreyfuss's *Measure of Man* ("Are you still designing for this body?"). The newsletter was both chatty and informative, and the meetings it announced were fun. Monthly gatherings were strategically held at such places as the Ridge Winery in the foothills overlooking Silicon Valley, and tours of the Stanford Linear Accelerator Center or the *Klamath*—the moored ferryboat that served as the San Francisco headquarters of Landor Associates—invariably ended up in a local tavern.[7] The social dimension must not be underestimated, however, for it contributed materially to the formation of a diverse but self-conscious community of professional practice. Indeed, it was the cohesiveness of a spirited, energetic membership that emboldened the SF chapter to make a bid to host the annual meeting of the national organization.

The gathering—held at the Asilomar Conference Grounds on the edge of Monterey Bay—rattled a professional association already under siege from the left for contributing to capitalist excess and from the right for its failure to contribute more.[8] Moreover, the demand for greater social and ecological relevance converged at the landmark Asilomar conference with a movement for democratic reform that had been rising within the organization itself. It was transformative for the IDSA—"the precise moment," in Gantz's view, "that IDSA leadership began to shift from autocratic control by non-elected elders to democratic governance by rank and file members"[9]—and instrumental in thrusting the West Coast design community into a position of national and even global prominence.

Peter Lowe and Darrell Staley, who cochaired the steering committee that organized the Asilomar meeting, brought to the program a note of urgency and optimism and a characteristically Bay Area perspective that embraced technology but in a manner that was distinctively against the grain. "We were of a mind that we wanted to create something earth-shattering, mind-blowing, consciousness-raising," and they used the design process itself to get there: brainstorming over reams of butcher paper taped to the walls; letting their thinking diverge around bold themes and then converge around specific speakers who might address them; endless prototyping of promising ideas. They first considered calling the conference "Options," but dismissed that title as uninspiring. Then, with a breathlessness reminiscent of Marinetti's account of the founding of Futurism seventy years earlier, someone said, "How about this word: Thrival?!"

> We all must have spoken that word to ourselves and each other a mil-lion times in the next 24 hours. We went to sleep saying it and woke up saying, calling each other on the phone. "Thrival?" YES. Then we had to come up with a modifier . . . . It seemed to need an explanation. It needed to sound good with Thrival, to have the right rhythm, to not preach, to have the right tone. We tried on several dozen . . . . "Beyond Survival" seemed to do it.[10]

"Thrival: Beyond Survival" was meant to suggest that we have come to a crossroads and that designers must now decide whether they are to be part of the problem or contribute to its solution. "It is time to redirect our-selves, because, although technology and mass-production have increased the quality of life in some ways, and places, the current direction is life-threatening."[11] Designers can do more than pull us back from the brink; with their ability to humanize technology and visualize alternative scenar-ios, designers can help us not only to survive, but to *thrive*.

The all-volunteer effort was undertaken by a steering committee of Sili-con Valley design professionals, most of whom had day jobs.[12] The days' events were bracketed by yoga and meditation in the morning and kite fly-ing at the beach at the end of the day; the radical architecture collective Ant Farm, already famous for its *Cadillac Ranch* installation in Amarillo, Texas, displayed its *Phantom Dream Car*, festooned with TV monitors, at the first-ever IDSA auto show. James Ferris—who would soon join the upstart Apple Computer as its first creative director, designed a conference poster that depicted the earth as a fragile, glowing orb suspended between two sheltering hands. Instead of a conventional program they created a sixty-page *Thrival Manual*, dedicated to Charles Eames, who had died a few weeks before the opening.

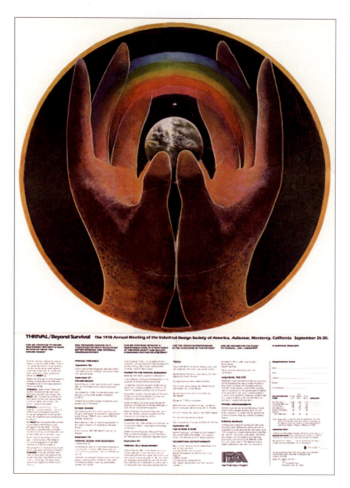

Figure 3.1

Poster announcing "THRIVAL: Beyond Survival," the 1978 IDSA National Conference. Collection of Marnie Jones.

Most important was the cast of invited speakers, many of whom had never appeared before an audience of designers. Sim Van der Ryn, appointed by Governor Jerry "Moonbeam" Brown to the position of state architect, explained the concept of "appropriate technology." A team of social scientists from the Stanford Research Institute laid out three future scenarios—"dynamic status quo extended," "economic disappointment," and "cultural transformation"—as a framework for long-term planning.[13] The keynote address was delivered by Ralph Nader, who opened the conference with a blistering attack on the design profession for its complicity in fouling the planet with products that are unnecessary, unhealthful, and unsafe at any speed—and was jeered and heckled by those in the audience who made their living doing so. The emerging generation felt that Nader had given them a voice, however, and Jay Wilson was among many Bay Areans who "left with the impression that he was on our side."[14]

In the faint California afterglow of the sixties counterculture, *Thrival* exposed deep fault lines within the national organization and announced a radical agenda that shocked many of the four hundred design professionals in attendance. Delegates from the Japan Industrial Designers' Association, the British Design Council, and IDSA members from across the United States, Mexico, and the Pacific Rim wrote to the organizers to express appreciation—or, occasionally, outrage—for their effort to broaden the perspectives of a profession that had grown complacent, conservative and overly commercial in its outlook. The members of the San Francisco Bay chapter—scorned by the national leadership as "hippies" afflicted with "the apparent disrespect of youth," came away focused, energized, and determined to seize the day.

The Asilomar meeting, held in the last days of September 1978, was, in many respects, a defining moment for a nascent design community that was beginning to find a distinct regional identity. Where they had previously clamored for recognition, activists now came to dismiss the national organization itself as parochial, self-absorbed, and irrelevant. The boundaries of the profession seemed to be dissolving, and new formations were taking shape. Spurred by an invitation from officers of the Western Art Directors' Club, a group of midpeninsula professionals began to discuss how they might leverage their common interests at a weekly picnic in Palo Alto's downtown Lytton Park. And in summer 1977, as the planning for *Thrival* was getting under way, a San Francisco graphic designer named James Stockton conceived the idea of an intimate, multidisciplinary gathering where professionals could explore ideas at the margins of their respective fields; out of this initiative the Stanford Design Conference was born.

At a time when the venerable International Design Conference in Aspen and the annual meetings of the various professional societies were almost the only opportunities for creative comingling, the Stanford Design

Conference quickly became yet another touchpoint for a community whose intellectual appetite had been whetted. Over the course of fourteen consecutive summers the organizers went out of their way to stretch the boundaries of the disciplines to the point of questioning the very concept of "design." Indeed, it was less a *design* conference than a *designed* conference: physicists and geneticists rubbed shoulders with architects and urban planners; engineers and inventors shared box lunches with photographers and cartoonists; writers and critics hiked through the foothills with dancers and musicians, while graduate students, in a bizarre saturnalian reversal, shielded their professors from the out-of-control, flame-throwing robots unleashed by Survival Research Labs. Victor Papanek, purged from the IDSA and persona non grata at most professional gatherings, was the first of the invited speakers. A barefooted Steve Jobs sat on the grass and captivated a circle of fellow twenty-somethings with his vision of the seamless integration of design and engineering. Because it favored process over portfolio, was limited to three hundred participants, and was structured to allow internationally venerated luminaries to mingle not just with one another but with students, young professionals, and visitors from outlying fields, the impact of the Stanford Design Conference was catalytic, viral, and rhizomatic, and folded into Silicon Valley's larger design culture.[15]

These were among the overlapping initiatives that led Peter Lowe and Marnie Jones to launch the Center for Design in spring 1979, with a $25,000 grant from the National Endowment for the Arts, a frightening injection of their own money, and "a liberal amount of arm twisting, chanting, and praying." From modest beginnings (a name registered with the California secretary of state, a logo, unpersonalized business cards, and a telephone line). the center soon employed five paid employees and drew upon the good will of another two-dozen volunteers who included industrial and graphic designers, a landscape architect, a photographer, an exhibition designer, an art tour director, and two practicing attorneys. Their inspiration resonated with one of the themes that had echoed across the *Thrival* conference: "Why not let the clients and users in on the design process? Why not let the children and the dogs on the set?" The next logical step, once the democratization of the IDSA got underway, was the democratization of design itself: "It's time design came out of the closet and was shared with those it is meant to benefit in the first place."[16]

The Center for Design hoped to focus the energies of a community of design professionals that was beginning to reach critical mass, to raise public awareness of the role of design in everyday life, and to foster interaction between these two constituencies.[17] Although the British Design Council had been operating the Design Centre in London since 1956, the *Internationales Design Zentrum* had opened its doors in Berlin in 1969, and national design centers could at that time be found in another sixteen countries around the world, there was no comparable institution in the United States. Rather than develop a national center, however, the founders saw this as an opportunity to explore a local model, which they described as "grassroots and humanscale." The Center for Design was expressly conceived as a prototype, viewed both by its founders and its funders as a model for similar initiatives in other cities.

Although the idea proved unsustainable in the long run, over the course of its lifetime the center—managed by what Peter Lowe described as "a core of well-intentioned dyslexics"—worked tirelessly to create a forum that would catalyze the exchange of ideas across disciplines and among disparate constituencies: *Centerline*, its monthly newspaper, announced lectures and exhibits. There were classes for specialists, the interested public, and kids. The tiny premises on Forest Avenue housed a reference library, a model shop, and a retail store that displayed "Design to Go" products on corrugated cardboard shelves. The center sponsored public service opportunities such as a special energy initiative and Project Enable, inspired by the example of Arden Farey, which set out to discover and respond to the needs of people with disabilities.[18] The partners were passionate in their desire to engage designers, clients, and the public, and at its peak reached out to some 12,000 practitioners and friends of design throughout Silicon Valley and the larger Bay Area. As Jones wrote in an effervescent letter to the National Endowment for the Arts, "The Center for Design has to be one of the most exciting projects I've ever been involved with. It is limited only by our imaginations and it seems to be coming of age."[19]

Such was the state of affairs that prevailed when Bill Moggridge walked in off the street in 1979. The Europeans—starting with Moggridge and Mike Nuttall from the UK, followed by Hartmut Esslinger and his team from Germany—did not find in the new world a trackless desert but fertile soil

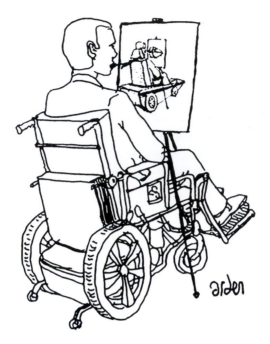

Figure 3.2
Arden Farey, by himself. Courtesy of Gwen Farey.

that had been worked by many hands. Peter Lowe nevertheless remembers asking himself, "Why are these guys coming here? What opportunities did they see in Silicon Valley that the American designers did not?"

Moggridge Associates was a respected industrial design consultancy in London, with a decade's worth of notable products in its portfolio: a prototype desktop minicomputer for Computer Technology had him thinking about ventilation, connectors, and interfaces already in 1973; a data entry terminal and a computer memory program recorder for ITT-Madrid; and a domestic fan heater for Hoover whose fluid, wind tunnel–like form expressed the flow of air through a heat exchanger and into a chilly English bedsit—or would have, if it had ever been manufactured.[20] Indeed, it was a growing competence in handling the aesthetics and ergonomics of technology products, together with the frustration of Britain's drift away from manufacturing and toward a service economy, that prompted Moggridge to begin exploring his American options. In 1979 he announced to his clients that the company would soon be opening an office in California:

"We have chosen the Bay area of San Francisco for its electronic technology and hope that this will enable us to transfer technical knowledge to our UK office."[21] Although he implied that "ID Two" was essentially a colonial outpost intended to support the imperial capital, Moggridge knew exactly what he was doing when he installed his family in a glassy, midcentury modern house Palo Alto, laid a carpet of green Astroturf in his garage, and went looking for work.

In contrast to old Britain—beset by restive trade unions, declining productivity, factory closures, and low profit margins—Silicon Valley seemed to Moggridge to be an unreal paradise. Where the European design culture was elitist and hierarchical, in California he quickly found himself embedded in "information networks," enrolled in "invisible colleges," and enjoying an unheard of level of cooperation between industry and academia, between individuals working for competitive companies, and sometimes between competing companies themselves.[22] If it was a land of opportunity, however, it was also a land of stupendously missed opportunity. Nothing in the American romance with what his compatriot Reyner Banham had called the "great gizmo" seemed to acknowledge that not just new products, but whole new product categories were emerging. In short, the space between the refined tradition of European design and the boldness of American engineering remained largely unexplored. "Here was a blank sheet of paper to work on, instead of the usual one already covered with product precedents, manufacturing equipment, and distribution channels."[23] It was a designer's dream.

Over the next few years, Moggridge steadily built up a staff, a network, and a client base, and learned to play by a different set of rules. "In an established company lots of time and effort is spent on persuading management to accept an idea after it has been formulated by the design team," he noted. In the startup adhocracy of Silicon Valley, by contrast, "when an idea was agreed on we were able to act on the decision immediately."[24] As clients like GRiD and Convergent Technology began to ensure a steady flow of work, he summoned Mike Nuttall, a graduate of the Royal College of Art, from the London office, and began to hire selectively from within the community of native born and recent arrivals. The result was a rigorous body of work that brought the technical into line with the human: "We shared a common feeling that engineering design and industrial design could be compatibly blended," stated one of his first clients; "I saw that his work married form and ergonomics with solid engineering design; and that's what I wanted."[25]

Although the marriage was indisputably historic, the courtship was not always a happy one. Convergent Technologies was founded in 1979 to supply intelligent computer workstations to original equipment manufacturers—so-called OEMs—such as Burroughs, RCA, and Honeywell. Their first offspring—a complete range of display-based computers and peripherals—was well received and Convergent grew rapidly. Three years later the company spun off an advanced information products division (AIPD) to develop and market its own line of tools for mobile professionals. Under the leadership of Matthew Sanders, whom Moggridge had met while doing some part-time teaching in the Stanford product design program, AIPD committed itself to a frenzied, twelve-month sprint to build a tablet-sized computer capable of running an integrated suite of business-oriented spreadsheet programs. The design of the proposed WorkSlate—which the Brits codenamed "Ultra"—was taken over by Moggridge's partner, Mike Nuttall.

The WorkSlate illustrates the unique set of challenges facing designers in the feverish startup economy of the period. Money was abundant—Convergent had just concluded the largest IPO in the valley's history—and the technological hubris immense. Thirty years later we think nothing of carting around an ultrathin, 8 1/2 × 11-inch tablet running an assortment of specialized apps, but in the early 1980s nearly every aspect of mobile computing was untested and unproven. The task of the designer, as Nuttall's saw it, was to balance a multitude of competing objectives to achieve a result that was "not too big, too heavy, too ugly, or too expensive." There were no precedents to guide them, and as one engineering manager conceded, "It was the blind leading the blind."[26]

This space of uncertainty, ambiguity, and compromise, however, is the native habitat of the designer: An engineer will typically focus on the technology and ask, "How does it work?" Designers, in this climate of open-ended innovation, were learning to start with the human being and ask, "How will people use it?"—a question that had been of only marginal relevance in the receding era of audio oscillators and gas analyzers. This human-centered approach, informed by an aggressive program of user-testing, helped impart to the WorkSlate both the functionality of a computer and the simplicity of a calculator.

Nuttall's restrained, classically proportioned exterior belied the insurmountable problems within. In order to achieve unprecedented thinness—under one inch—and still accommodate ports for a full range of peripherals, the circuit boards were assembled with expensive and relatively untested surface-mount technology, which drove the manufacturing cost far above the $499 target price. The marketing budget had to be slashed, denying the product full media exposure. But it was ultimately the impossibly compressed twelve-month development cycle, which drove the WorkSlate from engineering to production without an adequate test phase in between, that doomed it. Sales were dismal, quality was poor, and the product that CEO Allen Michels had boasted would "blow the GRiD Compass out of the water" sank beneath the waves.[27]

The tidal current that would drive the transatlantic sea change in Silicon Valley design originated not in Britain, however, but in the iconic, garage-based startup founded in 1976 by the unlikely team of Steve Jobs and Steve Wozniak. Everybody now knows the lore of how the supposedly introverted "Woz" cobbled together a circuit board, connected it to a keyboard and his black-and-white television set, and carted the "Apple I" over to the Stanford Linear Accelerator Center (SLAC) where the Homebrew Computer Club held its semiweekly gatherings. While the crowd studied Wozniak's innovative microcomputer, so the story goes, Jobs studied the crowd.[28]

The Homebrew hobbyists and *Popular Electronics* tinkerers who ordered Apple's fully assembled printed circuit boards from the Byte Shop in Mountain View took them home and packaged them in mitered wooden boxes and riveted metal shells. Wozniak continued to work on technical refinements—color, high-resolution graphics, faster speeds with leaner code and fewer chips—while Jobs pursued the idea of a computer as an integral, self-contained product more akin to a household appliance than technical instrument: "I got a bug up my rear that I wanted the computer in a plastic case," he admitted to the first of Apple's many chroniclers.[29] Inspired by self-contained appliances like the recently introduced Cuisinart, Jobs and Wozniak began the search for an industrial designer who could provide it.

They had already seen a preliminary design proposed by Ron Wayne, a product development engineer at Atari whom Jobs had come to know during a six-month interlude soldering circuit boards.[30] This appears to have whetted their appetite for a more refined concept, so the pair began making the rounds to the best-known local consultancies. After Noland Vogt of GVO and John Gard of Inova both declined to take the job on spec, they found their way to Manock Comprehensive Design, one of a growing number of one-person shops that had begun to spring up in the midpeninsula.

Jerry Manock was a local designer whose touchpoints included the Stanford product design program, a graduate student internship with Carl Clement at Spectra Physics, and stints at Hewlett-Packard and Telesensory Systems, a company formed to develop an assistive device that enabled the blind to read by translating optical characters into tactile stimuli.[31] Inspired by Buckminster Fuller's vision of a "comprehensive anticipatory design science," and grounded by a couple of business administration courses, Manock was building a practice with clients such as Philco-Ford, Trimble Navigation, and other technology-intensive Silicon Valley companies. The buzzword at the time was *concurrent engineering*, a model that called upon the designer to function as a systems thinker who worked hand-in-glove with tooling engineers, electronics suppliers, and everybody else who might be involved in bringing a portable radar installation or a satellite guidance system from conception to completion.

In January 1977, having installed himself in an 8 × 16-foot closet in downtown Palo Alto that he shared with a drawing board, a couple of straightedges, a hot glue gun (for prototyping), and his beloved HP-35 calculator, Manock received a telephone call summoning him to the next gathering of the Homebrew Computer Club. In a throwback to the receding era of timesharing, he arrived at SLAC to find the twenty-one-year old Steve Jobs juggling four or five simultaneous conversations. The two were nonetheless able to come to terms (Manock demanded to be paid in advance), and over the next three weeks he developed a set of mechanical drawings for a compact enclosure capable of dissipating the heat given off by Wozniak's circuit board, accommodating an internal power supply, and presenting to the user an angled, integral keyboard.

Manock proposed a sleek, wedge-shaped slab design, but it was not his intention to make a statement: "The dimensions of a standard keyboard decided the width. The dimensions of the motherboard and the power supply decided the depth. The vertical orientation of the peripheral boards decided the height. If people are typing on it the angle is going to be pretty damn close to 12º."[32] The design considerations that remained—color, radii, chamfers—allowed him to give the enclosure a softer, more approachable, more psychologically appealing look, but even these refinements were constrained by the fact that it was all drawn by hand and complex shapes would have been prohibitive. Manock arranged for the production of twenty hand-finished, reaction-injection molded plastic cases, and a proto-type Apple II made its debut at the West Coast Computer Faire in April, looking for all the world like a high-volume mass-produced product of an established computer manufacturer.

The hugely successful Apple II came fully assembled and was the first personal computer to be sold in anything other than a rectangular sheet metal box—a seemingly mundane detail whose significance, both for the computer and the design industries, can hardly be overstated. It is best captured by Steve Jobs himself:

> It was our belief that for every *hardware* hobbyist who was capable of assembling his own computer there were a thousand *software* hobbyists who were not. We thought that if we could make a computer that people didn't have to assemble you could sell a lot more—and we were right. So we wanted to put the Apple II in a housing that would reflect more of a humanistic point of view. Once we found a way to do that, the next question was, "What should it look like?" "What should it express?" "How should it work?" And that led us down the path of having to think about those things.[33]

Jobs's alleged fixation on "design," in other words, was a *function* of a strategic objective, not—as innumerable commentators have wrongly supposed—the primordial force driving it. Having committed himself to the idea of the computer as a sealed, self-contained consumer appliance, questions of design necessarily followed: the aesthetic statement of the enclosure; the software interface; the experience of unpacking the box or browsing through the user's manual—in short, the emotional valence of the entire product in all its details. Within a year Manock was billing 80 percent of his time to Apple and had more work than he could handle.

This is not to say that Steve Jobs did not bring to this program a strong aesthetic predisposition: He spoke to his closest friends of watching his father, a machinist at Spectra Physics, restore cars in their garage in Cuper-tino, and admired the post-and-lintel transparency of the Eichler houses in their suburban neighborhood; he recalled to the Stanford graduating class

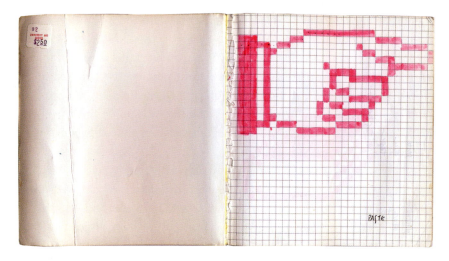

Figure 3.3

Susan Kare notebooks—icon study for Macintosh computer (1982). Courtesy of Susan Kare.

of 2005 the liberating experience, after dropping out of Reed College, of enrolling in a course in calligraphy; and he learned to appreciate the elegant geometry of Wozniak's circuits.[34] The idea of an accessible "personal" computer certainly had its origins in Alan Kay's Dynabook, but Jobs's actual education in design can be traced more directly to his association with James Ferris, who handled the Apple account at Regis McKenna, Inc., the valley's iconic marketing firm. As evidenced by the "design tours" he and Peter Lowe had organized in the earlier decade, Ferris was deeply immersed in European design culture and proved to be a knowledgeable guide and mentor. After he moved over to Apple in 1979 to become the first director of creative services, the two spent endless hours debating what made certain products great, pondering the impact of good and bad products on their users, and arguing volubly about whether the original Macintosh should be more like a Porsche or a Ferrari ("We ultimately decided the Mac could be better than either!"). Those discussions happened wherever they found themselves—at work, driving somewhere together, at meetings, at parties, flying to New York or Hawaii—and eventually evolved into a mature philosophy: Ferris recalls that "for Steve it was not just a focus on product or even brand design, but a complete design mindset, a way of thinking and making sense of things."[35]

Steve Jobs enters the picture precisely at midpoint in the history of Silicon Valley design, and is the hinge on which the entire story pivots for the simple reason that he accorded to design a place it had not heretofore occupied in any major technology corporation. This occurred both at the level of product design, but also—and of equal importance—in the design of the company itself and the image it sought to project: "Looking back," remarked Clement Mok, who in 1984 assumed leadership of Apple creative services, "I learned from him *how to design an idea*: you design the inside, the outside, and everything around."[36] As Apple's design philosophy matured, it came to encompass hardware and software, communication and advertising, annual reports, trade show booths, and Apple's famous concept of "event marketing." "When Steve Jobs used the word 'design,'" continued Mok, "he was advocating everything from hardware, software, advertising, communication, and user experience design . . . . Projects large and small were given the same level of scrutiny and attention, whether it was warranted or not."

Even with his fabled willfulness, his invasive management style, and the impenetrable "reality distortion field" that hovered about him, however, Jobs could not have done it alone. To the contrary, it was a propitious moment in which to seek out talented partners. The semiconductor era, which had defined Silicon Valley in the 1970s, was rapidly evolving into the era of what PARC's resident visionary, Alan Kay, had envisioned as the "personal computer." Core technologies were beginning to migrate out of corporate R&D centers, university labs, and suburban garages, where they were being met by a new generation of "product designers" who sought to distance themselves both from the industrial designer's preoccupation with external form and the engineer's restrictive focus on measurable performance. Individuals formed themselves more or less spontaneously into groups to work on a specific problem—vibration, for instance, or adhesives— then disbanded upon completion without further commitment and went out looking for the next opportunity. "It did not fundamentally matter who owned the client relationship," recalled Davis Masten, one of the pioneering design researchers in the region; "what mattered was the opportunity to work on products that were literally new to the world."[37]

This was the climate in which Dean Hovey and David Kelley recruited a handful of fellow graduates of Stanford's product design program: Jim Sachs, Douglas Dayton, Rickson Sun, and an MFA student, James

Yurchenco, who had taken up more-or-less permanent residence in the student shop to work on his intricate kinetic sculptures. In July 1978, with a trickle of small projects in the pipeline—a differential cell counter for Chemetrix; a modular computer housing for Zilog—they formed a partnership and rented studio space on the second floor of a downtown building occupied by a motley assortment of painters, fiction writers, dressmakers, and a consulting mathematician. "We all thought that this was an interesting gig and we would ride it as long as it worked," recalled Yurchenco, "but expected we would all be doing something else in a few years."[38]

One day Kelley walked down the street and introduced himself to Jerry Manock, and their collaboration began almost immediately: first a joystick; then the industrial design of the ill-fated Apple III. Once they had established a credible track record, Hovey felt emboldened to arrange a meeting with Steve Jobs to pitch some new ideas: "I started running down my list, and he said, 'Stop, Dean. What you guys need to do—what we need to do together—is build a mouse.'"[39] He had no idea what a mouse was.

As is so often the case, the macrocosmic world of Silicon Valley design is discernible in this seemingly granular detail. The three-button, $500 "mouse" Jobs had seen at his storied visit to Xerox PARC two days earlier was the input device, based on Engelbart's "x-y position indicator," engineered for the Alto and refined for the STAR workstation.[40] What PARC's researchers saw as a sensitive laboratory instrument, however, Jobs perceived as a key component in an emerging vision of how novices might work with computers in a way that was personal, comfortable, and even intimate (during a subsequent conversation with Hovey he ran his hand along his thigh and said that he wanted a device that would work on his jeans). The members of the Hovey-Kelley team, for their part, accepted the challenge with aplomb, although as Jim Sachs confessed in retrospect, "If he was willing to pay us $25 an hour to do this, we would have designed a solar-powered toaster for him."[41]

This episode speaks to far more than simply the cheekiness of a bunch of smart, young designers who did not even know what a mouse was, what people were going to do with it, or how it would be used. Indeed, what motivated them was precisely the challenge of working not just on a new product but a completely new product *category* for which there were neither standards nor precedents, and out of this ad hoc process a new and highly improvisational design methodology emerged. They scavenged surplus electronic parts from shops like Haltek in Mountain View and Weirdstuff in Sunnyvale, bought cheap prototyping materials from University Arts around the corner and cannibalized their own kitchen appliances when doing so was more convenient than running down to the local hardware store. Across the street from their studio was a Walgreen's, which Dean Hovey visited following his meeting at Apple; over the weekend he hacked together a spatial prototype of what would become the first commercial mouse using a plastic butter dish and the ball from a tube of roll-on deodorant.

The technology was new, but not so advanced as to be over the heads of overconfident generalists who had been taught by their Stanford professors to think of themselves as "little Leonardos." In the course of the following year Jim Sachs worked on software and developed a system of x-y optical encoders; Rickson Sun experimented with a spring-loaded roller that eliminated the heavy bearings of the Xerox mouse and allowed the ball to float freely; James Yurchenco designed an ingenious injection-molded "ribcage" that made it possible for all of the precision components simply to be snapped into place in minutes. The effect was to eliminate issues of tolerance, precision, and alignment that had made the Xerox mouse unreliable and expensive, and to deliver a design that was mass-producible for around ten dollars.

In contrast to the one-hundred-year-old automobile industry, with its test tracks and crash dummies, no equipment existed for testing the first generation of computer peripherals, nor even a clear idea of what to test for. They opted for a "miles to failure" approach, and attached their various designs to the tone arm of a phonograph set to 33 1/3 rpm, and simply measured how long it took for the mechanism to fail. They discovered Fitts's Law, which predicts the corrections made by the human brain and spared them having to achieve extreme levels of precision. David Kelley, in the meantime, created dozens of wooden models, inspired by everything from sanding-blocks to bicycle handles. "Today I'd bring in hand surgeons to make sure that no muscle groups were used unnecessarily," he reflected, "but then, we were just blasting it out." Once the general form-factor was resolved, Douglas Dayton completed the industrial design of the "hide," and by May 1980, Hovey-Kelley Design had built a working prototype.[42]

At Apple the Hovey-Kelley mouse underwent several successive refinements under the direction of Bill Dresselhaus (styling, color, and texture control) and Larry Tesler (functional performance), but no additional engineering. It was created for the Apple Lisa, a business computer designed in 1981 and introduced two years later as the first desktop system to offer a point-and-click, icon-based graphic user interface. One of the unsung heroines of the computer revolution, Lisa offered sophisticated hardware design, the first practical graphical user interface, a functional, one-button mouse design and numerous other innovations.[43] It was, moreover, a foundational experience in comprehensive product development at Apple, integrating every detail of the design process from concept through cardboard mockups and rubber-molded prototypes to manufacturing and postmarket service. Even the intemperate Steve Jobs seemed to appreciate Lisa's innovative fusion of industrial design and engineering. Pre-empting the formal unveiling, he ripped the cloth cover off the professionally machined appearance model, glanced at it briefly, and declared, "This looks like shit." Since nobody was summarily fired that day, the team interpreted this as high praise.[44]

Lisa sold poorly, however, and was eclipsed in the following year by an under-the-radar project, code-named "Annie." The inspiration for that initiative can be traced to a series of witty papers composed in 1979–80 by Jef Raskin, the idiosyncratic manager of Apple's publications department. In these explorations Raskin visualized an "anthropophilic" machine that would weigh under ten pounds, sell for under $500, and appeal even to people who took what he described as "a perverse pride" in knowing nothing about computers: "Seeing the guts is taboo. Things in sockets is taboo. Billions of keys on the keyboard is taboo. Computerese is taboo. Large manuals . . . (a sure sign of bad design) is taboo." Above all, "The computer must be in one lump." Disliking the ritual use of female names to refer to computers, Raskin's papers came to known internally as "The Book of Macintosh."[45]

Even as the Lisa advanced toward its launch date, Raskin was assembling a stealth team that included a gifted programmer, an electronics autodidact, a self-described "software wizard," a marketing specialist, and an industrial designer—Jerry Manock—who was tasked with configuring the "lump." The demands of the new program soon overwhelmed his private consulting practice, so in February 1979 Manock finally closed his office and went to work for Raskin as Apple employee no. 246.

In his new role as "corporate manager of product design," Manock set about building a team that was equal to the considerable challenges that lay ahead. Jim Stewart, who had studied industrial design at San Jose State, was the first hire. Next came Terry Oyama, who had graduated from Art Center College of Design in Los Angeles and then bounced around in a series of three-year jobs on both sides of the Bay. Manock's approach to design was shaped by Stanford's emphasis upon engineering, manufacturability, and marketing. Oyama, by contrast, had been schooled in the Art Center culture of surface, styling, and flawless presentation. Once he moved to the Bay Area he began to appreciate what was required to take an idea from concept to full-scale design layouts, and their different backgrounds merged into a close and complementary partnership. Jobs had stipulated only that the Macintosh have a vertical configuration to preserve valuable desktop real estate, and for the same reason that it be equally presentable whether viewed from the front, back, or sides. Beyond that, the designers were given a free hand, and in March 1981, Manock and Oyama presented their first design for a compact, self-contained desktop computer. With its wide forty-five-degree chamfers (to reduce visual bulk), angled top, and U/V-resistant beige-brown color (PMS 453), the Macintosh built on the design language announced by the Apple II and III but extended it in a less businesslike, more consumer-centric direction. Oyama designed the front of the case and Manock was responsible for the back; symbolic of their seamless working relationship, the screws that hold the two main parts together are concealed within the underside of the handle.[46]

The Macintosh computer had achieved iconic status even before it was released; it has often been noted that the famous Ridley Scott commercial that interrupted the Super Bowl on January 24 with the announcement that "1984 won't be like '1984'" did not even bother to depict the machine itself.[47] Long before the launch of the Macintosh, however, Manock had already begun to feel that the existence of independent and even competing product teams posed a threat to the integrity of Apple's emerging brand. His personal notebooks contain musings about an "Apple family look" already in January 1981,[48] a concern that led him to form an informal Product Design Guild that met monthly to share information across Apple's seven divisions. The roots of Apple's reputation as a "design-driven" company lie in the ongoing campaign waged by the Product Design Guild to win formal recognition (which it never did) and executive-level support (which it never got).[49]

The guild—so-named to emphasize their overriding commitment to craftsmanship—served as a clearing-house for ideas and a forum for peer critique, and a platform from which to pursue Manock's call for "a new unified appearance for the '80s."[50] At one level, the absence of a set of uniform design specifications made it seem as if Apple's products had come not just from different divisions, but from different companies. At another, this "visual chaos" was beginning to create problems for peripheral products that must live comfortably across all platforms and in all product combinations. Finally, the success of the Apple II had transformed the company from a scrappy startup to a global presence, and the time had come to shed its roots in a two-car garage in Cupertino and develop an internationally recognizable identity on the order of Olivetti, Braun, and Sony.

Several initiatives converged at this pivotal moment to raise the profile of design at Apple, both internally and externally. One proposed that the five-year-old company inaugurate a corporate design center, described by its advocates as "a dedicated facility for design" that would centralize resources, facilitate planning and communication, promote consistency across Apple's growing product line, and—not least—serve as a showcase for the interested public (Apple was by this time receiving hundreds of requests per year for tours of its facilities); the idea appears to have gotten nowhere.[51] A second was the creation of an integrated corporate identity program, driven by Tom Suiter, who in 1982 had become head of Apple Creative Services. Third was Manock's bold and personally risky proposal to launch a search for a world-class consultant to help Apple create a unifying product design language. Project "Snow White," as this initiative was called, would ultimately stretch far beyond Apple's seven divisional dwarves to complete the sea change that transformed Silicon Valley from a provincial outpost to the imperial capital design.

The Snow White competition was driven by Rob Gemmell, an industrial designer working in the Apple II Division. Although he could scarcely have been aware of it at the time, Gemmell was instrumental in bringing European design to the shores of the New World. Following his studies at San Jose State University and a stint building Star Wars spaceships for Industrial Light and Magic in San Rafael, Gemmell had secured an entry-level position with RichardsonSmith in Columbus, Ohio, the first of the national consultancies to integrate human factors, cognitive research, market analysis, and strategic planning into the design process. Within that expansive environment Gemmell had been able to work on projects that ranged from consumer electronics to landmark corporate identity programs for National Cash Register and Xerox. He also benefited from Richardson-Smith's close relationship with the design department at Ohio State University where he came into contact with Reinhart Bütter, one of the architects of "design semantics," the post-Bauhausian idea that "form follows meaning, not function."[52] From deep in the American heartland Gemmell began to read the Italian *Domus,* where he was exposed to the refined elegance of Mario Bellini and the flagrant eroticism of Ettore Sottsass, and the German *Form,* where he encountered the *"weniger, aber besser"* ("less, but *better*") minimalism of Dieter Rams and the emotion-driven formalism Hartmut Esslinger.

By December 1980, Gemmell had entered the master's program at OSU and was working on a thesis on "The Use of Computers for Creative Professionals" when—with much fanfare—Apple Computer went public; a couple of months later he found himself in Cupertino being interviewed by Jerry Manock and Terry Oyama. Emboldened by his global perspective and corporate branding experience, Gemmell embarked almost immediately on a campaign "to get Apple thinking bigger." Manock was receptive, Oyama was enthusiastic, and Steve Jobs—who had announced to the Product Design Guild that, "I want our design not just to be the best in the personal computer industry, but to be the best in the world"—approved a budget to send the three designers to Europe to assess the state of the art.[53]

In April 1982, traveling first class (as if to put themselves in a suitable frame of mind), Manock, Oyama, and Gemmell stopped first in London where they met with principals at Pentagram and Moggridge Associates, and then to Paris to see the industrial designer Roger Tallon. In Milan they interviewed the iconoclastic Ettore Sottsass, who had lately jolted the European design establishment with the undecipherable products of his Memphis studio. Mario Bellini declined on account of potential conflicts of interest with Olivetti, as did Dieter Rams because of his work for Siemens. Within two months they had narrowed the field to Esslinger Design, located in the tiny village of Altensteig on the edge of the Black Forest, and BIB, the London consultancy run by Nick Butler and Stephen Bartlett. Each firm was presented with an eleven-part brief, a set of product specifications covering everything from radio frequency interference shielding to cable management, and a description of the seven product categories to be unified under a common "Snow White" design language: a business work station based on the Lisa computer ("Doc"), a home computer based on the Apple II ("Sneezy"), an entry-level Macintosh ("Happy"), a "book" computer imagined as an electronic clipboard ("Bashful"), a mouse ("Sleepy"), a desktop dot matrix printer ("Grumpy"), and an external floppy disk drive ("Dopey"); there was also "Flower," a 5.25-inch external hard drive named after the fragrant little skunk in *Bambi*.[54] Each firm was given six months, and a budget of $50,000.

BIB was representative of a growing effort among design firms to gain access to strategic decision-making at the boardroom level. Many companies perceived such initiatives as a threat to the personal fiefdoms of their middle managers, and there were (and remain) gifted formgivers within the design community itself who felt that to reach beyond the singular object was to venture into alien territory where they had nothing to contribute. Apple, however, seemed to be inviting precisely that level of engagement. Stephen Bartlett, who led the initiative for BIB, likened the opportunity to Pirandello's *Six Characters in Search of an Author:*

> The absolute fascination of the Snow White challenge was that in Apple we found a set of characters in search of their identity. What were these products for? What were they going to become? How could we develop a visual language that would be functional but at the same time capture the romance and poetry of what would be seen as an extraordinary episode of innovation?[55]

Both designer and client understood themselves to be exploring territory that was largely uncharted under rules of engagement that had yet to be written.

If Steve Jobs sent his three emissaries across the Atlantic in search of "European sophistication," he most certainly got what he paid for. BIB developed a family of models in dark anthracite gray in defiance of "the blandness of West Coast beige." Their slab forms intersected with a dramatic angularity that referenced the edgy software they delivered rather than what Butler called the "soapy forms" and "unadventurous style" of contemporary American office equipment. Chamfers—Manock's signature device for reducing the visual bulk of an otherwise blocky machine—were nowhere to be seen. A dimpled "golfball" texture served both to confirm the kinship among the disparate products and to compensate for the limitations of injection molding, which at that time resulted in disfiguring flow lines, drab surfaces, and a film of grubby static. Finally, recognizing that flat screens were on their way, BIB rendered the monitor "future safe" by allowing the enclosure to scale down as new technology became available without requiring new tooling or compromising the overall design language.

The visual rhetoric of BIB's submission spoke more to the brooding sultriness of the Black Swan than the naive innocence of Snow White. Indeed, so different was it from Esslinger's that there was speculation that the two firms had not been given identical briefs (Jobs was known for his strategy of "management by conflict"). Whereas BIB aggressively embraced the technological edge, Esslinger retreated into a collection of soft forms and light colors that were more approachable and—recalling the terminology Jef Raskin had used in conceptualizing the Macintosh—"anthropophilic": tightly rounded radii, zero-draft tooling, an off-white palette, and keyboard graphics executed in a slanted Garamond typeface combined to extend the user-friendliness of the Mac software to its hardware as well.[56] On March 13, 1983, the Apple executive staff gathered for a formal presentation of the competing concepts from England and Germany; the row of identical Porsche 911s in the parking lot, plated "Apple 1" through "Apple 10," foretold the outcome, and contract negotiations with Esslinger Design began.

Hartmut Esslinger had approached Snow White less as a design competition than a world-historical clash of *Weltanschauungen*. The Americans had gotten stuck, he felt, because they had defined the problem in the reductive terms of design language, whereas the stakes were actually much higher: "Olivetti never had a design language; they had a design *philosophy*. Braun had a *philosophy* behind it. At Sony we had a *philosophy* of how to do things." It was not that his American counterparts were not competent designers, but that they had been trained to approach their work either as stylists or as engineers. This discipline-bound parochialism prevented them from seeing the larger challenge, which was "to find a way to give cultural expression to a new technology," and to do so in a way that captured the essence of the new company: "simple, white, innocent, sexy, and a bit more radical."[57]

Figure 3.4

"Snow White" competition. Top: BIB Design, bottom: Esslinger Design. Courtesy of Stephen Bartlett and Hartmut Esslinger.

The language of "culture" and "philosophy" may seem eccentric in the mundane context of product design, but it is crucial to appreciating the "fusion of horizons" that would impart a European character to the products, process, and profession of design in Silicon Valley.[58] Esslinger's roots in the spiritually dense environment of Swabian Pietism show up clearly in his uncompromising manner and his postfunctionalist philosophy that "form follows emotion." His education at what was then the craft-oriented *Werkkunstschule* in Schwäbische Gmünd grounded him in the history of aesthetics—from the Babylonians to the Bauhaus—to a depth that was uncommon in American art schools and unheard of in the American engineering curriculum. Finally, in the charged political climate of post-Nazi Europe the example of America's popular culture provoked a level of conscious engagement with democratic ideals that inspired both the accessibility of his design concepts and his notoriously antiestablishment demeanor. The day after he saw *Rebel Without a Cause* the thirteen-year old Esslinger took a bus to the American military base at Stuttgart where he was able to score a couple of authentic Fruit-of-the-Loom T-shirts.

Esslinger Design was formed in 1969, and quickly gained recognition for its work for German clients including the consumer electronics company WEGA and the dental equipment manufacturer KaVo. In 1975 Esslinger negotiated a long-term contract with the design magazine *Form*, where his striking back-cover ads were seen by a small population of worldly Americans, including Rob Gemmell. Contracts with Louis Vuitton in France, Texas Instruments in the United States, and especially Sony gave the company an increasingly international presence, and Esslinger in turn began to hire talented designers from abroad: Stephen Peart and Ross Lovegrove, both from London's Royal College of Art, followed by Jack Hokanson, a young Californian who showed up broke at his studio in Altensteig in search of an internship. Hokanson brought the technical skills he learned in Germany back to the Bay Area where he opened a model-making business, and was soon working for companies such as HP, Atari, Sun Microsystems, and Apple. Esslinger traveled regularly between Germany and Japan, and in January 1982, during a stopover in California, Hokanson threw a small party in his shop where he introduced him to Gemmell. A year later, fortified by an unprecedented $2 million retainer, Esslinger began shipping precision shop equipment from the Federal Republic of Germany to the newly formed frogdesign USA.[59]

Less than a decade separates the naive idealism of the Palo Alto Center for Design and the founding of the professional consultancies that would become the signature of Silicon Valley design. IDEO, formed out of the merger of Moggridge's ID Two, Mike Nuttall's Matrix Design, and David Kelley Design, was literally a union of European design and American engineering. frogdesign brought to California a tradition of Continental design theory with roots in the Bauhaus and Ulm, if not Kant and Schiller. And these were only the largest of an expanding ecosystem of ever-greater diversity and complexity. If their beginnings were small, however, their ambitions were large, and the future seemed full of promise and prosperity. As Ariel sings, in *The Tempest*,

> Nothing of him that doth fade
> But doth suffer a sea-change
> Into something rich and strange.

4   THE GENEALOGY OF DESIGN

A famous poster hangs in the lobby of many a Bay Area company (and, not incidentally, the library of Stanford's Graduate School of Business). It depicts an electrical engineer's version of a genealogical tree in which roots and branches are reinterpreted schematically as the gates and switches of an integrated circuit. The signal originates in a cell labeled "Shockley Transistor" and propagates first through Fairchild Semiconductor; from there it pulses outward into Intel, National Semiconductor, Advanced Micro Devices, and a rectilinear maze of third-, fourth-, and fifth-generation technology companies that turned the orchards of Santa Clara County into the macroprocessor of Silicon Valley. We can visualize the design firms of the valley as a subsystem within this densely integrated network. At its source are IDEO, frogdesign, and Lunar, the friendly rivals that begat much of the complex ecosystem of studios, partnerships, virtual consultancies, and one-person boutiques that place the Bay Area at the global epicenter of professional practice. Their offspring, and the offspring of their offspring, continue to propagate.[1]

In terms of sheer numbers, the proliferation of design offices located or headquartered in the Bay Area is unequalled anywhere in the world, but that is only one part—albeit a very large part—of the story. The other concerns the continuous expansion of the field of professional practice itself. New product categories—interactive video games, educational software, telepresence surgical equipment—called forth new methodologies and even whole new fields of design practice. Industrial design, having exhausted the modernist dogma that "form must ever follow function," incubated the field of interaction design. Market research was supplanted by user experience design. Ergonomics, with its preponderant focus on physical affordances, evolved into human factors, which extended the field of analysis to the cognitive, emotional, and behavioral dimensions of product use.[2] In successive waves, a new cast of specialists trained in the social and behavioral sciences took their seats alongside the artists and engineers who had already laid claim to the title of "designer."

To be sure, the expanded field of professional practice is not specific to Silicon Valley. What is unique, however, is the intimacy and immediacy of the relation between the new technologies and the designers who were enlisted to render them accessible, meaningful, and pleasurable. The migration of the personal computer from research lab to retail outlet—to take only the most obvious example—can be traced within the circumference of an easy bicycle ride.

The groups around Bill Moggridge, David Kelley, and Hartmut Esslinger were nourished, as we have seen, by the computer industry; clients such as GRiD Systems, Convergent Technology, and Apple Computer provided them with long-term retainers or at least a steady supply of work that allowed them to expand rapidly within the Bay Area and ultimately to plant colonies across the nation and overseas. Kelley, who had simply wanted to work on "cool stuff with a few friends," found that he was forced to grow his firm because the work kept coming: "You were just inundated in those days. Somebody comes in the door—you don't know who his is—saying, 'Could we put a case around their computer boxes?' and they turn into 3Com or Rolm or Zilog. Jim Clark [founder of Silicon Graphics] comes in; I don't know who he is—*he* doesn't know who he is yet! We just couldn't keep up with the frantic pace of how fast things were moving."[3]

They also expanded functionally, adding new capabilities to meet the requirements of new technologies, new companies, and new industries. It is one thing to improve upon an existing kitchen gadget, but quite another be asked to design a mouse or a modem. The Silicon Valley consultancies, accordingly, were forced to develop new competencies to deal not just with new products, but with new product *categories* in which precedents did not exist and the shopworn homilies about form and function no longer applied, and in which cognitive and behavioral issues were as critical to product success as line of sight or lumbar support.

Even as they grew, however, the young consultancies worked hard to sustain internal cultures that would support creative problem-solving, right-brain thinking, and—not the least of it—an atmosphere that was sufficiently entertaining to keep underpaid designers from being lured into the corporate design offices of their clients. Awards ceremonies, sponsored by the IDSA and *Business Week* and fueled by ample supplies of Absolut vodka and Ghirardelli chocolate, created opportunities for intermingling. "Thirsty Thursdays" became an after-hours ritual for the multitudinous community of designers working within walking distance of Palo Alto's University Avenue, and teams from competing firms still hop on their mountain bikes and make the twenty-five-mile trek to the ocean. Despite the volatile environment of Silicon Valley the design consultancies experienced surprisingly little cross-company raiding, but the entrepreneurial nature of the business encouraged ambitious individuals to peel off and start their own firms, which they did on a regular basis.

The GVO partnership was probably the first to calve off an independent group when Peter Lowe, who had joined as marketing manager following the demise of the Palo Alto Center for Design, rallied three of his younger associates—Jeff Smith, Gerard Furbershaw, and Robert Brunner—and created Interform in 1982.[4] Ironically, GVO's success in positioning itself as *the* regional consultancy seemed to Lowe to have narrowed the firm's focus just at a point when "Silicon Valley" was poised to become a global brand. Running a VisiCalc spreadsheet on his Apple IIc, Lowe persuaded his prospective partners that by pooling their complementary talents, they could create the first Bay Area consultancy with a truly international presence.

Interform's first years were challenging, but the company gradually began to win projects from national clients: General Motors, which was already beginning to think about embedding computers in cars; the *6000* series cabinet system through which Steelcase hoped to emerge from the shadow of the design-driven Herman Miller Company; a concept car for John DeLorean (who never paid) and a programmable universal remote for CL 9, the company started by Apple cofounder Steve Wozniak (who did). Within three years, *ID Magazine* was reporting on "a pace-setting California design firm [with] a million-dollar-a-year success story."[5] Lowe courted prospective clients by promising them "West Coast eclecticism," while Peter Müller, who had moved over from frogdesign, lectured visiting journalists about Interform's ability to meld Silicon Valley technology with "European" styling. Having worked in the diverse environments of Germany, Italy, and England, Müller knew perfectly well that "in Europe there is no such thing," but to their American clients it made for a good story.[6]

Although he himself had instigated the defection from GVO, nobody was more surprised than Peter Lowe when he returned from vacation to the news that his partners had conspired to follow in the tradition of the "Traitorous Eight" who had deserted William Shockley's lab twenty-five years earlier. Lowe's business plan had been to grow the company rapidly by investing heavily at the front end: an edgy space designed by Ace Architects; top-tier photographic, legal, and public relations services; ads in the *Wall Street Journal*; and a corporate ID program directed by the prominent San Francisco graphic designer Michael Vanderbyl, who created the stretched-out *inter f o r m* logo. The aim was to project the image of a mature and successful firm, despite the fact that Interform was still, in the words of one of the partners, "operating on vapors." Smith, Furbershaw, and Brunner, by contrast, believed that the more prudent strategy was to pursue slow, organic growth, build a reputation for excellence, and preserve their dwindling supply of cash. In the end, the two strategies proved irreconcilable. Robert Brunner had done some moonlighting while completing his studies at San Jose State and the idea had occurred to him to print up business cards depicting a lunar eclipse. The name stuck, and in December 1984, the three defectors sent out announcements of the "Lunar Launch."[7]

In comparison with the methodical strategy Peter Lowe had mapped out for Interform, the business development efforts of the Lunar team were amateurish at best—a salesman who worked out at Furbershaw's gym had an idea for a device to help warehouse employees carry large boxes; an advertising guy he ran with during lunch breaks offered to make an introduction to one of his clients. This was not unusual, however, as nearly all of the firms operating at that time were small-scale operations, led in many cases by idealistic MFAs who had little patience for such pedestrian concerns as a "business plan." Even the larger consultancies operated on a bare-bones, time-and-materials model that had not changed much since the glory days of the 1930s. The partners had closely monitored the impact of frog, ID2, and Matrix, however, and in a spirit of what Brunner would later call "oblivious optimism," they decided that "if they could do it, so could we."[8]

In time, the content-driven "organic growth" strategy paid off: Jeff Smith learned to become an effective project manager, Gerard Furbershaw deepened his knowledge of small-scale manufacturing, and Robert Brunner emerged as the obvious design talent in the group. At one strategic moment, their nonexistent financial margin even yielded an unexpected benefit: To save money, the partners agreed to swap studio space to a couple of engineers in return for training in AutoCAD, the first generation of computer-assisted design tools capable of running on a desktop computer. At a time when most design work was being done with mechanical pencils on drafting tables, Lunar became one of the earliest adopters of the software tools that would soon become the price of entry to the field.[9]

Serious project work eventually began to trickle in. Zehntel hired them to work on a large chip-testing machine, and Droidworks, a subsidiary of Lucasfilm, gave them a lucrative contract to design the furniture, hardware interaction, and modular controls for an audio- and video-editing console. Such high-profile, widely published projects gave them a degree of stability, exposure to engineering-intensive programs, and the opportunity to develop their newly acquired CAD skills. The decisive opening came from Bill Dresselhaus, however, a Stanford design graduate who had worked with Peter Lowe in the early seventies and had advised the Interform group on engineering processes. Having joined the Lisa team at Apple, Dresselhaus tapped his friends at Lunar for assistance in a minor subassembly—not a particularly memorable job, but it proved to be their entrée to the most coveted client in the valley. With the dethronement of Steve Jobs in 1985, Apple's exclusive relationship with frogdesign had begun to chill, and Lunar was positioned to assume an increasingly important role over the next several years.

Too important, as it turned out: by the end of the 1980s, Bob Brunner was spending nearly three-quarters of his time on Apple projects, including a low-cost computer geared to the education market and conceptual studies for a portable, and he had developed a well-articulated point of view: the Snow White language was aging, and needed to evolve if the company was to move forward. This inevitably caught the attention of Richard Jordan, director of product design at Apple, who invited him to move from consultant to employee. After declining twice, Brunner finally yielded to the inevitable and in 1989 agreed to join with the understanding that his role would not be to manage Apple's network of outside contractors but to build an internal industrial design group within the company. He remained at Apple from 1989 to 1996—"between Jobs," as he later quipped—during which time he hired the core of what would become the most widely admired (and obsessively secretive) corporate design group in the world.

With the departure of Brunner—or, more accurately, his transition from partner to client—Lunar had to come to terms with a changed landscape that posed challenges and opportunities. The most obvious expression of this was the recognition that if the partners were to attract clients that were operating at the leading edge of technology, they would have to deepen their own engineering capabilities. The first move in this direction was to strike an alliance with a high-level engineering consultancy, Product Genesis in Cambridge, Massachusetts—a relationship that proved difficult to sustain for both geographical and cultural reasons. With the end of this partnership Lunar took the plunge and in 1996 began to build its own internal engineering group under the leadership of Robert Howard, who moved over from Apple's printer group.[10] The combination of strong industrial design and growing skill in computer-aided rendering and complex surface modeling allowed them to move beyond simple enclosures ("panel-and-hinge" jobs, in the vernacular of the trade) and resulted in award-winning work that helped to define some of the innovative product categories of the nineties: the PowerBook, with Apple Computer, which was the first commercially viable laptop; the O2 Workstation for Silicon Graphics, whose curvilinear surfaces referenced the modeling capabilities that would be made possible by the machine itself; the acclaimed Velo 1 Personal Digital Assistant for Philips; and—probing the outer limits of medical technology—the paradigm-shifting da Vinci robotic system for Intuitive Surgical.

Medical instrument design operates under an entirely different framework from consumer electronics, where development times are impossibly short and the closest thing to a regulatory agency is the annual COMDEX show in Las Vegas. Both, however, are revealing of the dense professional networks that are a defining feature of the region, and in which it is often possible to track the entire developmental cycle of a new product—from laboratory science to engineering prototype to design, testing, and marketing—all within a fifteen-mile radius. The personal computer is the most obvious example; remote or "telepresence" surgery is another.

In his 1990 grant application to the National Institutes of Health, Philip Green, director of the Bioengineering Research Laboratory at SRI, had made a radical claim: "Through telepresence we can create a 'virtual reality' by which we can project our full motor and sensory capabilities into remote or hostile environments, into microscopic and macroscopic environments, and even into environments that exist only in a computer memory."[11] NIH was interested in enhancing the effectiveness of minimally invasive laparoscopic surgery and seemed to be the logical source of funding, but the proposed technology was conjectural at best. After the second of his NIH grant applications was rejected as impractical, Green resubmitted it unchanged, but added a video showing him using the system to slice a grape; it was immediately approved.

With support from SRI, NIH, and subsequently DARPA (which was exploring means of providing emergency medical intervention in battle zones or in space), Green led a medical engineering team that exploited recent advances in stereo imaging, telecommunications, sensors, and robotics.[12] By 1995 they had built a prototype telepresence workstation and demonstrated that an operator, wearing stereographic glasses, could manipulate a robotic arm equipped with "wristed" microsurgical tools without having to overcome the counterintuitive fulcrum effect of a human hand wielding an inflexible surgical instrument through a cannula.

Just as Douglas Engelbart had sought—a few years earlier and a few doors down—to augment the human intellect and not simply to automate it, the goal of the SRI telepresence concept was to enhance the skill of the surgeon rather than to replace it. From fostering collaboration among geographically distributed knowledge workers to enabling robot-assisted surgery, SRI clearly had no shortage of gifted visionaries, but as a divisional administrator reluctantly concluded, "In the case of Doug [Engelbart] and Phil [Green], the vision exceeded their capacity to realize it."[13] The concept underlying the SRI Telepresence System was ultimately licensed to a trio of medical entrepreneurs—John Freund, Frederick Moll, and Robert Younge—who founded Intuitive Surgical Devices to bring it to market. Within two years they had built a first prototype of the da Vinci robot, nicknamed "Lenny."

A team of world-class engineers at Intuitive evolved the technical platform to include an immersive haptic environment for the surgeon, a four-armed electromechanical actuator, and scalable software capable of stabilizing a beating heart or neutralizing the tremors in the hand of a skilled but aging physician. What they did not have were the ergonomics, usability studies, or a clear idea of the "statement" they wanted the system to make. Freund and Younge both came to Intuitive from the Acuson Corporation, which had worked with Lunar on its pioneering Sequoia digital ultrasound system: "We were 'on the list,'" surmised Jeff Salazar, now Lunar's vice president for design, when he learned that they had landed the job.[14]

Since 1543, when Andreas Vesalius first made it acceptable for the medieval doctor to descend from his academic chair and operate—"ex cathedra"—on a human subject, surgeons have been inching closer and closer to their patients. In the da Vinci system, they were suddenly being asked to reverse this five-century trajectory of hands-on practice and retreat to a workstation in the far corner of the operating room, outfitted with stereoscopic goggles and force-feedback manipulators. This was a wholly unfamiliar environment for physicians trained largely in a craft tradition in which touch, smell, and sound were paramount. The engineering challenge was to make it work. The design challenge was to make it usable.[15]

The team at Lunar approached the problem in the way that designers throughout the valley were learning to approach highly constrained, technically complex, systemic problems: at the Stanford University Hospital they studied the temporal "workflow" of an operation as procedures passed between doctors, nurses, and technicians. At the client's premises in the Stanford Industrial Park they analyzed the spatial dimensions of the operating room environment, where real estate runs to $600 per minute. To gain empathy, they spent hours learning to suture up a pig.

While the engineers at Intuitive perfected the mechanics and informatics of the system, the designers at Lunar developed a process that focused on the human experience. This began with a series of "immersion studies" intended to engage the client in a discussion of possible operator environments, from a fully enclosed module to an open frame that fell somewhere between a racing motorcycle and an exercise machine. Back in their Palo Alto studio they built adjustable mockups of an interactive console that both male and female surgeons would find approachable, comfortable, and that allowed them sufficient freedom of movement. They ultimately developed a swoopy design language that transformed the robot and monitoring equipment from an assemblage of scary technology into a visually integrated suite. Although there was really nothing with which to compare it, in 1999 the IDSA conferred upon the game-changing, paradigm-shifting, $1.5 million da Vinci Surgical Robot System its highest honor: a gold medal in the medical equipment category.

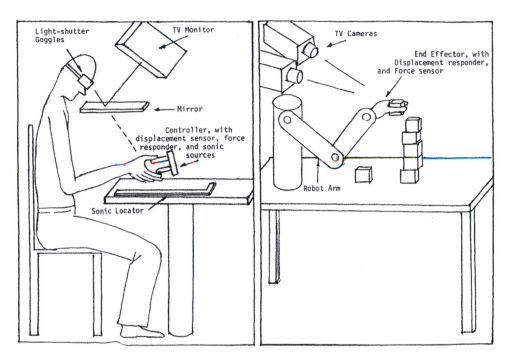

Figure 4.1

Philip S. Green, Preliminary sketch for a remote manipulator with Telepresence (1984).

The original da Vinci system was designed without any useful precedent and there were inevitable learnings as it came to be deployed in hospitals in Germany, Belgium, and the United States. Laparoscopic surgeons, who previously had to stand for hours over a patient while staring upward at an overhead video monitor, loved it, but nurses tripped over the cables and banged into the robotic arms and dreaded the herculean task of cleaning it. Intuitive CEO Gary Guthart readily acknowledges that the first pass at ID was something of an afterthought: Lunar's designers had not been brought in early enough, and when they were it was with the instructions, "Give us some aesthetics so we can sell it as a commercial product." In the second iteration, therefore, Intuitive's engineers worked closely with an independent designer, Ricardo Salinas, to shift the focus to the overall experience not just of the surgeon, but of the entire surgical team: fiber optics replaced the fat copper cables that had snaked along the operating room floor; Salinas advised them on how to contain space to reduce collisions, decrease

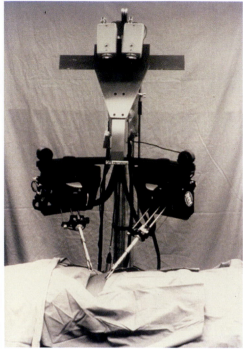

Figure 4.2
SRI Telepresence prototype: dual remote manipulators and stereographic cameras
(c. 1995)

weight, and further reduce the overall visual mass; they returned to a more subdued language appropriate to a medical environment and a product with low turnover and an exceedingly long life expectancy.[16]

The major consultancies were thus well positioned to capture work that explored the fringes of late twentieth century product development. Functionally diverse, technically proficient, and equipped with state-of-the-art prototyping equipment, they created practices attuned to the fast-paced, high-pressure startup mentality of the companies that hired them. None of them had anything even approaching a rigorous design methodology: frogdesign offered a program of "strategic integrated design" in order to shift their clients' thinking from discrete objects to integrated systems. Lunar rallied behind the slogan that "Form Follows It All" to capture the idea that a product's "function" had to include emotional appeal, ease of use, manufacturability, and the integrity of a brand. The iconoclasts at

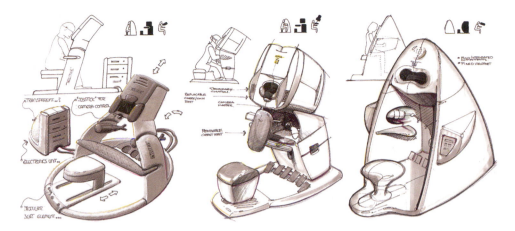

Figure 4.3
Intuitive Surgical and Lunar Design: "levels of immersion" (1998). Courtesy of Lunar Design.

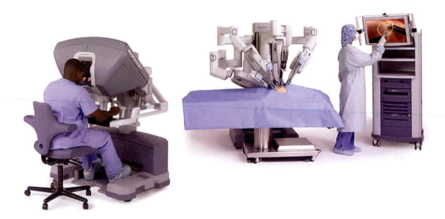

Figure 4.4
Intuitive Surgical and Ricardo Salinas: Da Vinci System (2002–2012). From laboratory science to commercial product in a fifteen-mile radius. Courtesy of Intuitive Surgical.

David Kelley Design learned to *FLOSS* regularly, using "an effective decay-preventative design methodology" that had proved to be of significant value: *Fail sometimes, be Left-handed, get Out there, be Sloppy and Stupid.*[17] Many a client would make the rounds of the three firms looking for the best price and the best fit.

ID Two, which had decamped by this time from Palo Alto to the decidedly hipper environment of San Francisco's North Beach, may have taken the boldest stride in conceptualizing the emerging class of hardware/software artifacts. Bill Moggridge had experienced something of an epiphany while working on the GRiD Compass in the early eighties: The idea of a hinged "laptop" computer in which the screen folded down over the keyboard was a radical innovation (one of forty-three that were named in the patent award), but as soon as he began to experiment with a working prototype, he found himself drawn to the *other* side of the screen: "Almost all of the subjective qualities that mattered most to me were in the interactions with the software, not with the physical design." For half a century the Bauhausian framework of "art + engineering" had helped designers deal with complex mechanisms. It could not, however, address the issues involved in designing a complex interaction. "My frustrations and rewards were in this virtual space."[18]

Although the designers at ID Two—principally Moggridge and Bill Verplank—may have earned what Nietzsche called "the lordly right of giving names," the foundations of the new discipline of interaction design had been laid at least a decade earlier by a familiar cast of players. Emblematic of the incestuous lineages that populate the genealogy of Silicon Valley, the corporate legacies of Ampex and Xerox converged in the anarchic culture of Atari and the freewheeling world of interactive gaming.

Atari was founded in 1972 by Nolan Bushnell, one of the more colorful technopreneurs of Silicon Valley lore. Bushnell had supported his engineering studies at the University of Utah (which, under the leadership of Ivan Sutherland, had built one of the world's pioneering computer science departments) by working at an amusement park outside of Salt Lake City—an oft-cited detail that neatly captures his lifelong fascination with the intersection of high technology and popular culture. Unable to land his dream job at Disney, Bushnell settled for Ampex, which provided him with enough spare time and spare parts to experiment with inexpensive transistor-to-transistor logic (TTL) circuits that he attached to a modified black-and-white television set. In 1972, together with fellow Ampex engineer Ted Dabney, he launched his own company.[19]

Atari was, at that time, almost the only major Silicon Valley technology company oriented expressly toward consumer products: where HP and Intel had stumbled, Atari skyrocketed to success with the release of *Pong*—the hypnotic, utterly mindless, but spectacularly popular diversion that is credited with launching today's $12 billion video game industry.[20] Bushnell's business model was predicated on the migration of the video game from the garish demimonde of pool halls and carnival midways to the more respectable milieux of student unions, shopping malls, and ultimately the family den. Like other social climbers, from Jay Gatsby to Vito Corleone, electronic gaming never fully shed its lowly origins in what Bushnell called the "cacophony and dissonance" of the pinball arcade. But to the extent that designers of consumer products must reach beyond technical solutions and address a multitude of human factors, this subcultural phenomenon decisively affected the trajectory of Silicon Valley design.

The first designer to work in the nascent video game industry was none other than George Opperman, the "O" in the original GVO consultancy, whom Bushnell hired to create the Atari logo—a stylized letter "A" whose arms were meant to suggest two combatants locked in a mortal game of *Pong*. During the formative period in which Opperman worked on the cabinets of its coin-operated machines, Atari's sales roughly doubled every year, its offerings expanded from *Pong* to some twenty-four hard-wired video games, and the machines themselves continued their relentless march from pizza restaurants and bowling alleys into the suburban home, where they would initiate millions of adolescent males into a virtual world in which, in the caustic estimation of an early industry observer, "the eye seemed to short-circuit the brain and deal directly with the hands and the adrenal gland."[21]

As Atari's product line grew and diversified, so too did its stable of designers. In 1973, Chas Grossman, one of the original members of the design team at Ampex, moved over to become the first manager of an internal design group that included Roy Nishi, George Faracco, and Regan Chang. Corporate I.D. worked first on particle-board "coin-ops" and then on the first generation of home video consoles, most notably what can only be called the game-changing Atari Video Computer System, the third version of which was skinned in a simulated wood-grain cabinet in order to assert its place among the furnishings of the domestic interior.[22] It was the designers of the games themselves, however, who formed the head and heart of the company. Many of them—beginning with Al Alcorn, creator of the original *Pong*—became high priests of a cult-like community they were conjuring in real time. Long before undergraduates could major in game design at USC or the Academy of Art University in San Francisco, these sorcerers practiced a dark art for which precedents did not exist and parameters had yet to be defined. Accordingly, their eccentricities were tolerated to a degree that was unusual even within the permissive culture of the valley. In 1975 Bushnell negotiated a deal by which Sears became the exclusive distributor of *Home Pong*, the industry's first foray into the home entertainment market. During a visit to Atari's manufacturing facility in Sunnyvale, one of the suits from Chicago peered at the hyperkinetic visuals of a game called *Video Music* and innocently asked, "What were you guys smoking when you did that?" The designer, obligingly, reached into his desk and showed him.[23]

Although it paid them poorly, Atari held the developers of its driving, shooting, and sporting games in awe and treated them with respect. In 1976, however, in need of an infusion of cash to finance his vision of a home computing business, Bushnell agreed to a buyout by Warner Communications and Raymond Kassar, a well-tailored marketing vice president at Burlington Industries and Harvard MBA, replaced him as CEO. Kassar's attempt to transfer his management skills from textiles to technology was contentious in the extreme. Profits soared during his five-year tenure, but relations between the designers and management began to deteriorate almost immediately. He publicly derided them as "high-strung prima donnas" and dismissed a delegation of supplicants by telling them that, "Anybody can do a cartridge. You are no more important to that game than the guy on the assembly line who puts it together." Alan Miller, the first of what would become a wave of defectors, recalled being summoned to a gathering in the company cafeteria in which Kassar introduced himself and explained how he intended to straighten out Atari's erratic course:

> The question just came up, "What's your background?" He said it was from the textile industry, importing fabric and stuff like that.
>
> Somebody asked him, "Well, how are you going to interact with electronics designers?"

He said, "I've worked with designers all my life."

I remember saying to myself, "What does he mean by that?"

He went on to say, "The towel designers . . ."

I was like, uh-oh, we're in for a lot a trouble. This is going to be a disaster.[24]

And a disaster it was. By the late 1970s games like *Gran Trak 10*, *Battlezone*, and *Adventure* were selling in the millions, and "designer" at Atari was coming to be recognized as something other than "the glorified term for programmers."[25] In the early years, the same individual was responsible for everything from concept to execution: "You had the idea, wrote the program, created the graphics, did the sound effects, chased down bugs, tested the game on kids, revised it until you were satisfied, and wrote a draft of the game manual."[26] Once they had figured out how to display pixels on an 8×8-inch screen, color them, and move them around, however, game design began to follow the same trajectory of professionalization as industrial design, which became progressively disengaged from manufacturing, and graphic design, which separated itself from the craft of printing.[27] As the underlying technology progressed, design became an increasingly distinct function. And as had been the case of its neighbors in adjacent disciplines, the professionalization of game design brought with it the expectation that game designers be treated like professionals.

Of the first generation of polymorphs and polymaths, a few, like Warren Robinett, were trained in computer science; others, like Alan Miller and Rob Fulop, had studied electrical engineering; Dona Bailey, the only woman in an original group of about thirty, was a software engineer; as their numbers swelled they would be joined by artists, musicians, zoologists, or college dropouts who simply had a gift for conceiving a primitive story and crafting it in code. None of them, obviously, was trained in the field they were collectively inventing. Indeed, it was largely a desire to be recognized as masters of a new art—rather than "dime a dozen" hacks, as Kassar had called them—that led almost all of the original superstars to take flight: Alan Miller, Dave Crane, Bob Whitehead, and Larry Kaplan—the "gang of four"—left Atari in 1980 to found Activision, the first third-party game developer; Howard Delman, Roger Hector, and Ed Rotberg—the "three stooges"—launched the electronic entertainment company, Videa. Bill Grubb, Bob Smith, Denis Koble, Mark Bradley, and Rob Fulop—the "Numb Thumb Club"— founded the short-lived Imagic; Warren Robinett recalled that "those of us who stayed at Atari called ourselves the Dumb Shits Club."[28]

The most remarkable of the Atari spinoffs, however, went not in the direction of entertainment but education. Robinett had always been interested in the capacity of interactive graphical media to simulate complex phenomena—"vehicles which move cargo through spaces, kayaks in swirling river currents, planets orbiting their stars, competing creatures in evolving ecologies, human thought darting across a tangled network of knowledge." His parting gesture upon leaving Atari had been to hide an "Easter egg" (his signature) in an obscure corner of *Adventure*, following which he turned from "large lumbering dragons [and] slow slithering snakes" to math education. Together with Ann McCormick Piestrup, an educational psychologist, Teri Perl, who had just completed a PhD in math education at Stanford, and biologist Leslie Grimm, Robinett secured a grant from the National Science Foundation to study "Early Learning of Geometry and Logic using Microcomputers." For their first product, *Rocky's Boots*, he developed an interactive graphical simulation that used the familiar elements of an adventure game—connected rooms and moveable objects— to teach second- and third-graders how to solve problems in Boolean logic. *Rocky's Boots* was clearly not the usual sort of adventure game, however; in fact, he wrote, "It was not an adventure game at all. Rather, it was educational software set in an adventure game world of rooms and objects."[29] Although the designer took some liberties in order to render difficult concepts accessible to eight-year-olds, *Rocky's Boots* represented one of the earliest forays into the field of educational software opened up by the availability of inexpensive microcomputers, particularly the Apple II. Once their NSF grant ran out, the partners secured venture funding and it became the flagship product of the Learning Company, the most prominent among the first generation of educational software publishers.

The spectacular growth of game design has produced an unending torrent of books, fanzines, websites, conferences, lawsuits, and degree programs, as well as a slew of learned journals (*J. Games and Culture*, *J. Gaming and Virtual Worlds*). It has also generated a body of theory whose roots lay unexpectedly close to the source. John C. Wakefield, Atari's first president, insisted from the very outset that game development involves more than coding and storytelling and requires "an in-depth understanding of human behavior to determine what challenges, frustrates, gratifies, and motivates

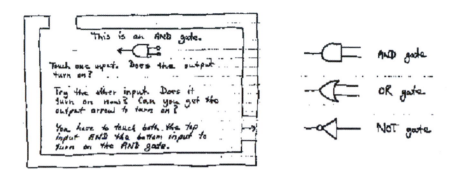

Figure 4.5

Warren Robinett, sketch for *Rocky's Boots* (1980): connected rooms and movable objects. Courtesy of Warren Robinett.

people." This would have been unusual language coming from an engineer or an MBA, but was lingua franca for Dr. Wakefield, a clinical psychiatrist whose training included a medical residency at the famous Menninger Foundation in Topeka. Wakefield was running a practice in Los Gatos specializing in "organizational diagnostics" at the time he was tapped—by his brother-in-law, Nolan Bushnell—to lead the company.

Wakefield recognized that in contrast to the passive, inflexible, and nonprogrammable character of broadcast television, video games are inherently interactive. Indeed, to an extraordinary degree, the professionalization of interaction design at Atari can be traced to an intensifying scientific interest in the fundamental cognitive structures, behavioral processes, and learning strategies that are mobilized during creative play. In that respect, Atari's program ran almost exactly parallel to those of a cluster of advanced research centers including the Artificial Intelligence Laboratory directed by Seymour Papert and Marvin Minsky at MIT, the Stanford Artificial Intelligence Laboratory (SAIL), founded by John McCarthy, and the Learning Research Group (LRG) at Xerox PARC, led by the visionary Alan Kay. "Unlike conventional mediums," Kay had written in a special issue of *Scientific American*, "the computer medium is active: it can respond to queries and experiments and even engage the user in a two-way conversation."[30] When Atari's board of directors stressed to potential investors that "[their] games are designed with great emphasis on game theory and player psychology,"[31] they were tapping into not just a new market segment but an embryonic vision of the computer as a profoundly new medium of creative interaction.

Nor were these merely independent trajectories, for in the warped space of Silicon Valley, parallel lines inevitably meet. For the better part of a decade, Alan Kay and Adele Goldberg had been hauling Palo Alto middle schoolers into the LRG lab to gauge their ability to use his object-oriented programming language—Smalltalk—on what he called the "Interim Dyna-book" and what his colleagues in the neighboring Computer Science Lab called the Alto. Failing to inspire Xerox management with his enthusiasm for educational technology, in 1982 Kay joined the PARC Diaspora to become chief scientist at Atari Systems Research Labs. As surely as game theory pointed Atari's star designers to education, education theory led one of PARC's major luminaries into games.

The details, of course, are somewhat more complicated. In 1982, the year in which the video game industry crested and began its precipitous decline, the cash-rich company asked Kay to help set up a corporate research center with the mission of conducting basic research into the future of interactive multimedia. Kay acknowledged that this was a risky venture and that a respectable company such as Hewlett-Packard would have been a more logical career move. It was precisely Atari's consumer orientation, however, that appealed to Kay's populist vision of transparent interfaces and $1,000 computers that were simple enough to be used by children: "You cannot beat Atari's base," he told an interviewer in explaining his decision to join Atari Research Labs. "They are the very people I said I was interested in for 15 years, so it's really put-up-or-shut-up time."[32]

While Atari's industrial designers busied themselves with coin-ops and consoles, Kay set about recruiting a cadre of gifted young researchers from MIT's Architecture Machine Group, the computer science department at Carnegie-Mellon, and PARC. Mostly they required little inducement. By the early 1980s personal computers had begun to proliferate, but almost nobody at that time foresaw how deeply they would penetrate into every corner of daily life or grasped how they might be used as creative tools and not simply expensive calculating machines: "It is the first metamedium," Kay argued, "and as such it has degrees of freedom for representation and expression never before encountered and as yet barely investigated." Even more important, he felt compelled to add, "it is fun, and therefore intrinsically worth doing."[33] Here was the ultimate opportunity to engage in what

Douglas Engelbart had called "bootstrapping," to develop the conceptual tools of a discipline in formation.

From its two-story building in Sunnyvale, the Atari Research Laboratory provided a generously funded environment for a research staff distributed, like characters in an Evelyn Waugh novel, between "upstairs people" working on interactive software and "downstairs people" working on circuits and chips.[34] As prankish as some of their antics may have been (the creation of an avatar—"Art T. Fischell," loosely modeled on MIT Media Lab director Nicholas Negroponte—to run the lab during Kay's prolonged absences; the proposal for an interactive video game that dolphins and humans could play together), their investigations prefigured developments in voice and gestural interfaces, data visualization, and virtual reality that would become mainstream in the following decade. At its peak the lab employed around 100 researchers who roamed freely from theoretical physics to cognitive science to improvisational theater.

The overall mission of the Sunnyvale lab was to explore ways in which next-generation electronic technologies might engage the full range of intellectual, physical, and emotional faculties of the people who used them. Formally, this program was pursued within "visibility clusters" representing such hybrid practices as interactive animation, a games research group under the erratic guidance of ludiologist Chris Crawford, and information environments, which included a media room outfitted to study the integration of voice, touch, gesture, image, and sound. Additionally, the lab supported numerous "special projects" carried out by members of its talented but eclectic research staff. Randy Smith, who had been laboring to explain relativity theory to his undergraduates at U.C. Davis by means of equations, found that at Atari he could build interactive simulations that slowed the speed of light to ten or twenty miles per hour without otherwise violating fundamental laws of physics: "Here was a way to get a feeling *in your bones* for the meaning of relativity. Here was a way for people of any age to learn about what the universe is like and how it works." Brenda Laurel applied her background in theater to the study the poetics of narrative fantasy on the interactive stage of electronic games. Robert Stein, wishing to understand how people will navigate the coming world of ubiquitous information, designed an imaginary question machine and recruited a twelve-year-old faculty brat from Stanford to record every question that occurred to him in the course of an average day; Michael Naimark, not to be outdone, conducted a parallel experiment with the twelve-year-old descendant of an Ifugao headhunter in the Philippines.[35]

The program that most ambitiously embraced the lab's interests in education and entertainment was a collaborative effort to build an "Intelligent Encyclopedia"—an idea first broached by Vannevar Bush in his 1945 vision of the "Memex," driven forward by ARPA's Information Processing Technology Office (IPTO), and given its first incarnation in Project Xanadu, the hypertext protocol conceived in 1960 by Ted Nelson.[36] In 1981, Bob Stein, a streetfighting political activist who had been bitten by the technology bug, rather brazenly sent Kay a 125-page paper describing a future collaboration among such dissimilar entities as the Encyclopedia Britannica, the Xerox Corporation, and LucasFilm. Although linkages among high culture, mass media, and the technology industries had not even entered the realm of cyberpunk fiction, Kay read it through in one sitting and announced, "This is exactly what I want to do." Within a year a group of Atari *philosophes* was laying the conceptual foundations of an infinitely scalable, self-correcting, richly interconnected *Encyclopédie*. Stein's original, still inchoate vision was of a book that was somehow augmented by audio and video, but it evolved under Kay's prodding into a form that was not just multimedia but interactive. "This 'intelligent encyclopedia' you're so interested in," Kay chided him: "Don't you think the *readers* might have something to contribute?"[37]

It is no small undertaking to reinvent a genre that has existed, in one form or another, since Pliny the Elder: questions had to be resolved at the level of overall system architecture down to details of graphical icons and whether to indicate a link by means of font, color, or boldface; text, graphics, animation, and sound needed to be integrated in such a way that an entry on, for instance, the theory of harmonic motion might allow a user to flow seamlessly from reading a text to viewing an image to the experience of hearing, and even swinging a virtual pendulum or plucking a vibrating string. Insofar as it was driven neither by technology nor markets but by a focus on the user's experience, the encyclopedia project exemplifies yet another passage from science and engineering to design and design research. Staggering in scope and unprecedented in scale, it challenged the patience of innovators who knew that their reach exceeded their grasp. It also challenged the patience of the executives at Atari's parent company,

Figure 4.6

"A third grade class studies various aspects of space travel. The group on the right is running a simulation of a Mars landing while the students on the left are studying a design for a spacecraft."[69] From a series of scenarios created for Warner executives to show how the Intelligent Encyclopedia might be used, rendered by Disney animator Glenn Keane (1982). The kid in the back row is doing what kids in the back row always do. Courtesy of Robert Stein.

Warner Communications, none of whom had a computer on his desk or grasped the potential of the lab they had bought.

As Alan Kay became increasingly removed from the day-to-day operations of the lab—memos to him routinely concluded, "If we do not hear from you we will assume . . ."—Kristina Hooper Woolsey, who had joined the migration from MIT's Media Lab to the West Coast, was anointed de facto director. Woolsey rallied her troops with the prediction that "within a year or two we can really establish ourselves as a first class research outfit, out of the traditional ilk and onto the most important problems of the times,"[38] but it was not to be. In 1984, beset by plummeting stock prices, riven by internal scandal, and with the catastrophic overproduction of Pac-Man cassettes munching into its profits, Warner Communications abruptly sold off the company to Jack Tramiel, who shifted Atari's focus from video games to home computers, summarily fired a large part of the research staff, and closed the lab. Woolsey, who had the thankless task of presiding over its demise, put a brave face on it, assuring the various project teams that their work was cutting edge and that "it is Atari that is in trouble right now and not us," but to no avail. The end came swiftly and without notice: reminiscent of the final days of the Bauhaus fifty years earlier, security guards pulled up in vans, ordered the creative staff to gather up their personal belongings, and marched them out of the building.[39]

The cyclone that tore through Atari Labs scattered the seeds of interaction design to the far corners of Silicon Valley, whose boundaries were already spreading beyond the narrow peninsula of Santa Clara County. Some drifted north across the Golden Gate Bridge to LucasFilm in Marin, others over the Santa Cruz Mountains to Plantronics in the south; a significant number landed in a converted garage in downtown San Francisco where Apple Computer had established a skunkworks dedicated to the future of multimedia education.

Apple had just released the groundbreaking Macintosh (1984), but despite the familiarity of its desktop metaphor and the friendliness of its "icons," the interactive possibilities of the new medium remained largely unexplored. A road map, of sorts, had been sketched out in a visionary project called the "Knowledge Navigator," conceived by Alan Kay and CEO John Sculley during a year of brainstorming, and executed over an intense six-week period by a team headed by Hugh Dubberly, director of Apple creative services. In this futuristic dramatization, a tweedy Berkeley professor uses voice, gesture, and an interactive touchscreen device (mocked up by Gavin Ivester of the industrial design group) to plan a multimedia lecture on deforestation for which he summons up current research data and extrapolates it dynamically into the future, all in collaboration with a remote colleague (who chides him for doing everything at the last moment); a bow-tied intelligent agent meanwhile reminds him of impending meetings, appointments, and his father's upcoming birthday. Members of Apple's various design groups recall walking out of the first internal screening of the Knowledge Navigator, scratching their heads, and asking one another, "How are we going to do that?"[40]

If the Knowledge Navigator suggested a vision of a fully interactive multimedia experience, the HyperCard application and programming tool, provided multimedia designers with a tool for realizing it.[41] Developed by Bill Atkinson of the original Macintosh team, HyperCard used the visual metaphor of stacked index cards and allowed designers to address a set of challenges that had been incubating throughout much of the preceding decade: How might new technologies support creative investigation and expression? How might technology and media companies collaborate to create products that enliven the educational experience? How might multimedia help "smudge the line" between teaching and learning?

These were among the questions taken up by the Apple Multimedia Lab, whose mission was to ensure that as the computer migrated from the office to the schoolroom it embodied "sights and sounds" and not simply text- and data-processing capabilities. Codirected by a cognitive scientist (Atari's Kristina Hooper Woolsey) and an educational psychologist (Sueann Ambron), the Multimedia Lab became a magnet for the first generation of Bay Area designers seeking to enhance the educational potential of the computer through image, sound, and video.[42]

In pursuit of answers the lab formed partnerships with organizations including LucasFilm, National Geographic, the Smithsonian Institution, the Audubon Society, and the Bettmann Archive, as well as a network of contractors and volunteers that ultimately grew to over one hundred people. Using methods found in every designer's toolkit—storyboarding, scenario-building, iterative prototyping—the lab generated some two dozen "design examples" intended to illustrate the possibilities inherent in the new medium to internal constituencies within Apple as well as potential partners and developers.

The design examples were typically three-month, $50,000 exercises in sketching out rough product ideas: "Voices of the Thirties," designed by Nathan Shedroff and Abbe Don in collaboration with a team of local school-teachers, brought to life first-person narratives of Steinbeck's America; "Life Story" was a program for learning about the structure of DNA. The signature achievement of the lab, however, was a sprawling Visual Almanac that can be seen as a first step toward fulfillment of Atari's unrealized vision of an electronic encyclopedia. Consisting of a videodisc, CD-ROM, and companion volume, it brought together a vast repository of information, graphics, video clips, images, and sounds, encoded onto 7,000 hyper-linked "data cards" from which students could build their own dynamic presentations. In contrast to the quick-and-dirty design examples, the

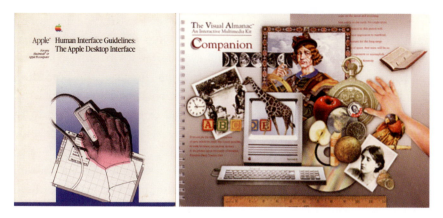

Figure 4.7

Left: Apple Human Interface Guidelines (1987); right: Companion volume to the Visual Almanac (1988–89).

Visual Almanac was an extended two-year project undertaken by the core Multimedia Lab staff but supported by another thirty people recruited from the Bay Area's nascent community of interaction and interface designers. In the years before the famously impenetrable veil of secrecy descended over Apple, this noncommercial project played a crucial role in defining the community that would soon populate the city's so-called Multimedia Gulch. As Charles Kerns, one of the lab's core staff, noted in retrospect, "Since everyone I meet these days . . . calls himself a designer—and no one did in 1988 – the Lab was part of the movement to make design a common word/act."[43]

Of at least equal significance is the fact that the Visual Almanac, like the Multimedia Lab itself, was research-based and design-driven. Although nobody doubted that computers would continue to get faster, smaller, and cheaper, by the mid-1980s the basic technology platform had sufficiently matured to allow the conversation to shift from "Can we make it work?" to "What should we do with it?" This is, as we have seen repeatedly, the type of question that designers are better positioned to answer than scientists or engineers, even though those identities might reside within the same lab, and even in the same person. "Engineers know how to lay the technical foundations," Woolsey remarked at a roundtable discussion at UCLA. "Designers . . . are people who have the beginnings of ideas about things and the intention to make these things real."[44] The strategy underlying the lab's methodology, accordingly, was to allow the core design team to create a set of experiences, and then present these as goals to be met at the corporate level. At a time when most internal design groups were still clamoring for recognition, the idea that design might drive engineering and marketing decisions—rather than be driven by them—represented a dramatic reversal of the sequence that prevailed in even the most progressive companies.

The Multimedia Lab never found a viable business model for its new media creations, and the closed world of the videodisc was soon to be overtaken by the infinite universe of the World Wide Web. The experiment concluded, nonetheless, on a note of accomplishment, with a grand party at its premises on Sacramento Street that attracted a significant percentage of the San Francisco design community. In contrast to the unceremonious demise of the Atari Research Labs, the "Golden Age of Multimedia" ended not with a whimper but a bang.[45]

The designers who worked in the Apple Multimedia Lab described themselves as scouts whose mandate was to explore new territory, plant an outpost, and try to attract a wave of pioneers who would settle it: "We stick around for the transition," declared the authors of the Visual Almanac, "but then we're off to find the next outpost."[46] Indeed, even before the lab was absorbed into Apple's educational technology group, its priorities were shifting from the creation of professionally authored products to handing authorship over to the users themselves. "I am not that interested in products right now," Woolsey told an interviewer in 1992; "I am more interested in [people] being able to make casual media themselves."[47]

This populist ethos resonated with the work Woolsey had already done in developing a set of guidelines for the Apple desktop interface, which was based on the self-evident idea that while people may not have years of experience with computer systems, "what they do have is years of experience with their immediate world."[48] As computers passed from the rarefied domain of programmers and kit-builders into the hands of nonprofessional "casual" or "discretionary" users, the ability of designers to understand and work with fundamental cognitive structures became increasingly central to their overall process.

The task of theorizing "the interface for the rest of us" was dispersed among numerous units at Apple, including the Human Interface Group (HIG), managed by S. Joy Mountford, a human factors expert recruited from the aerospace industry. Mountford had been working on cockpit displays for military aircraft, where tolerances are exceptionally tight and the consequences of error potentially catastrophic. Coming from a highly technical background she was bemused by the smiley-faced little Mac and puzzled by the idea that anyone would deliberately purchase a computer with such limited power. Her professional training had given her a deep empathy for the human subject, however, which she brought to her work at Apple. Capturing the nature of the interface as computer use expanded beyond the workplace and the restrictive desktop metaphor became the defining mission of her lab.[49]

As the HIG grew and diversified, it also evolved: from "design police" enforcing the newly codified human interface guidelines against the crimes and misdemeanors of the various engineering divisions, to prototyping and testing its own demonstration products, to a growing emphasis on interdisciplinary collaboration and original user experience research. Mountford believed that if computers were to gain truly widespread appeal, computer scientists and designers would need to overcome their mutual mistrust, and interface designers in particular would need to understand the mental models people brought to them. To do so they would have to turn outward and develop research methodologies attuned to the behaviors of people other than themselves, but this was not so easily done. Usability testing, while not unknown in the software industry, was in its infancy and there were few protocols to be followed or trained investigators to be found.

Mountford's solution was to leapfrog the narrow field of computer professionals and seed the next generation, which she did by sponsoring the annual University Workshop Interface Program: beginning in 1990, some 500 students at eight selected universities were given a design brief and challenged to respond with working interface prototypes based on observed needs and continuous user feedback. Students had the opportunity to work on real world problems with real-world constraints, and the Human Interface Group was able not just to survey the field of emerging talent, but to play a formative role in bringing it into being.[50]

Indeed, the enduring legacy of the Apple HIG was not its contribution to the QuickTime video editing program, the QuickTake digital camera, or WalkAbout, a project for a personal annotatable audio recorder. It was, rather, its role in cultivating a community of interface designers, more than 100 of whom worked on its projects as full-time researchers, student interns, contractors, or consultants. Nor was this simply a question of critical mass, for there is a point at which a quantitative increment sets off a qualitative shift. Laurie Vertelney captured this critical phase change in her contribution to a pioneering collection of essays whose scope was hammered out in the course of an intense three-day HIG retreat in December 1988: "In the 1970s there were hardcore mainframe programmers who wrote programs for other programmers; at the other end of the spectrum, there were graphic designers who were steeped in print media. In the Human Interface Group at Apple we begin to see the first new members of the rare species of eclectic interface designers." By bringing together graphic designers and computer programmers, the HIG played a decisive role in forming what was, in effect, the latest in an ongoing progression of new design disciplines. "The next step," Vertelney predicted, "will be designing the whole-product user interface, which can more elegantly be described as Interaction Design."[51]

Vertelney's insight was prescient. Only a few years earlier, Bill Moggridge and his associates at ID Two had concluded that a new framework was called for that could humanize the digital experience, just as he had been trained to do in the weighty realm of the physical: "Like industrial design, the discipline would be concerned with subjective and qualitative values, would start from the needs and desires of the people who use the product or service, and strive to create designs that would give aesthetic pleasure as well as lasting satisfaction and enjoyment."[52] At a conference in 1984 Moggridge proposed the term "soft-face" design, but the appearance that season of the puffy-cheeked Cabbage Patch dolls upstaged him and he thought it best to reconsider. "Interface design" had already been claimed by the software community even before the landmark Gaithersburg Conference on Human Factors in Computing in 1982, and "dialog design" seems never to have left the hillside redoubt of Xerox PARC. "Interaction analysis" was an increasingly popular field among anthropologists, but for the design community it represented a postindustrial terra incognita. For that very reason they settled, ultimately, upon "interaction design."[53]

By the time of its canonization in the San Francisco studios of ID Two, then, interaction design had endured the trauma of birth at Atari, a carefree childhood at Apple, and—as we shall see—was about to enter a promiscuous adolescence at Interval Research. The outlines of a mature design discipline were taking shape, even if its boundaries remained indistinct, its core concepts unformed, and its practitioners few. This lack of definition translated into a huge field of opportunity, however. Just as the pioneering work of Henry Dreyfuss in anthropometrics only came to fruition when Niels Diffrient codified it in *The Measure of Man*, Moggridge wrote in an unsuccessful attempt to recruit Vertelney, "you are capable of becoming the Niels Diffrient of Interaction Design."[54]

Recapitulating the process by which "game design" evolved out of the enforced cohabitation of computer scientists, software engineers, and hackers, "interaction design" had to be cobbled together out of existing specializations: Starting with the multifaceted Verplank, whose work on the Xerox STAR interface has earned him widespread renown within this emergent community, Moggridge went on a hiring spree that ultimately netted Tim Brown, a recent graduate of the Royal College of Art; psychologist Jane Fulton Suri, who would move "human factors" from ex post evaluation of defective products to a proactive role in the design process itself; Naoto Fukasawa, who had left the corporate design office at Seiko Epson and was en route to becoming a superstar in the Japanese design firmament; and Peter Spreenberg, among the first to have put the words "Interaction Designer" on his business card. By the end of the decade a diverse and talented team was in place. All that was needed was a client with big ideas and a big budget to support them.

They did not have long to wait. As the newly hired manager for human factors and industrial design at the Xerox Corporation, Arnold Wasserman had watched in shocked disbelief as the company's sophisticated copiers lost 50 percent of their market share in the previous five years to cheap, single-function retail machines from Japan.[55] The response from Xerox's engineers was to add features and functionality, which only made matters worse: service calls from their customers' office managers continued to rise, as did calls from their procurement officers to Canon, Ricoh, Minolta, and Sharp.

Determined to grasp the problem at its roots, Wasserman launched what would become a benchmark in the evolution of user-centered design research. From his base at corporate headquarters in Rochester he sent his human factors experts out into the field to find out why ruinously expensive service calls were increasing. Statistically, they determined that most of them were made by an office secretary, typically young and 95 percent of the time female. Confronted with a paper jam or an empty toner cartridge, she approached a control panel that resembled the flight deck of a DC-10 and searched through a flip-card deck of instructions (assuming nobody had walked off with it). If she managed to pry open a discretely engineered service panel with no visible affordances without breaking a nail, she had the option of thrusting her arm into a tangle of oily gears and inky rollers or doing what any sensible, smartly dressed, underpaid office assistant would do: place a service call.[56]

Wasserman recognized that if Xerox hoped to get anything out of its $50 million annual investment in research it would have to move from the invention of individual technical artifacts to the development of a coherent design language to unify them and a formal design strategy to guide their development. With his focus shifting from Xerox's vaunted technology to the "environment of use" in which it was deployed, he first enlisted the support of John Rheinfrank at the respected Fitch RichardsonSmith consultancy in Ohio to lead the development of a comprehensive design strategy based on these insights.[57] He also began to spend increasing amounts of time on the West Coast, slouched in the iconic bean-bag chairs and pecking away at the desktop Altos that could be found in every cubicle at PARC, and mingling with a tribe of Berkeley anthropologists who had penetrated the sanctum sanctorum of one of the world's most technology-intensive research labs.

It had been a point of pride among the first generation of PARC's researchers—which at one time claimed fifty-eight of the world's one hundred leading computer scientists—that they were seen as oblivious to the copier side of the business that paid their salaries. That began to change during the tenure of John Seely Brown, who arrived at the lab in 1978 and was thrilled to find that "a suit from corporate" had taken an interest in the cadre of anthropologists, sociologists, ethnographers, and linguists he had hired into his cognitive and instructional sciences group (CIS). Thus began a new collaboration between "JSB's" social scientists and Wasserman's industrial and interface designers in the form of the Operability Project. As the lab entered its second decade, the questions raised by some of PARC's most forward-thinking researchers shifted from "How do we build them?" to "How do they use them?"[58]

To be sure, a subliminal design orientation was discernible at PARC even from the beginning. In January 1971 Allen Newell—who was serving as an external consultant to Xerox—drafted a proposal in which he noted that the first generation of computer scientists, having regarded their field either as a natural science or a technological discipline, had been almost completely indifferent to matters of human and organizational behavior. To the cofounder of the field of artificial intelligence this represented more than simply a lacuna in information science, for as Newell hinted, "There is a substantial payoff (in dollars) to be had by really designing systems with detailed understanding of the way the human must process the information."[59] He went on to suggest that "a psychological research unit within a computer science-oriented industrial research laboratory" might be the ideal context in which to redress this imbalance.

Three years of difficult negotiations followed, but in 1974, with sympathetic lab directors Bert Sutherland and Robert Taylor providing political cover, PARC director George Pake agreed to fund a ten-year effort to build a theory for predicting human behavior in symbolic environments and a methodology for designing human–machine interfaces based on that theory. The Applied Information-Processing Project (AIP), jointly led by Stuart Card and Thomas Moran of PARC, and supported by Newell from his base at Carnegie-Mellon University, sought to provide a conceptual foundation for the design of interfaces such that, as Newell dared to imagine, "the tasks of programming and even coding can conceivably be viewed as design tasks (if design is taken, e.g., as the devising of artifacts to attain goals)." Significantly, in the final chapter of their foundational text, *The Psychology of Human–Computer Interaction*, Card, Moran, and Newell stepped down from their scientific empyrean to offer "Advice to the Designer."[60]

The untested notion that the social sciences might profitably be brought to bear upon such esoteric fields as machine intelligence and systems architecture marked a dramatic inflection point in design research—"It is rather close to becoming a new Zeitgeist," Newell predicted. But the importation of psychology and linguistics—albeit a heavily mathematicized cognitive psychology and a rigorously computational linguistics—was only the beginning. A nucleus of PARC's computer scientists had grown impatient with what Austin Henderson described as "the mismatch between the rigidity of computer technology and the richness of human life."[61] Prominent among them was Jeff Rulifson, who had joined the migration from

Engelbart's Augmentation Research Lab and was managing PARC's office research group. Seeking to escape the myopia of both marketers and mathematicians, and inspired by his reading of Piaget and Lévi-Strauss, Rulifson organized a study of office procedures at a Xerox sales center in Santa Clara in hopes of identifying the sorts of underlying regularities that computer scientists are trained to recognize. Dissatisfied with his own results, however, and feeling the need for an epistemological counterpoint, Rulifson took the highly unusual step of recruiting a coterie of young Berkeley anthropologists to approach the problem from the perspective of irregularities, discontinuities, and adaptations. The contrast between the schematics of the computer scientists and the narratives produced by the social scientists—informed by ethnomethodology, symbolic interactionism, actor-network theory, and the ascendant field of interaction analysis—is striking. Where the programmers had represented the office in terms of the linear flow of discrete information packets, the anthropologists shifted the analysis from the task environment to the social environment, drawing their data from office chatter, unorthodox workarounds, and the spontaneous "natural conversations" that are intrinsic to complex human organizations.[62]

It would be wildly misleading to suggest that PARC executed a ninety-degree "behavioral turn" during this period, or that a band of mutinous "ethnoids" had seized control of the ship; to the contrary, the anthropologists—Lucy Suchman, Jeanette Blomberg, Brigitte Jordan—often felt themselves to be occupying contested turf and in a gesture that might be dubbed "West Coast Story" at one point took to rumbling down the corridors of the lab in satin gang jackets emblazoned with their group's colors.[63] It is indisputable, however, that a shift in the center of gravity was taking place that would open up an entirely new era of design research—at Xerox PARC and beyond.

In summer 1980, as Arnold Wasserman's industrial design and human factors group in Rochester was conducting field observations among Xerox customers, the researchers in Palo Alto were turning their reflexive methodologies inward—in Suchman's words, "the imperative of innovation doubled back to take as its object PARC itself."[64] Anticipating that Xerox would sooner or later put a display on its machines, and concerned that no fundamental understanding of the human side of human–machine interaction prepared them for this paradigmatic shift, Suchman and Austin Henderson installed an 8200 copier in their lab, mounted video cameras above it, and readied their clipboards. As laboratory personnel used and abused the complex machine, the observers recorded hours of videotape, which they analyzed according to their respective disciplinary predilections: the computer scientist saw regular patterns as subjects adapted to the fixed protocols of the apparatus; the anthropologist saw in the same data particularities, noting the idiosyncratic manner in which users interacted with one another and with the machine.[65] Suchman and Henderson presented their findings internally, and also to Arnold Wasserman's product designers in Rochester, with whom they formed a long and fruitful collaboration that only deepened as Wasserman's own center of gravity shifted increasingly to the Bay Area.

In July 1982 Wasserman announced a new, "user-oriented" design strategy that heralded a major shift not just within Xerox but within professional practice generally. It was becoming increasingly clear that informational or computational artifacts could not be evaluated in the same terms as the previous generation of typewriters and adding machines, and that they posed challenges that went far beyond such routine ergonomic considerations as standardizing the size of buttons and the height of work surfaces: "User-oriented means nothing less than a paradigm shift in the way we think about products: from the machine side to the user side of the user/machine interface; from machine architecture to configurations of people; from machine logic to human logic; from the engineer's understanding of how machine systems work to the operator's understanding of what it takes to get a task done."[66] The strategy pointed to a wholly new conceptual orientation, which Xerox initially called "dialog design." The name did not stick, but the key insight did: "The user operates the interface, not the machine."

Increasingly drawn into the Bay Area's culture of experiment and innovation, in 1986 Wasserman engaged ID Two to work with RichardsonSmith and PARC on an innovation strategy for Xerox, with a time frame projected to extend into the early years of the twenty-first century. Bill Moggridge personally led a team tasked with creating a prototype document creation workstation that integrated hardware and software in a manner designed to optimize word processing, networking, and information management. The significance of these conceptual explorations was to move from invention to innovation, from technology to design, in a pattern that was becoming emblematic of Silicon Valley. Just as game design began as a forced cohabitation among programmers, engineers, and artists, Moggridge built his team out of the existing specialized fields: one had a background in information design, another in graphics and a third in industrial design. By the end of the decade they were calling themselves "interaction designers."

Conclusion

In 2010, en route to his new role as director of the Smithsonian's Cooper-Hewitt National Design Museum, Bill Moggridge paused to reflect upon the expanded field of design, which he characterized as a hierarchy reflecting the increasing complexity of the constraints imposed by the new class of objects that designers in Silicon Valley were being asked to address: surgical robots, interactive games, multimedia teaching resources, document creation workstations, and more. Parallel to the "technical factors" that remained the domain of the established design disciplines—industrial design, mechanical engineering, software engineering—corporate design groups and independent consultancies were learning to incorporate a growing number of "human factors":

Anthropometrics: the sizes of people, for the design of physical objects
Physiology: the way the body works, for the design of physical man-made systems
Psychology: the way the mind works, for the design of human–computer interactions
Sociology: the way people relate to one another, for the design of connected systems
Anthropology: the human condition, for global design
Ecology: the interdependence of living things, for sustainable design[67]

Nor was this simply an abstraction, for the hires the consultancies were making during the 1980s and '90s corresponded exactly to this ascending hierarchy of constraints: Moggridge first worked with fellow industrial designer Mike Nuttall; he hired a mechanical engineer to work alongside him on the GRiD Compass and then, in 1986, added the first human factors professional to the team; in the following year, interaction designers began to come aboard; and as the firm came to work increasingly on strategic issues for the companies of the scale of Xerox and NEC, systems designers who worked specifically on integrating the multifarious elements of complex sociotechnical systems. The growth of the firm reflected the concentric growth of the design professions in Silicon Valley generally. It would be followed—with an infinite number of permutations and combinations— by most of the consultancies that had begun to proliferate in the region.

A designer, in the context of this densely populated ecosystem, was more likely to be a design *team*, composed of "T-shaped" people, vertically grounded in their respective disciplines but possessed of the horizontal ability to work with people from radically different ones. How else might one approach the design of a device that allows commuters to download MP3 files from the Internet and play them back through their car radios while stuck in traffic on the Bay Bridge? Alongside CAD software and rapid prototyping equipment, the designer's toolkit came to include mental models, mind maps, futuristic forecasting, bodystorming, and an epistemological arsenal drawn from the study of human behavior.

By the time the twentieth century drew to a close, designers in Silicon Valley had learned—despite the caustic admonitions of W. H. Auden—to "commit social science."[68]

5   DESIGNING DESIGNERS

Tom Matano, who led the North American team that designed the ragtop Miata roadster, had acclimated to California and was unenthusiastic about being transferred back to Mazda's headquarters in Hiroshima. He decided instead to leave the auto industry altogether and take up a position as executive director of the industrial design program at the Academy of Art University in San Francisco: "I have designed enough cars," he reflected. "Now I want to design designers."[1]

Matano is hardly the first to cross the highly permeable membrane that both connects and separates academia and the world of professional practice. To the contrary, the diverse academic institutions of the Bay Area have played a crucial role in the formation of the region's tightly networked design ecosystem, just as design has occupied a major but neglected role in the formation of Silicon Valley generally. A cluster of institutions, ranging from elite research universities to state colleges to private art schools, has fed a steady stream of young talent into the region's established design offices and startups, while providing teaching (and scouting) opportunities for the area's working designers. At times they have led and at times they have followed, but by bringing together students and teachers, engineers and artists, theorists and practitioners, they have promoted exploration and experimentation in ways that client-driven consultancies or corporate design offices often cannot. They have also been among the most contentious, faction-ridden, and ideologically mobilized sites of local design discourse, which is as it should be. At the end of the day, the members of a design team must come together and present their client with a coherent path forward, but that is not the case in a seminar room, a midterm crit, or an interdisciplinary concept studio. Both within and among the Bay Area's academic institutions, educators have offered radically competing conceptions of how to design a designer. Like design practice, design education in the Bay Area matured slowly and erratically, as the experience of its three oldest and most prominent institutions suggests.[2]

Part One: The Founders

From its manicured campus, laid out by Frederick Law Olmsted in 1886, Stanford University dominates the academic landscape of Silicon Valley. It is an unabashedly entrepreneurial institution whose students have always been encouraged to carry their ideas out of the classroom and into the world: in 1938 Bill Hewlett and Dave Packard borrowed $538 from the chairman of the electrical engineering department to buy equipment; in 1999 computer science students Sergey Brin and Larry Page rode their bicycles to the Menlo Park offices of Kleiner Perkins and secured their first round of venture funding for Google. Most of Stanford's aspiring techno-preneurs seem to remain in the region, although a few, like the Italian office machine magnate Camillo Olivetti, class of '95, returned whence they came.[3]

It was only after World War II that Stanford began to emerge as a center of technical excellence, owing largely to the campaigns of Frederick Terman, dean of the School of Engineering and architect-of-record of the military-industrial-academic complex that is Silicon Valley. During World War II Terman had been tapped by his own mentor, presidential science advisor Vannevar Bush, to run the secret Radio Research Lab at Harvard and was determined to capture a share of the defense funding the federal government was preparing to redirect toward postwar academic research. Within a decade he had succeeded in turning the governor's stud farm into the Stanford Industrial Park, instituted a lucrative honors cooperative program that provided a *camino real* for local companies to put selected employees through a master's degree program, and overseen major investments in the most promising areas of research. Enrollments rose by 20 percent, and over one-third of entering class of 1957 started in the School of Engineering—more than double the national average.[4]

As he rose from chairman to dean to provost, Terman was unwavering in his belief that engineering formed the heart of a liberal education and labored to erect his famous "steeples of excellence" with strategic appointments in areas such as semiconductors, microwave electronics, and aeronautics. Design, to the extent that it was a recognized field at all, remained on the margins, the province of an older generation of draftsmen and machine builders who were more at home in the shop than the research laboratory—a situation Terman hoped to remedy with a promising new hire from MIT: "The world has heard very little, if anything, of engineering design at Stanford," he reported to President Wallace Sterling, "but they will be hearing about it in the future."[5]

As founder, director, and sole member of MIT's "Creative Engineering Laboratory," John Arnold had developed an acclaimed but highly idiosyncratic teaching methodology intended to jolt his students out of their routinized, formula-based problem solving habits. He introduced them to radical concepts such as "brainstorming" (borrowed from the advertising industry), "operational creativity" (borrowed from management consulting), and "applied imagination," derived from his own undergraduate studies in psychology. He lambasted the orthodoxy that located analytical reasoning in the technical disciplines and synthetic insight among creative artists, to the detriment of both. And as self-appointed general manager of Massachusetts Intergalactic Traders, Inc., he challenged his students to design harvesting equipment, two-passenger conveyances, and multipurpose kitchen gadgets for the beak-nosed, methane-breathing, bipedal extraterrestrials of the planet Arcturus IV.[6]

Although wildly popular among students, Arnold—who was largely self-taught and only later acquired a master's degree—had been viewed with extreme skepticism by his more disciplined colleagues at MIT: "Ours is a conservative profession," admitted engineering dean Richard Soderberg, "and there are many who think Arnold's course is a publicity stunt."[7] When he received an invitation from Terman (now provost) it took just a little prodding from Carl Clement, who had taken his summer course at MIT, to persuade him to move to Stanford. In 1957, as Sputnik beeped overhead and U.S. policymakers spiraled into a collective frenzy over the state of math-science education, John Arnold settled into an office in the Department of Mechanical Engineering with the somewhat incongruous title, professor of machine design. Squeezed between the thermosciences on one side and applied mechanics on the other, he soon took to answering his phone, "Design Division." Thus began a new era.

Elsewhere in the country, design—and design education—was becoming a recognized part of the midcentury academic landscape: the Carnegie

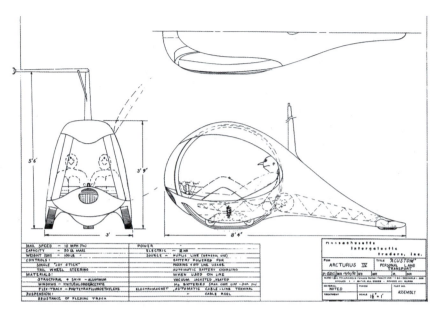

Figure 5.1

John E. Arnold, Massachusetts Intergalactic Traders, Inc. Personal conveyance for inhabitants of Arcturus IV.

Institute of Technology (later Carnegie-Mellon University) instituted the first industrial design curriculum in 1934, and by the time of Arnold's westward migration there were some forty-five degree programs in American colleges and universities; the Industrial Design Educators Association was formed in the very year of his arrival. Stanford, however, driven by its relentless focus on technical depth, was conspicuously lagging in its embrace of this inherently human-centered interdisciplinary field: "In the excited rush to expand scientific and technological frontiers," acknowledged a departmental newsletter, "one challenging area tends to be overlooked: The ever-growing design needs of people."[8] Stanford's engineering students could take a wide variety of theoretical courses, but product development, ergonomics, and disciplines related to the context of human use had not made it into the curriculum, much less the integrated, creativity-based approach to teaching and learning that Arnold espoused. In this respect, he had embarked on an educational mission that can best be described as quixotic. Finding few allies within the Stanford professoriate, he sought them from beyond.

Arnold's first recruit was Robert McKim, who had completed an undergraduate degree in industrial design at the Pratt Institute, followed by a stint in the New York offices of Henry Dreyfuss Associates; having begun his studies in engineering at Stanford, McKim had lately returned to California and was piecing together a livelihood teaching courses at various Bay Area colleges when Arnold invited him in. James Adams, who had sought relief from the equation-centric rigors of CalTech in the art department of UCLA, was enticed by Arnold's human-centered vision of "creative engineering," and signed on as a PhD student. A few other outliers joined the conspiracy, and together they began to assemble a radical, interdepartmental product design curriculum built around the core courses taken by all engineering students, but which then branched out into studio art, the social sciences, and the humanities. "The program is founded in science and engineering," they reassured a skeptical engineering community, even if "its goals are essentially humanistic."[9]

Stanford's fledgling product design program sought to awaken the dormant creativity of engineers and was rooted in John Arnold's conviction that creative problems invite "a spectrum of possible solutions." Analytical reasoning is suitable—indispensible, in fact—for solving discrete technical problems in which there is typically a single, correct answer: "What is the integral of $x^2\ dx$?" "What is the deflection in the center of an 18″ 70# steel I-beam, 20 feet long, uniformly loaded with 150 pounds per foot and freely supported at the ends?" In the design of an adding machine or an ensemble of playground equipment, however, the human context of needs, behaviors, judgments, and emotions enters the picture and the analytically driven search for "the one best way" is plainly inadequate. The first task of the program, then—borrowing tools from the humanistic psychology of Carl Rogers and Abraham Maslow—was to help students identify the perceptual, emotional, and cultural blocks to creative problem solving.

If the first pillar of creative engineering was to embrace complexity, the second was interdisciplinarity. Inspired by the "comprehensivist" philosophy of R. Buckminster Fuller, Stanford's design program sought to mobilize the arts and the social sciences and bring them into a fruitful alliance with physical science and engineering. Naively, perhaps, Arnold believed that comprehensive design provides "an almost perfect vehicle for experimenting in the effectiveness of bringing people of diverse backgrounds together in a creative effort,"[10] and he courted faculty allies from the departments of art, philosophy, psychology, and business.

Rounding out his vision of "comprehensive design" was a third component that anchored the program in the three-dimensional world of product design. Believing that a hands-on experience of manufacturing processes is essential to the education of designers, Arnold oversaw a revitalization of the outdated shop curriculum with the intention of shifting the emphasis from trade skills to leadership skills more valuable in the boardroom than on the factory floor. Canonical shop exercises overseen by journeyman machinists yielded to individual projects of the student's own conception and execution. Drafting was phased out in favor of sketching and other rapid visualization techniques. The goal of shop instruction shifted from executing a perfect weld to enabling students to express their ideas in physical form. When the electrical engineering and aero/astro programs outgrew the old "engineering corner" of the quad and moved into their own buildings, the insurgent design division seized the opportunity to expand its shop and turned a pattern loft over the foundry into studio space for graduate students. A vibrant loft culture soon developed in these cramped and airless quarters, populated by artists who wanted to use technology and engineers who wanted to make art.

Product design, it is important to note, was only one part of a larger design division that covered highly technical fields of teaching and research such as kinematics, control systems, analytics, and manufacturing. Its location in the School of Engineering distinguished the program from industrial design departments elsewhere—the Stanford program was never recognized by any of the national accreditation agencies—but also resulted in tensions within the design division itself. A graduate student working on the design of a turbine blade or a power transmission mechanism had little exposure to concepts such as end-users, ergonomics, or aesthetics; product design students, for their part, tended to begin with the assumption that issues of basic technology have been resolved and learned to direct their attention toward the totality of the finished product. The opportunities for turf wars were plentiful, both within the design division and between the division and the larger engineering community.[11]

In preparing to navigate these academic rapids, Arnold sought counsel from Robert McKim and James Adams. McKim's leading idea was that the designed, built, and manufactured environment serves as "a kind of

Figure 5.2
The Stanford Design Loft (1972), ten years before the Post-it Note. Courtesy of Dennis Boyle.

enormous classroom, or school, which we attend for life," and he felt that Stanford was preparing no more than 1 percent of its students to advance the "curriculum" of this non-verbal environmental education: "The remaining ninety-nine percent are, for the most part, receiving virtually no education to sensitize them to the impact of our man-made cocoon." McKim proposed an integrated, five-year curriculum that reflects the "wholeness of man" and balances the student's intellectual, physical, and emotional development. In deference to his own training at the Pratt Institute he initially called it "industrial design," but changed it to "product design" in order to emphasize the total creative act and not just the more-or-less elegant packaging of someone else's ideas: "Design is the inside and outside; sound and feel; everything you do."[12]

Adams, for his part, more carefully dissected the dissimilar constituencies that would be touched by such a program. Engineering design, he suggested, is theoretical and requires a logical, ordered, and precise thought process. Product design, however, operates in "the topsy-turvy world of emotion, public taste, mob psychology, and prejudice . . . . [It] is not theoretical design. It is commercial, practical, money-making design . . . which takes place only when factors such as ease of operation and mainte- nance, appearance, and economy of production become important."[13] If product design was to survive within Stanford's technology-based, research-driven School of Engineering, students would have to demon- strate that they were capable of designing from the inside out as well as from the outside in: "One of the greatest dangers is that it will be infiltrated by incompetent persons operating on a pumped up ego and a good com- mand of the English language."

John Arnold succumbed to a fatal heart attack while on sabbatical in 1963, and the mantle of leadership passed to his stunned acolytes—McKim, Adams, and Peter Bulkeley—who set about to transform the ideals of cre- ative engineering into a robust graduate and undergraduate curriculum. They were not alone, however. As the Stanford product design program settled uneasily into its home in the Department of Mechanical Engineer- ing, developments were taking place thirty miles to the south that would anchor the emerging culture of design education from a quite different direction.

The San José Teachers' College was founded in 1857, the moment at which land-grant colleges were being chartered to address the social and techni- cal transformations of industrializing America; a century later, as San José State College, the institution had embarked on an ambitious campaign to enhance the rigor and diversity of its academic curriculum, while adher- ing to its mission of serving a local community whose members may not have access to expensive private colleges and universities. Many departments found themselves poised uneasily between the older normal school tradition of the college and its emerging future, and were further buffeted by a raging national debate over what had variously been called "manual," "vocational," and "technical" education: Should the primary task of education be to prepare students for socially useful careers, or to help them realize their individual potential through a rounded, liberal education?[14]

Dr. Herber Sotzin, who had led the division for applied arts since the 1930s, straddled this cultural divide and found himself on the front lines of an internal debate with national implications. Recognizing that the ground was shifting under its once-progressive agenda, Sotzin had begun to advocate for the transformation of the industrial arts into a rigorous academic discipline.[15] A relic of the depression, however, his time had passed, and it fell to his disciples to complete the journey from the intellectual desert of vocational training into the promised land of professional education.

The most promising of these, Wayne Champion, had taken a leave from his SJSU teaching duties to pursue a doctorate in education at Stanford. To satisfy the fieldwork requirement, Champion developed a two-semester, four-day-a-week experimental course that he proposed to teach back in the Industrial Arts department of his home institution during the 1955–56 academic year. Sotzin approved, and the neophyte instructor was assigned to a twenty-by-forty-foot Quonset hut on the outskirts of the campus, substandard in every respect but with the unexpected benefit that nobody cared if he scratched the floors dragging a piece of equipment across the room or hammered nails into the beaverboard panels that covered the corrugated steel walls: "If the facilities are not suitable for a particular activity," he shrugged, "then it will probably be possible to modify the facilities."[16] Module B-31, as it turned out, proved to be the ideal space for prototyping the future of design education.

Champion's findings were sobering, but also inspirational. In contrast to the privileged young men who populated the engineering classes at Stanford, two-thirds of his sixty-one students were employed outside of school; a third of them were married; many were vets; and measured against the norm of the college, their academic records were markedly below average.[17] His hypothesis, however, was that given confidence in their own abilities and the belief that they could make meaningful contributions to society, the requisite skills would follow. The key was to develop a repertoire of teaching methods that would jolt them out of their trade school mentality, ignite their intellectual curiosity, and orient them toward meaningful social tasks. Accordingly, the course began—to the alarm of more than a few of the enrollees—with a discussion of Aldous Huxley's *Brave New World,* through which Champion sought to explore the implications of an educational system biased in favor of the skilled technician over the creative designer. Likewise, the exercises he created had a speculative character that deliberately departed from the practical, real-world situations encountered by electronics technicians, auto mechanics, and printers. By the conclusion of his experiment Champion was persuaded that "the fine arts and general education are crucial to the training of the designer as a thoughtful, critical, independent thinker who knows not only *how* to design but *what* to design."[18]

With his freshly minted doctorate in hand—and fired by the insights gained during a Fulbright year in Germany in which he was exposed to the Bauhaus model and its impact upon German, and British, and Scandinavian design education—Champion returned to the San José State faculty in 1957 with a mission: "How can we achieve an intelligent balance between the considerations represented by our Art Departments and those represented by our Industrial Arts and Engineering Departments? How can we teach the techniques of the present without suppressing the innovations of the future?"[19] The timing could not have been better.

During his absence, an interdivisional commission had been studying the state of design education on the West Coast and how best to serve the South Bay's socially diverse community and burgeoning industrial base. Their recommendations, in this seismically sensitive region, were literally earth-shaking: "Because of the rapid development of industries in the Santa Clara valley it has been determined by the planning committee that there is a need for college graduates trained in the field."[20] The California state legislature agreed, and groundbreaking began on the northeast cor- ner of the downtown campus that was still, unimaginably, bounded on one side by open farmland. On May 7, 1960, the *San José News* reported on the opening of "what is believed to be the largest college or university building devoted to training industrial arts teachers in the world." With its two lec- ture rooms, twenty-three laboratories, twelve planning centers, and dedi- cated shops for electronics, metals, automotive technology, ceramics, and print, the new Industrial Arts Building stood as a milestone in the evolution of the college. At the dedication ceremonies, the keynote speaker struck a defiant tone against those hidebound academicians who questioned the state's $3 million investment in a discipline as "soft" as the industrial arts:

> The library is thought of as a quiet place, whereas the shops are decid- edly noisy; the classroom is clean whereas a lab is dirty; books are read sitting down, whereas we work standing up, with sweat on our brow.[21]

Industrial arts at San José State comprised two main areas of instruc- tion, the largest of which—not surprisingly, given the normal school roots of the college—was the training of elementary, high school, and college shop teachers, and at the graduate level, the study of issues in teacher education per se. The other was broadly characterized as "occupational instruction," and included an existing program intended to channel graduates into business and industry and a new one, approved following a two-year study conducted by an interdepartmental faculty group and a nine-person advisory group drawn from local corporations and consultancies, in the "exacting" but ill-undefined field of industrial design. Insofar as the stated mission of this program was "to achieve a balance between an education in the humanities, science, business, engineering and art [with] proficiency in technique," Wayne Champion emerged as the obvious person to lead it. In reality, he soon found himself at the center of a community composed of "dissatisfied engineering students, art students with a too-practical bent, missionary-types, salesmen unsure of what to sell, and craftsmen growing up in an age when individual craftsmanship was dead or dying."[22]

Precisely because he was not a trained designer, Champion was able to introduce two radical innovations into his program. First, he was unwavering in his insistence upon a comprehensive approach: to meet the challenges of the present, he argued, "A designer must first of all be a creative thinker. He must think broadly and flexibly and must be aware of the physical, psychological, social needs of man in a rapidly changing and perplexing environment."[23] Second, recognizing that his own relation to the field was that of a "tourist," Champion befriended as many local practitioners as he could: Carl Clement lent him a member of his team at Hewlett-Packard to teach senior product design two afternoons a week; Frank Walsh of Ampex arranged for Arden Farey to teach the first-year studio; IBM's Don Moore taught portfolio presentation, and other part-time instructors came from FMC, Lockheed, and elsewhere. The embryonic design program at San José State gradually became one of the hubs of a professional design community that was just beginning to coalesce on the peninsula.

As the outlines of a viable program began to take shape, Champion was given authorization to hire a full-time faculty, and his own humanistic bent was soon complemented by the no-nonsense professionalism of Jack Crist and the creative eccentricity of Nelson van Judah. The triumvirate worked tirelessly to develop a practice-based curriculum, build a robust internship program with local companies, and enhance the visibility of the program within the college: in 1966 the enigmatic Buckminster Fuller spent a six-week residency as a guest of the engineering department, and Van Judah gained local notoriety by commandeering a disproportionate amount of his time. By the time the inventor of "anticipatory design science" had departed on his next global adventure, one of Van Judah's students had constructed a fifteen-foot geodesic dome in the middle of their classroom, and the class spontaneously began meeting in it. As the dome was progressively tricked out with an array of multisensory enhancements, it was visited by groups of preschoolers, engineers, a hypnotist, and a psychiatrist hoping to model the experience of schizophrenia—not to mention Stewart Brand, who was researching the *Whole Earth Catalogue,* and Stanford's Robert McKim, who was hunting for images for his influential book, *Experiences in Visual Thinking.* One visitor to the Dymaxion Dome, overloaded with sensory input, exclaimed, "We're inside Bucky's brain!"[24]

Mainly, however, the faculty struggled to communicate the value of a field still poorly understood by corporate managers, and even less by students, parents, and university administrators. Although Champion would recall the seventies as "the golden age of industrial design" at San José State, in time he wearied of arguing for a comprehensive academic curriculum against the parochialism of the vocational arts. A new and edgier generation of talented design students—the likes of Robert Brunner and Gerard Furbershaw, future founders of Lunar Design, and Sohrab Vossoughi, the future founder of Ziba—was meanwhile bristling against the indignity of having to squeeze past the driver's ed simulation machines to get to their second-floor studio. "The new, state-of-the-art facility was becoming obsolete and irrelevant," recalled Pete Ronzani, one of the first generation of ID students and later an instructor. More important, a new professionalism was taking shape that tied industrial design more closely to emerging programs in graphic design and interior design than to the old industrial arts. Fearful of the ramifications of merging with the engineering or business departments, and driven by a vision of "a unified professional design program," in 1978 Champion surreptitiously moved his faculty, students, and two truckloads of equipment into new quarters in the Department of Art. The relocation was initially met with great excitement on the part of the designers, who saw it as the first step in their journey to academic respectability: complementing the private research environment at Stanford, San José State seemed positioned to become "one of the top schools of design in the public sector. It needs only adequate support and a profound kick in the ass."[25]

Figure 5.3

Silhouette of Robert Brunner, senior (Industrial Design). SJSU *Spartan* (March–April 1981).

For better or for worse, there was no shortage of people willing to deliver it. In their new home the designers no longer rubbed shoulders with aspiring auto mechanics and high school shop teachers but with painters, sculptors, and art historians robed in the PhD and skeptical of the "wayward philosophy" espoused by their new neighbors. As surely as the industrial arts establishment had questioned the inclusion of so many "academic" courses in the design curriculum, voices were raised among the fine arts faculty about "our catholicity, our universality, our trade school mentality, and our vocational predisposition."[26] In attempting to referee one particularly bitter tenure dispute, Dean Arlene Okerlund began by acknowledging the "basic and inevitable differences" that divided her two constituencies:

> [The candidate] is an industrial designer being evaluated by a departmentmental committee composed largely of creative artists .... Contemporary artists and sculptors tend to the abstract/impressionistic/ expressionistic/surrealistic as they apply paint to canvas or mold bronze into an idea; industrial designers draw precise angles and draft practical

shapes as they produce a dentist's drill or an ergonomically perfect computer console.[27]

The case escalated and ultimately the president of the university went head-to-head with the president of the IDSA over the nature of professional practice and the obligations of design education at a state-supported university strategically located at the epicenter of "America's postindustrial growth center." Like their counterparts at Stanford, the educators at San José State found that they inhabited contested territory and learned to evade the academic border police who patrol the boundaries of the disciplines.[28]

It was possible, however, for an aspiring Bay Area designer to steer a middle course between the research-driven engineering environment at Stanford and the public mission of San José State, with its regional orientation and its commitment to the South Bay's social and industrial base. Such a student would have to drive an hour to the north, however, from the vanishing "valley of heart's delight" to the cradle of fifties beatniks, sixties hippies, and their latter-day heirs, the militants of the dotcom revolution.

In the fiery aftermath of the 1906 San Francisco earthquake, a German-born cabinetmaker named Frederick Meyer gathered together a group of fellow craftsmen to discuss how they might rebuild their livelihoods once the embers of their former workshops had cooled and the ashes of their studios had been swept away:

> After the San Francisco Fire, I attended a dinner of the . . . California Guild of Arts and Crafts of which I was President. We were asked to speak five minutes on what we would like to be doing instead of what we were doing. I spoke about my idea of a practical art school, one whose graduates would earn a comfortable living, and instead of teaching only subjects like figure and landscape painting, sculpture, etc., to teach design, mechanical drawing, commercial art, and the crafts.[29]

Unbeknownst to Meyer, a reporter was present and the following day a newspaper article announced the imminent opening of a school that promised to provide "instruction in the industrial arts." In the ensuing days Meyer was inundated with inquiries about his nonexistent college, which moved him to translate what had been little more than a vaporous idea into an institutional reality.

The School of the California Guild of Arts and Crafts opened in 1907, as the last wave of the English Arts and Crafts Movement was washing over the United States and coming to rest in Pasadena, Carmel, and the Oakland hills. The founders were inspired by the movement's quest for a unity of the fine and the applied arts, believing, with William Morris, that "when they are so parted, it is ill for the Arts altogether."[30] They also inherited the movement's powerful political ethos, which tied the cultural elevation of the "lesser arts" to the social elevation of the tradesmen who practiced them.

Rather than serving as a refuge for aesthetes who did not need to make a living, Meyer believed that an arts education could be an enabler for craftsmen who did. In his original vision he imagined a college that would train a new breed of art worker who could apply the sensibilities of the artist to the mundane objects of everyday life—not in the sense of decorating them, but of capturing the aesthetic possibilities inherent in their use. Together with a cadre of similarly inclined zealots, he pursued this mission in a spirit of what came to be described as "practical idealism." Within fifteen years the college had shortened its name to the California School of Arts and Crafts, relocated to a handsome four-acre estate in the Oakland hills, and reorganized itself into divisions of fine arts, art education, and the applied arts of interior decoration, furniture design, costume design, and something called "Design in the Art Industries."[31]

As one of the few institutions anywhere that integrated the applied arts into its offerings, the school attracted some early innovators: Joseph ("Jo") Sinel, the flamboyant New Zealander who styled himself "artist to industry," began teaching at the college in the early 1920s, just at the point when—inspired by the example of the protean William Morris—he was transitioning from helping companies advertise their products to helping to develop them. Sinel's radical insight was that the artist—*qua* artist—had a constructive role to play in combating the "visual halitosis" that afflicted commercial products. He spent several years teaching lettering and graphics while launching his career in the field—"industrial design"—that he is credited with having named.

After an interlude spent among the celebrity designers in New York, Sinel reopened his San Francisco office in 1936 and briefly toyed with the idea of opening his own school—a plan derailed by the war. By the time he returned to teaching in the late 1940s, Frederick Meyer's school had evolved from a pastoral retreat for about two hundred young ladies in search of refinement and a few young men unfit for military service into the California College of Arts and Crafts. Although design education was in its infancy, the college itself was, in Sinel's estimation, "right up there with the leading institutions of its kind in the country."[32] A wave of returning GIs had spiked the enrollment to nearly 1,500, and the vets brought with them focused vocational goals that contrasted sharply with the genteel environment of the early years. Moreover, the field of professional practice was becoming more disciplined. Speaking to an audience of educators during the war, Sinel had predicted that "a heightened consciousness of the necessity of intelligently directed design . . . is very likely to emerge from the present crisis," and neither consumers nor manufacturers would henceforth tolerate "useless ornamentation and superficial simplification."[33] His return to teaching reflected his belief, as he wrote to prospective students, that "the craft age was the world of your grandparents . . . the machine age is *your world*."[34]

Sinel's prophetic destiny was to gaze upon the promised land of Silicon Valley but not to enter it. Although he consorted with the designers at Ampex and attended charrettes at the technology-intensive San José State, he belonged to a generation of creative artists whose conception of their role in industry, by his own account, owed more to painting and sculpture than to engineering and ergonomics. "I had very little comprehension of what was being done in engineering terms," he admitted in a 1969 interview with CCAC's librarian, Robert Harper, and then—as if to confirm this—groped for the name of the field that was on the cusp of transforming the fabric of everyday life:

Sinel: Other things come much faster, the whole field of . . . what do you call
   the modern . . .
Harper: Electronics?
Sinel: Yeah.
Harper: That did develop in a hurry.
Sinel: . . . Now it's big and for some reason or other there's this section in
   northern California where the whole development of that type of industry has taken place.[35]

Sinel's vision nonetheless helped to drive an incipient shift from the application of art to industrial products to an incorporation of art into the product development process itself. He was not, however, the person to realize it—in part because of his distance from the practicalities of modern technology, in part because, as one admirer noted, "like most men who are creative, he is too preoccupied with his creations to have much time left to agitate for them."[36] Others, however, were waiting in the wings.

The violence that had driven so many cultural figures to the United States in the 1930s affected designers no less than physicists, psychologists, and philosophers. Walter Landor settled in San Francisco in 1939 and taught briefly at CCAC while he was establishing what would become one of the most prominent branding firms in the nation. Another German refugee, Wolfgang Lederer, had been trained in graphic arts and typography in Leipzig, Paris, and Prague and had made his way to San Francisco as the noose was tightening around Hitler's Europe. When Frederick Meyer offered him a part time teaching job, he surreptitiously looked up the word *design* in his dictionary (there is no German equivalent) and then hurried off the public library to read up on it. Hastily versed in the American vernacular, Lederer reported for duty in 1941, at which time CCAC offered one basic design class and another in advertising. To this rudimentary curriculum he added his own "advanced" graphic design class, which enrolled exactly four students.[37]

Like Sinel, Lederer was a passionate advocate of the ideals of the Arts and Crafts Movement and envisioned an autonomous discipline that stood apart both from the effete self-indulgences of the fine arts and the servile dependency of the trades. When an interviewer innocently referred to his courses as "commercial art," he politely demurred: "May I correct you?" The phrase implied to him that design was a debased form of fine art, "something not quite decent."[38] To his students he insisted that a diploma is not the academic version of a union card, and that while a coveted position in a corporate art department might await a few lucky graduates, their real goal should be a lifelong process of continuing artistic growth.

The learning curve was steep for both teacher and students: Lederer never fully adapted to his American students' need for praise, downtime, and self-expression, and they in turn sought to enliven his austere Bauhausian restraint. He persevered, however, becoming director of the School of

Design in 1956. By the time the mannered and avuncular Lederer retired twenty years later the Beat Poets, the Free Speech Movement, the Summer of Love, and the Black Panther Party had all washed over CCAC's Oakland campus and left their mark, and the design curriculum evolved accordingly. Advertising and illustration merged to become a leading force in the "West Coast wave" of graphic design—more expressive, more experimental, but emphasizing an exceedingly high level of craft; interior decoration matured into environmental design, with a concern for the shaping of the total living environment; but industrial design languished and was eventually dropped when it became clear that the lack of facilities—not to mention its bucolic setting on a secluded estate in the Oakland hills—would prevent the college from meeting the industry-based and technology-intensive needs of the discipline. ID would return with a vengeance, however, on the other side of the San Francisco Bay.[39]

A confluence of unforeseen developments conspired in the mid-1980s to drive CCAC's migration across the Bay Bridge. First, the interior design program had already established a beachhead among the artists' studios, graphic design offices, and furniture showrooms that populated San Francisco's storied North Beach neighborhood, but rising rents were forcing them to seek out cheaper quarters in what was just beginning to become known as the South-of-Market "Design District." Second, in 1985 the college was invited to purchase for the symbolic sum of $1 the architecture program of the venerable Cogswell Polytechnical College—"We overpaid," quipped the trustee who negotiated the deal—which made the acquisition of a new space a matter of urgent necessity. Finally, and most ominously, during the previous academic year CCAC had been put on notice that its financial and administrative affairs were in such disorder that continued accreditation was seriously in doubt. Whereas Stanford had the clout simply to ignore the threats and overtures of the national accrediting agencies, and SJSU, as a public institution, was answerable in the first instance to the California State University system, loss of accreditation was a potentially fatal blow to a small, vulnerable arts institution.[40] This gathering storm served as the catalyst for a major restructuring of CCAC into a School of Fine Arts, which remained in Oakland, and Schools of Architectural Studies and Design, which moved into a disused industrial building where, according to doubtful urban myth, the cables for the Golden Gate Bridge had been spun a half-century earlier. Two architecture and five design programs fed off the region's rapidly proliferating culture of professional practice and within a few years had outgrown their cramped rented space.

The real denouement came in the early nineties, and as had been the case at Stanford and San José State, the contingencies of architectural space played a decisive role. As the Internet bubble was beginning to transform this seedy neighborhood into the epicenter of the dotcom revolution, the college had the astonishing good fortune to acquire a pristine gem of midcentury industrial real estate in the form of a vacant Greyhound Bus maintenance terminal designed in 1951 by the über-modernist firm of Skidmore, Owings, & Merrill. "It would be pretentious to think we are at the beginning of a movement like the Bauhaus or the Wiener Werkstaette," David Meckel had told an interviewer at the time that he and Michael Vanderbyl were recruited to serve as deans of architecture and design, respectively, but ten years later they had shed their diffidence: the oil slicks had barely been scrubbed from the floor of the 60,000-square-foot clear-span shed when Meckel and Vanderbyl invited the Bay Area arts community to a gala opening: "Bigger than the Bauhaus," they boasted.[41]

Part Two: The Builders

By the end of the 1970s, John Arnold, Wayne Champion, and Wolfgang Lederer had all left the scene and it fell mainly to their disciples to propagate their faith in, respectively, creative engineering, public education, and design as art and as craft. Arnold's heir apparent was the iconoclastic Robert McKim, who introduced a cluster of innovative methodologies into the Stanford design curriculum including needfinding, idea sketching, "ambidextrous thinking," and abductive reasoning, a pragmatic system of logic that abjures truth and even consistency and instead gives the designer license to forge ahead on the basis of data that will never be complete.[42] Channeling the work of theorists ranging from Charles Sanders Peirce and William James to Rudolf Arnheim and Jerome Bruner, McKim was able to forge an eclectic body of thought into an accessible methodology and to inspire students to execute it with Prismacolor pencils and tracing paper.

The chairman of the mechanical engineering department would often loiter at the door of McKim's lectures with a quizzical look on his face, for his teaching methods were as unorthodox as the theoretical principles on which they were based. While students elsewhere in the ME department

Figure 5.4
The Montgomery Campus, CCAC, shortly after acquisition (1993): "Bigger than the Bauhaus." Photo by Douglas Sandberg.

busied themselves with labs and problem sets, students in the product design program were taking sculpture classes in the art department, awakening their spirituality in the New Age vortex of "Esalen at Stanford," and prying open their doors of perception in the Imaginarium, a sixteen-foot geodesic dome that they entered through a trapdoor and then, lying on their backs with their heads touching and their bodies radiating outward like the spokes of a mandala, allowed themselves to be bathed in the guitar music of Windham Hill, soft blue lights, controlled scents, and projected images of inspiring structures and famous inventions. "The purpose of the IMAGINARIUM is to remind you of imaginative powers that you already possess," read an early script:

> The IMAGINARIUM is a physical metaphor of your sensory imagination. Imagine that it represents your inner sensory world. Your metaphorical mind's eye . . . . In the IMAGINARIUM, as in your own imagination, you

will be able to see, hear, taste, touch, and move with incredible freedom. You will move through immense space and traverse enormous spans of time. You will perform imaginative feats impossible to achieve in every-day, perceptual reality.[43]

With their slumbering creativity awakened and their consciousness suitably raised, students—the majority of whom entered the master's pro-gram with at least some engineering background—felt that they were being given license to be artistic, creative, and altruistic. In 1968 Jerry Manock worked on a device to assist in the therapy of patients with cystic fibrosis; David Beach, who graduated from the program and rejoined it as a faculty member, used current medical research and on-site fieldwork to design a system of playground equipment intended to improve the attention span of autistic children; David Kelley's master's thesis had its origins in a dis-arming interview with a professor at the Stanford Medical School: "You know what happens if we misfile this medical record?" the doctor asked, grabbing a folder from a chaotic heap on his assistant's desk—"*We never find it.*" This was the inspiration behind "Medical Passport," a microfiche-enabled device that allowed patients to retain control of their medical histories.[44]

As the design division evolved, an accommodation gradually emerged between its technical and more humanistic sides and they came to inhabit a contiguous intellectual space. Galvanized by the human potential move-ment, Bernard Roth, a distinguished researcher in kinematics and robotics, developed an abiding interest in the responsibilities of the designer in soci-ety; James Adams, who had spent six years at the Jet Propulsion Lab work-ing on highly technical aspects of the Mariner, Ranger, and Voyager spacecraft, began to explore the conceptual foundations of problem-solving and emerged as a leading figure in creativity theory; while remain-ing grounded in mechantronic systems design and neurophysiology, Larry Leifer, turned his attention to the internal dynamics of technical teams, and Rolf Faste, the only professionally trained designer in the design divi-sion, explored the outer limits of what he called Zengineering. Sheri Sheppard—for years the only woman in the department—made the politi-cally risky choice to conduct research into engineering education per se.

Moving in the opposite direction, Matthew Kahn, who came to Stanford from the Cranbrook Academy in 1949, managed to negotiate the academic minefields that surrounded his home in what was then the Department of Art and Architecture: in the mid-1960s, Robert McKim and James Adams sought him out in the hope that he would assist them in evaluating applicants whose engineering credentials were weak or nonexistent. Kahn agreed, but on the condition that it not be as a consultant to an engineering design program but as a full-fledged member of a joint program in design that would respect the aesthetic, the expressive, and the conceptual as much as what he called the "sensible."[45] For McKim, whose interest in aesthetics was primarily as a mode of cognition, this formed a necessary complement. The designer-engineer and the designer-artist formed a long-term partnership that formed the axis of the undergraduate and the graduate programs.

Design at Stanford has come to embrace many elements, including the Center for Design Research (CDR), formed in 1984, which sponsors research into such recondite fields as biomimetics, dextrous manipulation, and collaborative haptics and robotics, as well as inquiry into what exactly designers do when they design.[46] The teaching innovations introduced by the original product design faculty, by contrast, were decidedly low tech. Students took basic ME courses in materials and manufacturing where they learned about fatigue and stress—as do graduate students in every discipline—but the shop courses were intended to support expressivity rather than proficiency and McKim emphasized techniques of rapid visualization over the accurate rendering of objects. Whether it is CDR's focus on the designer or the product design program's focus on the user, however, the signature of the design division at Stanford was always its humanistic bent, and it never entirely shed its reputation as the soft and vulnerable underbelly of the School of Engineering. James Adams succinctly captured the mood of his colleagues: "We felt like embattled good guys in a kingdom that did not understand us."[47]

Industrial design at San José State, by contrast, developed a strong, technology-centric orientation in the years after Champion stepped down as chair. His successor, Ralf Schubert, made significant progress in introducing national standards into a program that had begun to drift. Even so, the dean of humanities and sciences noted with alarm that "ihe Industrial Design Program is faced with a serious dilemma in that it does not possess in the current staffing an individual with a proficient computer background," adding that "this deficiency is particularly embarrassing in that SJSU is located in the heart of Silicon Valley."[48] The situation began to be remedied with the hiring of Del Coates, a seasoned industrial designer who came to the college in 1983 with both academic and industry experience as well as deep expertise in computer-assisted design and manufacturing (CAD/CAM). While working at Ford's advanced vehicle concept division in the early 1960s, Coates had attended a presentation by Ivan Sutherland in which the MIT graduate student used his revolutionary Sketchpad program to rotate stick figures on a primitive display. In his mind's eye Coates found himself replacing Sutherland's simple shapes with cars, a reflexive gedankenexperiment that would lead him to view the computer not only as a drawing tool but, more importantly, as a design tool: When it is possible to peer "behind" a skillfully rendered 2-D surface, he asserted, "you can't cheat." Coates thus embarked on a thirty-year quest to apply computers first to automotive design, then to product design generally, and ultimately to a sophisticated academic pedagogy.[49]

It is difficult, nowadays, to capture the degree to which this was once a controversial stance. In the early 1980s, however, designers still viewed computers with suspicion, in part because the ability to visualize an object on a CRT screen was still a rarity, in part because—in the antediluvian days before InDesign and SolidWorks—students had to be taught programming before the computer could be used as an effective design tool. At a more subjective level, many designers felt affronted by the idea that aesthetic judgments might someday be driven by a machine, or anxious that their hard-won rendering skills were trending toward obsolescence. To counter this resistance, Coates launched what would become a regular column on the use of computers in the design office, warning the readers of *Industrial Design* magazine that, "like it or not, every industrial designer under age fifty almost certainly will have to face the decision of jumping in or being swept into the CAD/CAM stream, to sink or swim." He continued to press the case at professional meetings, where the reception—"uneasiness," "anxiety," "agitation"—led one observer to remark, "Audience responses were almost more interesting than the information presented." And returning to his academic chair he advised fellow educators that, "any school that sees the future of its industrial design program in traditional terms of drawing and rendering skills is doomed to irrelevancy." Rather than narrowing field of decision-making, however, Coates argued that by demonstrating what is rationally possible, the computer actually opened it up. The rendering and surfacing techniques he had learned as a student at Art Center served him well enough in the fifties, but looking to the future, "The emphasis will have to shift to skills of problem analysis, fundamental design, and above all, judgment."[50]

Over the next two decades the professionalization of design at San José State advanced in parallel with the growth and diversification of Silicon Valley itself. Under the direction of Brian Kimura, the interior design program responded to the growing interest among local tech firms in the "workspace" movement—open offices and flexible environments intended to promote collaboration and innovation. Randall Sexton, who came to San José State in 1990 after a six-year stint as art director for IBM, presided over the transformation of graphic design wrought by the Macintosh computer. In contradistinction to Stanford's product design program, which sought to liberate the latent creativity of engineers, industrial design at SJSU remained resolutely focused on preparing students for the rigors of professional practice—sometimes to their despair. "We were not academics," recalled Brian Kimura, who rose from part-time lecturer in 1980 to chair of an integrated Department of Design that comprised all three subdisciplines. "We were practical people."[51] There was little space in the curriculum for conceptual studies or theoretical debate, courses were mainly geared to what was required by the profession, and everything pointed toward the creation of a portfolio that students could confidently present to a design manager at a top Silicon Valley company.

Measured by the criteria of the California State University system, the programs had indisputable success, with SJSU graduates finding their way into coveted positions at Apple, Hewlett-Packard, and Oracle, as well as all of the region's major consultancies: IDEO, frogdesign, Lunar, Astro, Whipsaw, Ammunition, New Deal, and fuseproject. Still, design education at San José State—like design education elsewhere—remained precariously positioned relative to more established and well-defined disciplines. Having extricated themselves from the industrial arts in the 1960s and '70s, the three design programs now struggled to reposition themselves in relation to the fine arts, whose studio artists and art historical scholars had always viewed them with suspicion.

Accordingly, a few years into the new millennium, the dean of the College of Humanities and the Arts found himself on the receiving end of a barrage of draft proposals setting out the case for autonomy on the grounds that, "Fine Arts and Design represent opposed ideological or philosophical perspectives, with Design focused on 'professional' approaches to student education and Fine Arts devoted to personal development of student artistic consciousness." In fall 2010, the petitioners were finally granted their wish. Yielding to a growing consensus that their learning objectives and disciplinary goals differed fundamentally from those of the fine arts, interior, industrial, and graphic design were separated from art and art history and formally constituted as an independent department. Sixty years after it was introduced into the university curriculum, in what one administrator called "a case of arrested development," design at San Jose State came into its own.[52]

Graduates of Stanford and San José State were recruited by the local tech giants or absorbed into the frenzied world of startups and consultancies. The character of an art college made the prospects of CCAC's graduates more problematical, however—especially one whose arts-and-crafts pedigree was more readily associated with the diversions of hobbyists and summer campers, on the one hand, or the radical idealism of the nineteenth-century Artworkers' League, the Century Guild, and the Arts and Crafts Exhibition Society on the other.[53] Lacking the engineering resources of Stanford and independent of the California State University system that underwrote the design programs of San José State, CCAC made a virtue of necessity and seized the opportunity to reinvent design at an institution whose student body is composed entirely of makers.

Following Lederer's retirement the old industrial design department was resuscitated in the form of a general design program under the optimistic premise that "in the rapidly changing technological world . . . the generalist may be more likely to survive and succeed than the specialist."[54] Unstructured and untethered, the program gradually became a dumping ground for a motley assortment of more-or-less interesting courses that did not fit readily into any of the other departments.

The first signs of revival came in the mid-1980s, when Deans Vanderbyl and Meckel began to lobby for a more concept-driven, context-sensitive industrial design program that would resonate with the ethos of the school but also capture the technological insurgency emanating from Silicon Valley and the momentum generated by the creation of an architecture and design department at the ascendant San Francisco Museum of Modern Art in 1983. "The opportunity to create and build it at the new San Francisco campus was one of the main reasons I took on the deanship," stated Vanderbyl, whose graphic design students were already being snatched up by Adobe, Oracle, and *Wired Magazine* and were contributing to an emerging and distinctly edgy West Coast style.[55]

In fall 1986, Vanderbyl recruited Aura Oslapas, a Cranbrook graduate whose professional trajectory had led her from the offices of Henry Dreyfuss in New York and the Bruce Burdick Group in San Francisco to Esprit, where she was serving as design director. As founding chair of CCAC's new program in industrial design, Oslapas set about to build a faculty based on the idea that "Designers are the sign-makers of our times." A credible, professional skillset is of course vital, but since technical courses do not differ greatly from one institution to the next, it was necessary to establish a distinct identity. "CCAC's ID program is different," she wrote, "because we're taking the time to understand the context in which we're designing." By the time she returned to professional practice eight years later, Oslapas had built a curriculum balanced between "industrial design" and "product design" tracks, recruited a faculty composed in equal measure of local talent and a trickle of expatriate designers that was turning into a steady stream—Sigmar Wilnauer from Germany, Masamichi Udagawa from Japan, Tim Brown from the UK—and ushered the first crop of ID graduates out into the world.[56]

The move into a permanent home in San Francisco—effectively 4.5 acres of unobstructed space under a single roof—prompted a year of searching internal debate over the physical relation of the various design disciplines to one another in an era of shifting boundaries and permeable academic membranes. Design pedagogy was in fact one of the passions of the new chair of industrial design, Steven Holt. Having attained national prominence as editor of *ID Magazine,* and then as "strategic visionary" at frogdesign, Holt embraced the view that we are living in what Intel CEO Andy Grove had famously called a "strategic inflection point." The hyperinformation economy unleashed by Silicon Valley technology hasn't merely undermined cultural values, Holt had written, "it has abruptly created new values replete with a whole new visual literacy." The task of educators is to equip an emerging generation of designers to cope with a cultural regime in which "images have the weight of objects, and objects have the profligacy of images."[57] The ground is shifting beneath our feet, he noted, "and because of this we want a balance of industry supported projects giving the student real world experience and conceptual blue-sky oriented projects that allow the student to blow the doors off the creative process."[58] The reference points of CCA's design program evolved under his leadership from the lifestyle companies in the school's backyard—Esprit, Gap, Levi-Strauss, North Face—to the technology drivers to the south: "It's the Renaissance," he declared in reference to the ascendancy of the digital, "and they're handing out the marble!"

In 2005 the mantle of leadership passed once again, this time to Yves Béhar, founder of the acclaimed consultancy, fuseproject. Béhar's stated goal was to raise the international visibility of the college and of its design programs, and he lobbied hard for improvements that would achieve this level of recognition: enhanced prototyping capabilities; a publication program to expose students' work to the wider world; their representation at major international venues such as the Salone Internazionale del Mobile di Milano and the International Contemporary Furniture Fair in New York; entry into competitions sponsored by James Dyson and Intel. Although Béhar's firm had won widespread recognition for projects including the XO computer for the One Laptop Per Child Foundation, he discouraged the development of a curriculum focused too myopically around the region's signature digital technologies.

The inexorable spread of "Silicon Valley" to the whole of the San Francisco Bay Area affected other disciplines as well, and the design programs at CCA have to some extent converged around a common set of postmodern, postindustrial challenges. Architecture now includes studios dedicated to digital fabrication—the postmodern successor to the old tradition of *architettura di carta*. Graphic design faculty, during this period, have begun to work for tech companies such as Adobe, Autodesk, and IBM, and in the estimation of Professor Jeremy Mende, "It is difficult now to locate a studio that is not heavily engaged in online, screen, motion, interaction, app design, etc. in the Bay Area." Their teaching has undergone a comparable inversion, with the emphasis shifting from print to online media. Fashion design has forged alliances with the more technology-intensive disciplines: "After all," chair Amy Williams reminded her colleagues in the industrial and interaction design programs, "we're the ones who invented wearables."[59]

By the end of the millennium, mature design programs were in place at Stanford, San José State, and the California College of the Arts, as well as a dozen smaller (and larger) schools throughout the Bay Area.[60] A well-oiled revolving door was spinning Silicon Valley's practicing designers into adjunct teaching positions where they were able to scout out the next generation of talent, and simultaneously easing the best and the brightest of their students into entry-level positions. The professional networks that defined the region from its earliest days extend equally to academia, which, like all of its other constituents, is both cause and effect of the Silicon Valley ecosystem of innovation.

Although past results are no guarantee of future performance, the blaze of initiatives launched during the last decade suggests that the Bay Area's experiments in design education are far from over. The boldest of these is arguably the Hasso Plattner Institute for Design—the so-called "d.school"— at Stanford. Since their origins, the Stanford design programs have prided themselves on their catholicity in melding advanced engineering, studio art, and the behavioral sciences. This was at one time a radical position, but as the heresies of the 1960s and '70s became the orthodoxies of the '80s and '90s, a degree of complacency set in and the academic culture found itself conspicuously in need of renewal. The d.school, formally launched in 2004, was initially imagined as a "School of Design" alongside the university's Schools of Medicine, Law, or Engineering, but these ambitions were quickly scaled back to the status of an independent institute without dedicated faculty, labs, or degree-granting privileges. Although humbled by their demotion, this may actually have given the organizers just the freedom and flexibility they needed.

The reigning ideology of the d.school is "design thinking," an ascendant movement driven by the twin insights that one does not have to be a designer to think like one, and that in their drive toward professional respectability, designers themselves have unreasonably narrowed the range of their ambitions. In partnership with corporate sponsors, startup entrepreneurs, NGO's, foundations, and a tight-knit assortment of friends and family, the d.school seeks to redirect this energy outward toward problems not traditionally encompassed by the various professional subfields: social justice, education, global poverty, health.[61] Accordingly, the Institute gathers its students from almost every sector of the university *except* design, and introduces them to a range of design tools that it hopes will be brought back to their respective fields. Seeking to produce "innovators, not innovations," the d.school combines the eccentricities of the original product design programs (the institute employs a resident d.shrink and offers stressed-out graduate students a course in d.compression) and a growing demand for relevance (a sought-after, two-quarter sequence in "Entrepreneurial Design for Extreme Affordability"). In a few short years the d.school—the design school that does not teach design—has attracted widespread attention and emulation.

Whereas Stanford, buffered by its $16.5 billion endowment, can withstand all but the most brutal economic shocks, the fortunes of San José State have always been closely allied to those of Silicon Valley and the industries located there. As a state-supported, land-grant institution, the university has a mandate to provide educational opportunities for an exceptionally diverse local community, and the profile of its student body is a direct index of California's bewildering demographics, Byzantine politics, and the generally dismal state of K–12 public education. The obverse side of its mission is to support the local economy by delivering to it a skilled and educated workforce.

Whether despite or because of these constraints, SJSU's newly autonomous Department of Design has maintained a high profile in the community and, in the estimation of one external reviewer, "is a recognized cultural resource for the city of San José and the entire Silicon Valley."[62] It is more than a labor pool, however. As San Jose State itself evolved from a trade school to a research-driven university, design faculty have become actively engaged in the university's academic mission. A particularly fruitful collaboration has taken place between John McClusky, an industrial designer who in a previous life had been exposed to ethnographic research practices at Xerox, and Charles Darrah, who began in 1991 to organize a massive fifteen-year ethnographic study of Silicon Valley itself.[63] Describing themselves as "an anthropologist, albeit one who was sensitive to how designers approached their practice and who could frame his research in ways that supported it," and "a designer, but one who constantly tested concepts and images against the brute facts of how real people lived their lives and how they aspired to alter those lives," Darrah and McClusky have jointly explored a range of theoretical and methodological problems in such concrete practices as ATM use and white-collar office environments. Their collaboration let to the creation of the Human Aspiration and Design Laboratory, whose goal is "to develop a means by which design and, ultimately, anthropology students could be competent designers who simultaneously incorporate the findings and methods of ethnographic research into their practices."[64]

In 2003, in one of its more controversial moves, the California College of Arts and Crafts changed its name to the California College of the Arts. Although widely misinterpreted as a repudiation of the core values of the century-old Arts and Crafts Movement, this renaming—the third in the college's history—in fact reflected an ongoing effort to preserve the relevance of the craft tradition in an age of laser cutters, interactive websites, and open-source programming.[65] Printmakers and textile artists still flourish on the Oakland campus, but design in San Francisco has settled into permanent quarters in what the mayor of San Francisco has lately dubbed the Innovation Corridor. The college acquired—and lost—the respected journal, *Design Book Review*, but other initiatives include a new undergraduate degree program in interaction design and an MBA in design strategy, apparently the first to be offered within the context of an American arts institution. These programs, like most others at the college, draw liberally from the deep reservoir of expertise that resides within the Bay Area professional community and reflect the redirection of resources from the material to the human that characterizes the Internet era generally. CCA's design students continue to craft objects, images, and spaces, but as Brenda Laurel, veteran of Atari Labs and Interval Research Corporation and founding chair of the transdisciplinary MFA design program put it in a centennial address to the faculty, at the end of the day "It's all information."

Although constrained by resources and buffeted by the usual run of failed experiments and internecine conflicts, design at CCA has benefitted from its location within an arts institution. Product designers at Stanford have waged a decades-long battle to defend their legitimacy within the School of Engineering. The designers at San José State have only recently been granted autonomous departmental status and remain answerable to the whims of the California State Legislature. At CCA, however, design is recognized as simply one more medium for makers: "Design is not second-class art, asserted Michael Vanderbyl. "It is equal to the fine arts, not the commercial stepsister of something supposedly far greater. It is a way of creating art that functions. We want to change the world we live in, and the only way you can do that is to become part of it."[66]

Conclusion

At the end of the spring semester 1980, as another cohort of robed graduates marched, pranced, and cavorted across the stages of the region's academies, a conclave of notables gathered to discuss the state of design education in the Bay Area. Primo Angeli, founder of one of the oldest and most respected graphic design firms in San Francisco, opined that the major defect in design education in northern California is "lack of space for making mistakes." For veteran industrial designer Budd Steinhilber, the problem was that, "Most schools seem to over-emphasize the creative as opposed to the production aspect." Darrell Staley of Ampex agreed, noting that San José State graduates seemed better prepared in problem-solving abilities, whereas Stanford students, whether despite or because of their more theoretical training, "have poor visualization skills in both modeling and sketching and are somewhat arrogant." Bruce Burdick took the rather more generous view that, "It's not that one school is better or worse than another," but that "each school limits a student in its own way depending on the placement [of its design curriculum] in the university structure and how the faculty relates to this structure."[67]

Taken together, the character of Stanford, San José State, and California College of the Arts would seem to validate Burdick's assessment. In the world of professional practice at that time, designers were mainly viewed either as failed engineers or as artists who had sold out; within academia their status was even worse. John Arnold and his successors struggled to communicate to their Stanford colleagues that design was neither exact science nor simply a fashionable gloss on mechanical engineering. Bracketing the valley, both geographically and pedagogically, the industrial designers at San José State labored to craft an identity independent both of the vocational tradition of the applied arts and the academic standards of the fine arts establishment. The design disciplines may have fared best at CCA, although the socialist ethos of the college still prompts skepticism about concept studios sponsored by Intel, Samsung, or Ford, and there remains a subliminal tension between the artist's focus on signed work and the characteristically anonymous requirements of industry. As Silicon Valley companies offered employment to growing numbers of their graduates, however, all three schools ultimately granted their design programs a grudging accommodation. Designers in academia, however, like their counterparts in industry, continue to defend and even cultivate their status as strangers in what is often an even stranger land.

6 THE SHAPE OF THINGS TO COME

Crowded into a small office in downtown Palo Alto, elbow-to-elbow with the rest of Thefacebook's twenty-odd employees, Soleio Cuervo was dissatisfied with everything about the "Awesome" button. The green, sixteen-by-sixteen-pixel rendering of an upward-pointing thumb was poorly drawn. It was tucked away in an obscure corner of a random page. It was not translatable across the many cultures the ambitious startup hoped one day to reach. He worried that too few objects of its intended affection would rise to the lofty standard of "awesomeness." And it needed to be a confident (if understated) verb, not a second-class modifier. He simply didn't *like* it, so Cuervo redrew it, renamed it, and the product shipped in February 2009.[1]

A few months after the "Like" button was released, Facebook exploded out of its cramped headquarters and moved across town into an old Hewlett-Packard manufacturing building on the toxic site where Carl Clement had built Silicon Valley's first design team sixty years earlier. In the 1950s, decades before a single one of Facebook's 180-odd designers was even born, HP shipped signal generators, frequency counters, voltmeters, and oscilloscopes from a loading dock in the back of the building on North California Avenue. They still talk about "shipping product" at Facebook, but today that usually means a keystroke that fires a stream of electrons out to a select focus group for beta testing—Iceland, for instance, or Venezuela.

The passages of Facebook capture the arc of Silicon Valley design: Having emigrated, like so many tech pioneers before it, from Cambridge to Palo Alto, the social networking site set up shop on the second floor of a downtown office building across from the tiny studio in which Jerry Manock designed the housing for the Apple II. It then relocated to the Stanford Industrial Park where "Zuck" held court from a panoptic glassed-in

cube at the center of the old HP manufacturing facility, and most recently
to a sprawling campus on the edge of the San Francisco Bay lately vacated
by the remnants of Sun Microsystems. From a dozen buildings encircled by
Hacker Way, a parliament of around 9,000 millennials governs what is now
the third largest country in the world.

The intangible requirements of New Age companies from Facebook and
Google down to the most recent e-commerce startup have called forth the
latest iteration in the history of Silicon Valley design. New companies and
even new industries have arrived in order to tap the seemingly bottomless
reservoir of technical talent, and democratizing cultural trends—the makers' movement, hackathons, open source developers' initiatives—inject a
continuous stream of adrenaline into the Bay Area design community. The
changes they have wrought have called forth whole new disciplines and
have penetrated into every corner of life: time, as Paul Virilio predicted,
has displaced space as the principal vector of meaning, and connectivity
has eclipsed materiality. The so-called Internet of Things has blurred the
line between hardware and software. Highway 101 remains clogged with
chartered vans carrying legions of young dotcommuters from their SOMA
lofts to the campuses of Apple, Google, and Facebook, but the borders of
Silicon Valley now embrace the whole of the Bay Area and indeed, the universe. "Things," in the most literal sense of that word, have changed.

The latest chapter in the history of Silicon Valley design opened in the
summer of 1997 when Steve Jobs returned to Apple and began immediately
to reorganize a company that had fallen into disarray. Robert Brunner had
departed the previous year to lead the San Francisco office of the Pentagram partnership, leaving the industrial design group, by most accounts,
unfocused and adrift, but this was only a symptom of Apple's larger mal-
aise. Wielding a scalpel in one hand and a machete in the other, Jobs slashed
a product line that had multiplied into fifteen separate platforms down to
four—a desktop and a laptop for professionals, and a desktop and laptop
for the general consumer; he dismissed a dozen contract advertising agencies leaving only one, Chiatt-Day, which proceeded to mock IBM (not for
the first time) with the iconoclastic "Think Different" campaign; he ele-
vated Jonathan ("Jony") Ive to the position of senior vice president, entrust-
ing an art school designer with a degree of strategic responsibility
unequalled in American corporate culture; and in the belief that given the

parlous state of its finances Apple would be better served by buying existing technology than developing its own, he instructed Donald Norman,
vice president in charge of the Advanced Technology Group, to close it
down, disperse its 160-person staff, and, in effect, fire himself.[2] The demise
of ATG freed up a new field of talent just as the virtual hand that seems
sometimes to be directing the course of Silicon Valley design was pointing
to the next convergence.

Inspired by the fecundity of Bell Labs on the East Coast and Xerox PARC
on the west, Microsoft cofounder Paul Allen had a few years earlier put
down the first installment of a $300 million investment in a research labo-
ratory strategically located at the edge of the Stanford Industrial Park. The
mission, as he conceived it, was to explore the unspecified "interval"
between the adoption of the computer as a business tool and its inevitable
integration into the fabric of everyday life. In contrast to the fabled corporate labs, however, which often battled their own management for permission to drive their ideas forward, Interval Research Corporation would not
be tethered to a mother ship. To direct this unprecedented venture, Allen
recruited David Liddle, whose experience leading the development of the
STAR workstation led him to imagine a "PARC without the Xerox."[3]

As the Internet economy surged and the computer industry generated,
in the oft-quoted words of venture capitalist John Doerr, "the greatest legal
accumulation of wealth in history," the autonomy afforded by Allen's largesse allowed Liddle unusual latitude to gain insights from practices—art,
play, theater—that fell well outside the domain of business applications.
Offering them "a place to do research you won't be able to do anywhere
else," he recruited an extraordinary staff that included engineers, biolo-
gists, psychologists, computer scientists, linguists, anthropologists, journalists, musicians, and designers, many of whom had worked together in
the hothouse environments of Atari, Apple, or PARC. Their field of exploration was to be the intersection of electronic media, computation, and communication, and their marching orders were "to do to the personal
computer what the PC had done to the mainframe."[4]

It was not the computer per se that drove the lab, however, but the
forms computing power might take—embedded in walls? implanted in
ears? dispersed throughout our daily environment?—and how people
might be using it by the beginning of the twenty-first century. At their first
formal gathering, on Bastille Day 1992, each member of the core research

staff agreed to draft a vision of how Interval might storm the bastions of the establishment. Even for an organization financed by the owner of Jimi Hendrix's Woodstock Stratocaster, these statements are remarkable for their Jacobinism, which expressed itself as a populist mission that was less about what could be built than how information technologies could be used "to significantly enhance the lives of ordinary people in a meaningful way."[5]

To focus their thinking, set a course, and explore possible modalities for working together across so many disciplinary frontiers, Interval held an offsite retreat in the Santa Cruz Mountains, facilitated by a senior team from IDEO, the design-and-innovation consultancy formed a year earlier out of the merger of ID Two, Matrix, and David Kelley Design. Liddle himself opened the meeting with a "rave" in which he likened the present state of computing to the medieval profession of scrivening, practiced by skilled, content-neutral literati who were paid to compose letters, contracts, plays, apologies, offers of marriage, and threats of divorce before they were driven into obsolescence by an increasingly literate middle class. Similarly, he argued, computation is about to pass from the domain of a technical elite and into the rhythms of everyday entertainment, education, and domestic life. The task, in the revolutionary age that was dawning, will be to create analog experiences in a digital world, to design systems that enable people to interact with the "infosphere" more like the ways in which they interact with one another: "We have our work cut out for us," he concluded.[6]

Over the course of three days of intensive discussion, debate, and informational performances, or "informances," six teams of Interval researchers, each guided by an IDEO facilitator, created scenarios intended to explore a spectrum of future-oriented themes in an experiential human context: an aging grandmother interacting with a home monitoring apparatus (facilitated by Jane Fulton [Suri]); a rapidly unfolding geopolitical crisis in the Middle East as played out in real time on an interactive "Video Wall" in the prime minister's office (Bill Moggridge); the challenges of a working mother in Sophia, Bulgaria, trying to manage the affairs of her daughter and her husband with the aid of the family robot (Bill Verplank); scenes from the life of a pharmaceutical sales representative outfitted with an electronic "Med-Folio" (Dennis Boyle); a tightly scripted day in the life of "Sylvie," a schoolgirl sporting a futuristic but believable slate-type learning device (Mike Nuttall); and a gang of unemployed street youth in Birmingham whose self-appointed mission was to use the products of designers to subvert the systems of which they are a part (Tim Brown). Ranging in perspective from the close-in to the far-out, each of the scenarios addressed in its own way the question that was at the heart of Interval's mission: "How will people live and work in the future?" Not only were they uncannily prescient, they represented a profoundly new role for design.

The informances, which were among numerous innovative design methodologies applied at Interval, involved what Brenda Laurel called "multisensory computing"—improvisational theater, role-playing, and other techniques intended to demonstrate "the appropriateness of 'thinking with the body' as a research technique in our field." Although each of the scenarios involved an imagined technological artifact, it was the situations in which they were embedded, not the devices themselves, that guided their efforts. Interval would go on to build numerous functional prototypes during its short but brilliant lifespan, but as ethnographer Bonnie Johnson remarked at the conclusion of the workshop, referencing the oft-quoted quip of Alan Kay, "If the best way to predict the future is to invent it, then the best way to begin inventing it is to visualize and enact it."[7]

At a time when most designers were still clamoring for recognition (or sequestered, like the priesthood of the Apple industrial design group, in a locked building reserved for "blue-sky creatives"), Interval's decision to engage a design firm at this formative stage represented an important inflection point in the growth of a professional community. The strategy, however, was grounded in the realities of a rapidly advancing technology. As interactive computing spilled out of the office and into the homes, cars, pockets, and purses of consumers, design, not technology, was destined to become the significant differentiator—"Today everybody can do the pick-and-shovel stuff," Liddle remarked with only slight exaggeration. Accordingly, in addition to developing algorithms and conducting ethnographic research, "we study and experiment with the design process itself."[8] Building upon the momentum unleashed by the Santa Cruz retreat, Interval invited "top designers from a variety of disciplines" for residencies ranging from a few days to a few weeks so that their practices could be observed and studied. Bill Moggridge was the first "captive designer" to submit to the anthropologist's gaze, followed by Gillian Crampton-Smith of the Royal College of Art.

In time, design methodologies came to be incorporated more-or-less seamlessly into the processes and practices of the lab. "What we did at Interval," stated Liddle, "was to introduce design ideas at the earliest stage of the product development process," rather than bring them in for an inspirational jolt at the beginning or cosmetic refinement at the end. The designers—sometimes to their own chagrin—were integrated into the larger research community, treated just like everyone else, and held to the same expectations: "I never minded that people felt that they were artists so long as they filed their patent disclosures on time and got their work done."[9]

In its early years, Interval cultivated a reputation as a sort of intellectual Camelot, where the best and the brightest followed their passions unconstrained by the commercial imperatives that beset the rest of the valley. They explored topics ranging from the mathematical (physicist Richard Shoup's attempt to prove that "a universe can be constructed not from first principles but from no principles") to the mystical (Dean Radin's rigorous investigations of parapsychological phenomena). In a shop overseen by Lee Felsenstein, designer of the first portable computer, they built musical instruments, haptic interfaces, wearable computers, image recognition software, wireless communications protocols, and holographic stereograms. Researchers traveled with the Lollapalooza alternative music festival to test an array of immersive computer experiences on glazed-eyed rockers and to Zion National Park where they studied Anastazi petroglyphs for clues to placemaking in virtual environments. "Everyone out there is doing things in a one- to three-year time frame," noted Paul Allen at the peak of his optimism, "and so we're trying not to do that."[10]

If Interval did not conduct itself in the manner of a button-down corporate lab, however, neither did it follow the model of a traditional think tank. Rather than simply attend conferences and publish papers, the research staff was expected to generate original intellectual property. Although this was hardly an unusual stance in the entrepreneurial climate of Silicon Valley, in time Paul Allen became increasingly impatient that there was "too much R, not enough D," and a coterie of MBAs arrived to help shift Interval's priorities, and its culture, in the direction of viable enterprises. In November 1996, Liddle dutifully announced the first of a series of startup ventures intended to prove that its projects were not "apartment cats," domestic pets unable to survive in the wilds of the market: Carnelian, based in Mountain View, supplied software systems for Internet publishers, drawing upon research conducted at Interval on the role of software agents in locating and retrieving information. Studies of computer vision conducted by Subitai Ahmad, John Levy, and Meg Withgott led to the founding of Electric Planet, a game company in Palo Alto that sought—fifteen years before Microsoft Kinect—to free hyperactive children from the shackles of keyboard-and-mouse. A couple of years later Interval spun off Fantasma Networks, which proposed to use ultrawideband radio signals to integrate the components of home entertainment systems with one another and with the Internet. By 1999 each of them had failed.

By far the most spectacular failure, however, was Purple Moon, a website and CD-ROM developed by a team led by Brenda Laurel and grounded in an intensive, two-and-a-half-year program of quantitative and ethnographic research into girls, computers, and play. This effort, supported by Cheskin Research and funded partially by Interval, illustrates some of the fundamental differences between market research—typically data-driven, analytical, and present-oriented—and design research, which uses qualitative methods that help designers "observe the future in the present." In the words of Cheskin's Christopher Ireland, "A company can ship a product to any part of the world, but it cannot ship to the future."[11]

Purple Moon grew out of Laurel's parallel interest in the gender imbalance in technology and her arresting idea that entering the virtual world of a computer program is equivalent to entering the imagined world of the theater.[12] Building on a research base that included interviews with 1,100 children (boys as well as girls), a comprehensive literature review, and consultations with academic experts in gender psychology and spatial cognition as well as schoolteachers and playground supervisors, Purple Moon launched its first titles, *Rockett's New School* and *Secret Paths in the Garden*, directed to girls, age eight to twelve. It was, for all intents and purposes, the first social network.[13]

The demise of Purple Moon (which was ultimately acquired by its archnemesis, Mattel, and summarily dismembered) points both to the power and limits of design research. While more militant members of the company demanded that the twelve-year-old Rocket be gay and in a

Figure 6.1
Rockett Movado and her friends, characters designed by various artists. Courtesy of Brenda Laurel.

wheelchair, the researchers at Cheskin countered that the program must be grounded not in an ideological mission but in research-based design principles: the power of play lies not in didacticism but in developing a platform from which players can explore their own imagined scenarios.

On a chilly morning in April, a few months into the millennium, the president of Paul Allen's investment arm, Vulcan Ventures, flew down from Seattle in a corporate jet. Flanked by a contingent of security guards, William Savoy summoned Interval's 116 researchers and fifty-four staff members together and in a reprise of the final hours of Atari, ordered them to pack up their personal belongings and exit the building—permanently. Interval provided an intellectually intense environment and was wildly productive of ideas (the research staff generated 131 patents over the course of its eight-year lifespan), but there were also serious oversights: Referring to Stewart Brand's Whole Earth 'Lectronic Link, Liddle remarked in an unguarded moment that the World Wide Web was of little significance beyond "a few geeks and WELL-heads." Moreover, discipline was loose and constraints—which are the lifeblood of design—were often lacking. "Our Monday morning kickoff meetings started at 11:00," recalled one researcher, "and then we broke for lunch." Another observed that—for better or for worse—"There simply wasn't anyone in the room who represented a commercial imperative." A skeleton staff stayed on to work on

Figure 6.2
Visitor's badge, Interval Research Corporation.

problems related to Vulcan's broadband portfolio, but as the millennium dawned over Silicon Valley, Interval dispersed its design talent to the winds.

Although the popular press took a morbid pleasure in reporting on "the think tank that tanked," from the perspective of Silicon Valley design the story is arguably more positive and certainly more nuanced.[14] Liddle deliberately removed obstacles to creative learning and cross-disciplinary collaboration and fostered an environment in which there was effectively no hierarchy, a mix of age and gender was the norm, and everybody had access to everybody else. Colin Burns captured the experience of many of the younger researchers: while deepening his technical skills as an interaction designer, the chance to work shoulder to shoulder with computer scientists, ethnographers, artists, and production engineers "made my T-shaped arms longer and stronger."

But the long-term impact of this radical interdisciplinarity was structural as well as personal. Precisely because Interval was research- rather than product-oriented, Liddle was able to encourage a robust network of academic affiliations. Joy Mountford, who had joined the exodus from Apple's advanced technology group, brought with her the University Workshop Interface Program she had launched within Apple's Human Interface Group; at Interval she continued to offer internships, residencies, and exchanges with research universities such as Stanford and Carnegie Mellon, but also design schools including Art Center, the Institute for Design at IIT, and London's Royal College of Art, where Gillian Crampton-Smith was building a pioneering program in computer-related design.

The shared commitment of Interval was to the idea that computer interfaces should be shaped as much by cultural factors as functional requirements. Scores of researchers carried this influence back to their careers in corporate design offices, professional consultancies, and especially academia.

One the most enduring of the Interval-sponsored initiatives had its origins in a course taught by Liddle and Terry Winograd, a prominent Stanford University computer scientist with a decidedly humanistic bent. In 1990, Winograd had been invited to deliver the closing address at the annual meeting of CHI, which marked his transition from artificial intelligence to the emerging field of computer–human interaction. Influenced by the provocations of Mitch Kapor, who had just nailed his eight-point "Software Design Manifesto" to the door of the computer industry, and cognitive engineer Donald Norman, whose *Psychology of Everyday Things* (1988) had generated widespread debate about the consequences of ill-considered product "affordances," Winograd summoned a cadre of like-minded professionals to a three-day conference in Pajaro Dunes. Under the banner "Bringing Design to Software," they trained their artillery on yet another bastion of engineering that had rested comfortably on the pillars of functionality and profit.[15]

The common denominator in all of these efforts, and of Silicon Valley design generally, is the principle, as Winograd stated it, of "designing for the full range of human experience." History and language, he argued, are as important to software design as equations and algorithms. As such, the movement can be seen as an insurgency instigated from within the world of engineering itself, one that was prompted in part by the populist agendas of computer scientists ranging from Douglas Engelbart to Alan Kay to Terry Winograd, and partly by the demands of an expanding consumer market. In this respect, Interval Research Corporation can be seen as the last of the self-contained, multidisciplinary centers—SRI, Xerox PARC, Atari Research Labs, the Apple Advanced Technology Group—that have figured so importantly in the history of Silicon Valley design. The labs advanced their own programs while helping to redefine the field and position it within a distinctively Bay Area continuum that extends from basic research to the marketing of finished products. Even so, they formed only one part of a complex ecosystem that continues to teem with life.

SRI International and PARC—now a for-profit subsidiary of the Xerox Corporation—continue to flourish, of course, and internal corporate design groups still play a major role at companies throughout the Bay Area— although in a corporate setting, design is only as good as the leadership of the company allows it to be. The partnership of Steve Jobs and Jony Ive is the object lesson of "leadership by design."[16] Less well known, but equally instructive, is the case of Hewlett-Packard.

In 1996, Sam Lucente joined the migration from the East Coast—in this case IBM's Corporate Design Center in the Hudson Valley—to the west. While working with Richard Sapper on the IBM ThinkPad, Lucente became convinced of the trajectory toward hardware-software convergence and of the role of the Internet in driving it. On a hunch, Lucente tapped his cache of frequent flier miles, and bought a one-way ticket to Mountain View where he met with Marc Andreessen at Netscape, which had just launched Mosaic, the first successful web browser. Betting on the Web, Lucente joined Netscape as director of user experience.

With the eclipse of the Netscape Navigator, Lucente spent an interlude exploring the untamed frontier of the Web before joining Hewlett-Packard as the first vice president for design—a position of executive authority coveted by HP's internal designers for generations. There were at that time thirty-five people in HP's corporate design office, ninety-eight external ID firms doing contract work worldwide, and every business unit had its own graphical, interface, and instrumentation standards. By the time he left eight years later, the internal group had grown to some 300 industrial, human factors, and user experience designers; he had built an online design center; and had narrowed the circle of outside ID contractors to Lunar, IDEO, frog, Astro, and about half-dozen others. Rather than playing them off against one other, Lucente gathered together all of the internal and external designers under the shared umbrella of "HP Design Attitude." Each firm took on a different product category—desktops, notebooks, printers, and scanners—and then swapped over an intense three-month period of coordinated development. The new family of products hit the market in 2004–5, and proved extremely successful as well as personally gratifying: "It was just beautiful to work with these firms on the basis of a true strategic partnership," he mused. Less beautiful was working with an unresponsive leadership and an uncomprehending board.[17]

Hewlett-Packard thus played a decisive role in stabilizing the independent consultancies during a period of economic distress, and today they form the most prominent feature of the twenty-first-century design landscape; three generations of them now constitute an archipelago of innovation that stretches from San Francisco to San Jose. From their origins in industrial design and engineering, they have expanded their offerings and diversified their staffs in an ongoing effort to stay one step ahead of an ever-changing market, the industries that populate it, and the technologies that drive it. The larger firms have planted colonies in a dozen countries around the world.

With the return of David Kelley to Stanford, leadership of IDEO passed to Tim Brown, who oversees a global workforce of 650 creatives, about half of whom are distributed between locations in Palo Alto and San Francisco. In its formative years, IDEO had neither the resources nor the inclination to support its human-centered approach with quantitative data gathering or market analytics. Accordingly, the designers improvised a cluster of ad hoc practices that have matured into a rigorous methodology. Market research may yield data, but *inspiration* is more likely to come from statistically insignificant observations of "extreme users" and open-ended interviews conducted by researchers who are trained to listen as closely to what is not said as to what is. IDEOers are fond of quoting the tag attributed (without evidence) to Henry Ford: "If I had asked my customers what they wanted, they would have said, 'a faster horse.'"[18]

Over the course of its thirty-year history, IDEO has experimented with a series of organizational modalities in an ongoing effort to stay abreast of a changing world: interdisciplinary studios, then discipline-driven practices, "collectives" attuned to shared content areas, and most recently the notion that the design process itself may be conceived as a "platform." In the words of CEO Tim Brown, "It has always been about sending out probes to explore the edges," with the understanding that some of those edges will inevitably move to the center, and the certainty that today's center, as William Butler Yeats pointed out, will not hold.[19]

As the culture, the economy, and the competitive landscape shift, interdisciplinary teams at IDEO are now being asked to handle a range of problems that fall well outside the traditional concerns of design firms: reducing the incidence of teen pregnancy; reversing the epidemic of pediatric obesity; or designing strategies to encourage Americans to conserve energy, donate blood, or adhere to drug regimens. To remain relevant (and profitable), the company has responded with a wave of experimental programs: the nonprofit IDEO.org, IDEO Labs, and OpenIDEO, a web-based open-source program that invites the public at large to propose solutions to sponsored challenges deemed too vast for any single design team to handle: managing e-waste; restoring vibrancy to cities facing economic decline; promoting healthy aging; and imagining a new role for the media. A core team invites responses from a global community of "citizen-designers," then moves methodically through a process of inspiration, ideation, evaluation, refinement, and implementation. OpenIDEO has been compared to a brainstorming session of 40,000 people.

IDEO built its reputation on a creative synthesis of industrial design and mechanical engineering and continues to work on such tangible projects as injection devices for Eli Lilly and office products for Steelcase. Today's products, however, involve complex interactions and are located within a physical and virtual environment that extends infinitely in all directions, and design has become less about discrete objects than about systems and applications. Reflecting the arc of IDEO's recent history, Brown recalls that his own training in industrial design was oriented toward *stuff*: better, more efficient, more beautiful stuff, to be sure, but stuff nonetheless. That is changing: "We are still designing machines," he wrote in a commentary on the future of industrial design, "but also the ghosts that live inside them."[20]

The subliminal rivalry that once animated relations between IDEO and frog has largely abated since Hartmut Esslinger began to ease into retirement and the reins of leadership passed first to Doreen Lorenzo and then to Andy Zimmerman. Since its earliest work for Wega and Sony, frog had maintained a strong orientation toward consumer electronics; Esslinger in fact once bet—and almost lost—the company on a failed venture called "frox" ("frog electronics"), which hoped to integrate entertainment and computing within a single digital multimedia system. In 1994 Esslinger began working with a software group in Austin, which became the core of the global software team. Interaction designers now constitute the most numerous species of the 300 frogs who populate the creative pond, with about that many again distributed between strategy and engineering.

Like all amphibious life forms, frog is constantly metamorphosing and its center of gravity has shifted decisively in the direction of digital design.

In 1998 the company felt ready to take on a massive project to redesign the 250,000 page website of the German software giant, SAP, and as it crossed the threshold into the new millennium, digital design constituted about 70 percent of frog's overall revenues. Even so, frog remains committed to its governing principle of "integrated strategic design" and industrial design remains a core practice and has in fact grown steadily. A recent project for Disney World—the largest in frog's history—is emblematic of the trend toward convergence. At the most immediate, tangible level, it begins with an adjustable wristband that transmits visitor data to reading stations located throughout the park and allows Goofy to greet "Tommy" by name as the child approaches (and Tommy's parents to find him if he gets lost); the next tier includes physical signage and digital maps created by frog's interaction and visual designers to manage people flow; finally, leaving the material plane altogether, the visitors' accumulated data is transferred back to a family website that records the details of their visit.

As computing leaves the computer and such everyday objects as running shoes and eyeglasses become portals to an infinite cloud of data, a massive change is taking place in the ways in which we relate to our things. Mark Rolston, until recently frog's chief creative officer, observed that "People are understanding value through systems, through experiences, through brands, more than through the physical instance of the product." At the same time, information itself is moving from its anchorage in injection-molded desktop boxes and becoming pervasive and surrounding—"the collective ecosystem," as Lorenzo put it, "of all devices, networks, data sets, and people." The challenges to design organizations are enormous, and the stakes for their clients even greater, but the leadership is optimistic: "I used to have to persuade clients of the value of design," noted Lorenzo, but "the battle has been won. It is recognized at the C-level that a design strategy is at the same level of importance to a company's survival as a business plan."[21]

Although smaller than the two other first generation companies, Lunar Design has by no means been eclipsed by them by virtue of its more concentrated focus. Since 2001, when John Edson inherited the presidency from founders Jeff Smith and Gerard Furbershaw, the company has endeavored to ground itself in a sustainable and transferable operational model. Lunar has a strong heritage of combining design with engineering (as typified by Edson himself), and its core business remains tied to product development even as Silicon Valley moves relentlessly into bits and bytes and the industry into strategy and research: those parts of the business are nonetheless growing, and Edson stresses that "We can still watch a part come off the machine while having conversations about the fuzzy front end."[22]

Consumer electronics and lifestyle products remain strong practices, and have in fact merged unexpectedly with Lunar's core strength in the life sciences, as patients become better informed and more actively involved in their own healthcare. At the most highly professional level, a design team might still work to bring an ophthalmic surgeon's tools up to the same level as her BMW or her iPhone, but a product such as the Core 2, a stylish armband for BodyMedia whose sensors track some 5,000 physiological data points per minute, is a striking example of how the life sciences and medical technology are crossing over into the consumer economy.

In the first phase of its history, Lunar's founders viewed design as a means to help clients differentiate their products from those of their competitors, articulate a point of view, and—one hopes—create desire. Lunar's ongoing relationship with Hewlett-Packard, which now dates back some twenty years, is an example. The HP Pavilion family of home computers, first introduced in 1995, represented the company's first major effort to move computing out of the technical and business market at into home use, but to do so, the design language of the product needed to shift from "office equipment" to "home appliance." Lunar helped to domesticate the computer by reducing the footprint of the tower and—anathema to the PC world—adding a dash of style: "We aimed for a slim, elegant profile," stated Ken Wood, now Lunar's executive creative director. "And we noticed that as the design progressed, people found the PC much more approachable— almost like one of their favorite household products." The collaboration continued with the Touchsmart all-in-one PC and HP Patterns, a graphical intervention that uses texture and color to transform the laptop from a business machine into a personal accessory.

As the company matured the emphasis shifted upward from products to solutions, and as it prepares to seed the next stage of its evolution, the central challenge, as Edson puts it, is "understanding what people are all about." Lunar's core design and engineering practices, led by Jeff Salazar and Art Sandoval, respectively, remain close to the heart of the organization, but they have been augmented in recent years by a growing focus on strategy and insight, user experience design, and—particularly in the domain of the life sciences—emerging markets in India and China.[23]

Over the course of their thirty-five year histories, IDEO, frog, and Lunar have merged and acquired; their client bases have diversified; their business models have evolved; and their internal organizations can best be described as an ongoing prototype. Even as they outgrew their funky loft spaces, idiosyncratic work hours, and nonexistent dress codes, however, they continue to place great importance upon maintaining internal cultures that are sufficiently individualized to keep their most seasoned employees from being tempted by salary offers from Google and Intuit. They have also, during those formative decades, incubated nearly all of the second-generation consultancies that have helped turn the San Francisco Bay Area into the most concentrated field of design talent in the world.

Yves Béhar, Dan Harden, and Gadi Amit worked alongside one another at frog, and launched their respective firms as an express rebuttal to Hartmut Esslinger's unsettling pronouncement one day in 1999 that "ID is dead and everything is heading toward convergence." This did not sit well with a cohort of industrial designers trained at the top schools in Switzerland, Israel, and the United States and deeply committed to the irreducible physicality of the object. As the center of gravity at IDEO has shifted in the direction of strategic consulting, and frog's toward digital design, the second-generation consultancies remain resolutely focused on traditional product development.

But apart from some Spanish revivalist architecture and a popular classic car show, there is very little in Silicon Valley that can be described as "traditional." In the space of barely a decade the new consultancies have had to incorporate far-reaching changes into almost every aspect of their practice: visualization tools, especially 3D CAD systems, have become cheaper, more versatile, and more intuitive; rapid prototyping equipment allows a laptop-toting designer to complete the layout of a part before boarding a flight in Shanghai and have the "printout" waiting when she returns to California the next day; the technologies that drive the products they are asked to work on have become smaller and lighter, and the products themselves might need to balance physical, digital, and cloud-based elements. Most important, perhaps—and due in large measure to the success of "design forward" brands such as Apple, Nike, and BMW—there has been a dramatic spike in corporate America's perception of the value of design per se: "After all," as Whipsaw's Dan Harden points out to wary clients, "bad design costs just as much to tool as good design."[24]

The second-generation firms compete, cooperate, and sometimes collaborate, and all tend to know when Nike or Dell is in town shopping around a new project. To be sure, they differ from one another in significant respects: in the balance each tries to strike among designers, engineers, and strategists; the degree of immersion they maintain with their clients throughout the product development process; the number and fidelity of their deliverables (a data set, a stack of Alias renderings, an assortment of volumetric models, a fully engineered functional prototype); and even in their criteria for hiring (Brett Lovelady at Astro: "Can they sketch?" Gadi Amit at New Deal: "Can they learn?"). More important, each speaks in a distinctly different voice. Whereas IDEO has reorganized itself as a partnership and frog, in the post-Esslinger period, has evolved into a decentralized "hydra-headed" leadership structure, the second wave studios tend to be guided by the design philosophy of a single individual: Yves Béhar at fuseproject, Dan Harden at Whipsaw, and Gadi Amit at New Deal Design touch every project and personally sign off on everything that goes out the door. Although it is not a model that is readily scalable, it does enable them to articulate a cohesive point of view and to differentiate themselves from one another. Most would agree with Gadi Amit: "I truly believe that the competition is making us better."

In a graffiti-covered warehouse in San Francisco's ever-emerging, Mad Max-inflected "Design District," the entire staff of fuseproject is arrayed within a single, unobstructed space where each project can be worked on by an integrated team. The disciplinary fusion reflects Béhar's narrativist concept of "bringing stories to life." Everybody, in this age of hybridity—software and hardware designers, user-interface and user-experience, strategists and technologists—must be telling the same story and that story must be consistent from coding to naming and everywhere in between. The metanarrative has clearly resonated. After what Béhar describes as a "slow build," both the firm and its founder have attained celebrity status. A one-person show at the San Francisco Museum of Modern Art in 2004, a series of high-profile projects for the European companies Birkenstock and BMW Mini, and products such as the innovative LEAF lamp for Herman Miller have fueled the growth of fuseproject to some seventy-five creative professionals and an equity investment by the Chinese marketing firm BlueFocus.

A whipsaw, once a familiar artifact of Northern California's dwindling redwood forests, is wielded by two loggers whose reciprocal motions must be perfectly aligned. This is the principle underlying Dan Harden's thirty-five-person consultancy located at the opposite end of the valley in San Jose. Harden believes that design is as much about two-way relationship building as it is about product development. Achieving this alignment is not always easy—"most of our clients are left-brain, designers are mostly right-brain"—but by immersing themselves deeply in the client's problem, preserving a populist orientation, and supporting their work with rigorous engineering, the designers at Whipsaw have racked up a disproportionate number of awards, honors, and citations. A singular vision does not, however, translate into a house style. To the contrary, Harden asserts, "it's really about design getting out of the way" and finding the right statement for the product in question: bold for Eton's family of emergency equipment, unobtrusive for ApniCure's sleep therapy system, organic and inviting for Adiri's infant bottles.

Gadi Amit, who began his career designing precision medical imaging equipment in the "startup nation" of Israel, is arguably the most hardheaded among the cohort that leapt from the frogpond at the end of the nineties. Known for his impatience with the current rage for "design thinking" (he forbids the use of Post-it notes in the studio), Amit believes that by placing thought before action and analysis before creative ideation, design thinking has seriously compromised the professional skills needed for design *doing*. "In fact," he counters, "the real challenge designers face is the opposite: a recognition that action (prototyping, sketching) often precedes thinking and that many products, inventions and great companies were born out of a burst of creativity and not through a regimented thought process." New Deal's approach to the FitBit Tracker personal fitness monitor reflects Amit's contrarian philosophy: the design team conducted extensive research into female demographics, OLED technology, and options for embedding electronics, but at the end of the day the form of the device was inspired by a simple wooden clothespin.

Whether guided by pragmatism or Platonism, each of these designers has learned to navigate the void that separates the art and craft of design from the give and take of business. Yves Béhar had never heard the initials

"ROI" when he began his design studies in Lausanne, and even when he entered the Academy of Applied Arts in Belgrade, Branko Lukić, who leads Studio NONOBJECT in Palo Alto, had no idea that "there was a job that was to make things better." They have come to terms with the hard realities of running a business, however, and along with most of their peers, have recognized that the old fee-for-service model of the consultant designer has reached the end of its useful life. fuseproject has entered into long-term ventures with major clients including Herman Miller and Jawbone; Whipsaw has invested in promising startups, and Astro Studios spun off a separate gaming company under the leadership of founder Brett Lovelady. Each of these business model innovations is grounded in a revaluation of the service designers are offering, which New Deal's Gadi Amit put most succinctly: "We don't sell hours; we sell ingenuity."

The oldest of the second-wave consultancies is Astro Design, launched by Brett Lovelady in 1994, and the youngest is Ammunition Group, ignited by Robert Brunner in 2007. Lovelady was working on million-dollar, cleanroom disk storage systems at Tandem Computer but never lost the irreverent spirit of his undergraduate sideline as an illustrator and political cartoonist: "I was enamored of pop culture, street culture, youth culture—I wanted to start a company that embraced all the things that Silicon Valley was *not* paying attention to." To achieve this, it was necessary to be as edgy in designing a sustainable, scalable business model as it was to design the Microsoft Xbox 360 wireless console gaming system or Nike's first electronic product, the family of Triax sports watches. Some 15–20 percent of Astro's work is equity-based—stock exchanges, royalties, licensing agreements—which enables the studio to stay close to the ground while keeping its head in the stars.

Ammunition Group, the youngest of the mid-sized, second-generation firms, was founded in 2007 by Robert Brunner, who grew up listening to his father—an IBM engineer—rail against industrial designers ("All you guys do is spec. the paint and it usually peels off"). Brunner has been particularly aggressive in addressing the paradox that designers typically exit the product development cycle at precisely the point at which value (and profit) is being created. An evolving portfolio of partnerships with Williams-Sonoma, Barnes & Noble, and the spectacularly successful Beats by Dr. Dre family of audio products, which Ammunition developed as a joint venture with music producer Jimmy Iovine and the hip-hop artist Dr.

Dre, have served to vindicate Brunner's assertion of the role of designers in creating value and the legitimacy of their claim to be recognized for it— and not just by fellow designers.

As cofounder of Lunar Design in in 1984, founding director of Apple's industrial design group in 1989, and leader of Pentagram's product design group in 1996, Brunner has observed, participated in, and to a significant degree driven the changing status of his profession. In the early days, he recalls, the designer was seen as providing a service to engineering—the "art guy" in the product development process who was handed a list of constraints and told to navigate around them. Over the course of his long and variegated career Brunner has witnessed an inversion to the point that designers are increasingly in a position to define those constraints at the outset. His own epiphany came at Apple, where he sat at the same table with MBAs and PhDs: "At first I wondered what I was doing there, but I gradually came to the realization that I knew something that they did not."[25]

This reversal of fortunes corresponds to a new generation of hybrid products that cannot easily be accommodated by the industrial equation of centralized mass production and generalized mass consumption. In the 1930s, the first generation of American consultant designers became celebrities by streamlining refrigerators and pencil sharpeners to reflect the supposed dynamism of Machine Age America, abetted by a new breed of behavioral scientists who devised strategies by which to sell them. The challenge to today's designers is to give form to products that may be crowd-sourced or cloud-sourced, solar-powered or sensor-activated, portable, wearable, implantable, and of course networked. Devices such as the UP 24/7 personal monitor designed by fuseproject for Jawbone, the FitBit activity tracker (New Deal), and Nike's FuelBand (initiated by Astro and brought to completion by Whipsaw), are outfitting citizens of the era of Big Data and the Quantified Self. Adobe's first foray into hardware—Project Mighty, a cloud-based pen that is mightier than any sword; a digital straight-edge drawing device known as Napoleon (a "short ruler")—are part of a growing trend toward products that are inherently ambiguous: mass-produced but instantly customized; intimately personal but also aggressively social; tools of work that are also accessories of play. They are singular artifacts but they function only within an ecosystem of accessories, services, apps, and websites that call for new forms and new disciplines.

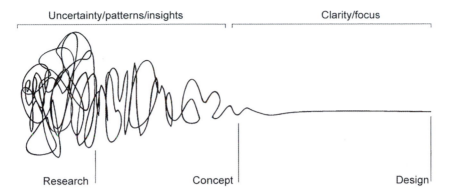

Figure 6.3

Damien Newman, "The Squiggle." Courtesy of Damien Newman, Central, Sausalito, California.

The San Jose-based Adobe Systems bridges these two generations. Adobe, it may be recalled, was founded by two renegade scientists from Xerox PARC—John Warnock and Charles Geschke—and earned its reputation as an engineering-driven software company. In December 2005, however, Macromedia's chief creative officer, Michael Gough, walked across Townsend Street, the main artery of San Francisco's "Multimedia Gulch," and became Adobe's first vice president of experience design. Gough—himself a trained architect—now oversees an XD staff of more than one hundred designers, a term he uses liberally to include the recognized fields (visual design, interaction design, industrial design) but also architects, sculptors, engineers, researchers, writers, and DJs. Designers have always had a place at Adobe—the eccentric Russell Brown, senior creative services director, has been with the company almost from the beginning—but XD is evidence of a cultural shift in which design is no longer merely a "creative service" to engineering.

It is not so much that Adobe was slow to embrace design; rather, the thirty-year old company had to wait until demand and supply were in proper alignment. On the one hand, multilayered products such as Photoshop 6.0 have now evolved to a level of complexity where, in Gough's words, "people who understand interaction and experience need to be involved." On the supply side, the design community itself had to mature to a point where it could go beyond superficial visual layout and really grapple with the internal complexities of digital publishing: just as

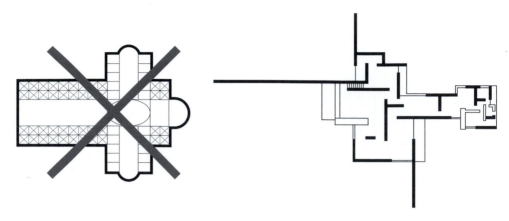

Figure 6.4

Adobe Experience Model. "We are modernists in our aesthetic sensibility." Courtesy of Michael Gough, Experience Design, Adobe Systems.

engineering reached a point where it needed design, Gough finds that "Today it's possible to hire designers with technical proficiency."[26]

The articulation of the Adobe Experience Model (AXD) represents a pivotal moment in the repositioning of design. At the heart of AXD is a set of attributes common to every design discipline: speed, flexibility, craftsmanship, appreciation for the choreography of an unfolding experience, and harmonization of the details with the whole. Most important, however, is an unusual relationship to the designer's absolute desideratum of empathy: "We want the same thing from our interactions with computers that we want from our relationships with people," Gough believes, and insofar as the designers of Adobe's products are in the business of creating tools for other creative professionals, they are in the unique position of being their own customers.

Adobe is an example of a second-generation company that has navigated the innovator's dilemma by transitioning from an engineering- to a design-driven model. An array of third-generation companies that were born into the new age, however, is transforming the postindustrial landscape of Silicon Valley as visibly as did their industrial predecessors in the 1960s and '70s. Just as Hewlett-Packard and Ampex provided a base for Silicon Valley's first industrial designers, Google and Facebook and an alphabet of smaller companies from Airbnb to ZYNGA are doing the same for an emerging generation of interface designers, interaction designers, and user-experience designers.[27] The ever-expanding Googleplex, whose solar panels, beach umbrellas, volleyball courts, and mobile haircut bus are visible from space (courtesy of Google Earth), exemplifies the changing face of design in the Age of the Search.

Google employs designers to take care of its visual assets including Search, Maps, and Gmail. In addition, as the company expands into hardware, a growing number of industrial designers are to be found working on Chromebook laptops and Nexus tablets powered by its Android operating system, public initiatives such as Glass, and "moonshots" fired from an undisclosed facility called Google[x] that include self-driving cars, high-altitude balloons capable of bringing Wi-Fi Internet access to disaster areas, as well as two to three confidential initiatives begun each year. "Design has no purpose in and of itself," states Astro Teller, who directs the operations of Google[x]. "Design drives everything we do."[28] This is a striking departure, however, as Google operated for a full seven years before hiring its first full-time, classically trained visual designer: "We let the math and the data govern how things look and feel," stated Marissa Mayer, then the company's vice president of user experience in an interview that left the design community profoundly demoralized.[29]

On June 21, 2011, Creative Director Chris Wiggins alerted the public in a blogpost to a new project intended to update the look and feel of its interfaces: "Starting today, you might begin noticing that things look a little different across Google products. We're working on a project to bring you a new and improved Google experience." Behind this understated announcement lay a profound shift in the character of one of the world's most powerful companies. Two months earlier, in the same week that he assumed the position of CEO, cofounder Larry Page had personally launched what became known as "Project Kennedy." Google's principal products—Search, Maps, Calendar, Gmail—had evolved organically but independently, and as these services matured and began to be used side-by-side it became increasingly evident that they bore little family resemblance and burdened users with redundancy, inconsistency, and too much "cognitive load." Project Kennedy sought to bring order to this unruly mess by balancing the engineer's devotion to "simplicity and speed" with the designer's quest for "beauty and cohesiveness." "We were let out of our cage," exulted Jon Wiley, design lead for Search and coordinator of the so-called User Experience Alliance, which includes every one of Google's design leads. Matias Duarte, design director for the Android operating system, agrees that the entire company is in the midst of a fundamental transformation: "For lack of a better word, Google is going through a design revolution."[30]

The design revolution is manifest in layout, typography, and other visual elements, but also in the full spectrum of functionality that falls under the category of "user experience." It was occasioned by multiple factors, not the least of which is an intense competitive environment in which design has come to be understood as the chief differentiator among functionally similar products. This has long been the case in the world of consumer goods, but it applies equally to a new generation of digital artifacts that have disrupted the rhythms of everyday life: Just as the citizens of the twentieth century came to expect their physical products to do more than simply function properly, citizens of the twenty-first century are making the same demands of their hybrid information appliances and ultimately of the software itself. Sound engineering is expected of any product entering the market, but so, increasingly, is sound design.

Four freeway exits to the north of the Googleplex, bordered by San Francisco Bay and encircled by Hacker Way, lies the campus of Facebook, where some 180 design professionals work to maintain the consistency of a website that serves well over a billion people of all ages, on all continents, and who may log on in Afrikaans, Tagalog, or Welsh. Facebook is, in effect, a single, longitudinal program of design research that moves at warp speed and on a global scale. Like the automobile industry one hundred years earlier, its design and engineering teams are building a product, its infrastructure, and its user base simultaneously and in real time, and it is not much of an exaggeration to say that they are making it up as they go along. As in so many other Silicon Valley giants—most notably Apple—designers at Facebook are in a position of considerable strategic importance. In contrast to Apple, however, whose overall design program is guided by the singular vision of Jony Ive, responsibility for design at Facebook is distributed among content strategists, UX researchers, communications designers, and a product design team that includes around one hundred web and interaction designers who became part of Facebook when it acquired the San Francisco digital design firm, Hot Studio, in 2013. What is remarkable about this burgeoning community is that almost none of these fields even existed a generation ago.[31]

Figure 6.5
Awesome button, early prototype. Courtesy of Soleio Cuervo.

Aaron Sittig, a product of the Napster-Friendster-MySpace shakeout, was the founding member of Facebook's design team, though it was not entirely clear, in the early days, exactly what that meant: "I had written some code, I knew something about layout, but I never really thought of myself as a designer," he admitted. This innocence served him well, however, for when Sittig set out to refresh the original site, he focused not just on visual appearance but on how it actually worked. Facebook was at that time still a tiny startup with only around a dozen employees, and the culture was, "Let ideas have a chance, prune them early, and redesign." One of these early ideas was of a "button" that would invite users to signal their approval with a single click, rather than type out a written commentary. Sittig's idea of an "Awesome" button was refined by Soleio Cuervo, who redrew it, renamed, integrated it into Facebook's "Universal Feedback Interface" and transformed into one of the most recognized graphical symbols in the world.

Facebook is governed by Zuckerberg's Law, which states that, "next year, people will share twice as much information as they share this year."[32] As it evolved from a closed, intrauniversity network to an open platform operating on five continents, Facebook has launched a progression of new "products" including Newsfeed, Timeline, Graph Search, and—as it makes its move into mobile—Messenger, in order to keep the system relevant, engaging, and growing. Each phase change has resulted in challenges on a scale that is unprecedented in the design profession: new features may be tested on a focus group of ten or twenty million users, results are processed instantaneously, and continuous modifications are made. According to Maria Giudice, one of four directors of product design, the process advances through "a healthy conflict between imagination and metrics."

In every project at Facebook, a designer sits alongside an engineer, a researcher, and a project manager, and the design directors sit at the same table every two weeks with the leadership of the company. While this is not yet the norm in technology companies, there is growing recognition that an enterprise cannot be successful if it does not have a designer on every team. This is in part due to the simple law of competitive advantage—designers have argued for much of the twentieth century that design can be the key differentiator among functionally comparable products. But it has also to do with the much-discussed "rise of the millennials," a generation born into a world in which technology is ubiquitous and therefore unremarkable. The reigning design principle at Facebook, therefore, is that people should feel that they are interacting with other people, not with the system.

In the world of Web 2.0, represented by Bay Area upstarts such as Google and Facebook but also Dropbox, LinkedIn, Instagram, Pinterest, Twitter, and Yelp, it is accepted that a well-engineered product is merely the price of admission to the market, and that it must be well designed—if not brilliantly designed—if it is to compete. It is also the case, however, that older industries are turning to designers for an extreme makeover, and not merely updated styling or refreshing an aging logo. Examples abound of Silicon Valley companies that have reinvented established product categories such as the book, the automobile, the telephone, or even the humble residential thermostat, and engaged internal or external design groups to assist them. Typically, it is not simply a problem of form-giving, but of conceiving a product, the infrastructure that supports it, and the business model that sustains it in one pass. Design, in Silicon Valley, is inextricably embedded in a complex ecosystem of innovation.

The most venerable of the traditional object-types is surely the book, which has experienced surprisingly little innovation in the five centuries since Johannes Gutenberg prototyped the world's first mass-produced information appliance. As the bearer of cultural memory, the book proved notoriously resistant to technological change until the late 1990s, when the SoftBook, designed by IDEO for Softbook Press, and the Rocket eReader introduced by the Palo Alto firm NuvoMedia, made their first, tentative steps toward market acceptance. Softbook founder Jim Sachs struggled to create a viable infrastructure for the three-pound, leather-covered, dial-up device, and the bursting of the Internet bubble finished it off. But the seeds of an electronic book, conceived on a hitchhiking trip through India and Nepal, had been planted: in 2007 Amazon offered the original Kindle, which sold out in five hours.[33]

Early in the new century it had become clear to CEO Jeff Bezos that the days of packing books into cardboard boxes and driving them to people's houses in smoking trucks were numbered, and he began to think about how Amazon's formidable brand, market, and content assets might be combined in something more than an online mail order house. Accordingly, in 2004, Amazon spun off a research and development skunkworks located 800 miles from Amazon's headquarters in Seattle but barely half a mile from the main campus of Apple in Cupertino. Gregg Zehr, a veteran of Apple and Palm, was tapped to lead Lab126, which he describes as "an upside-down startup."[34]

Situated in the strategic heart of Silicon Valley, Lab126 has developed all six generations of the Amazon Kindle and has been responsible for every detail of the design, from the Paperwhite display to the page-turn interface to the choice of inks and cardstock in which it is packaged. The design teams are mixed, in terms of discipline, age, and industry experience, and may include industrial, interaction, graphic, and UX designers; there is even a fashion designer who developed the colors for the ingenious "origami" cover of the Kindle Fire, which doubles as a stand that can support the tablet in either landscape or portrait mode. "We have evolved the full spectrum of design," explains Zehr, "starting with basic questions of 'what is an e-reader' and 'what should be in it.'"

Driving the evolution of the Kindle, from 2007 to the present, is the goal of "immersive reading"; new functionalities are added—cross-referencing, translation, word definitions—and extraneous "bells and whistles" are removed in pursuit of this singular objective. It is noteworthy that nobody at Lab 126 speaks about replacing the book, but only about how to enhance the experience of reading—by technology, and by design.

As a product category, the automobile has been as disruptive of transportation as the book has been of information—and like the book, innovation in this sector has been strangely incremental. Hardly oblivious to this record (and grudgingly aware of the uncertain future of the internal combustion engine) nearly every major auto manufacturer in the world has in the last decade established a presence in Silicon Valley: BMW, Volkswagen, and Mercedes; Fiat, Volvo, and Renault; Toyota, Honda, and Nissan; and GM, Ford, and Chrysler have all created research facilities staffed by a combination of auto industry expats and Bay Area locals who are engaged in primary research, technology scouting, recruiting, and limited product development; the same is true for a network of secondary suppliers such as Bosch, insurance giants including State Farm and Allstate, and, inevitably, auto-related software startups such as Waze, Uber, and Lyft. The Center for Automotive Research at Stanford (CARS) links many of them together in an industry affiliates program.[35] Only one company, however, has dared to build a production vehicle from scratch, but in doing so has taken the entire industry from zero to sixty in what seems like 4.6 seconds.

Tesla Motors was founded in 2003 and is led by the visionary entrepreneur Elon Musk, who serves as CEO and "Product Architect." Musk remains intimately involved with all phases of design, engineering, and manufacture, and it is impossible to distinguish clearly among them: the mechanical design of the powertrain, the interface design of the seventeen-inch flat-panel center console display, the ergonomic design of the interior and the styling of the body were developed in a dispersed but tightly integrated process that is without precedent or parallel in the automotive industry. Furthermore, the overall vehicle design is a direct expression of Tesla's innovative business model. The body of the original Tesla Roadster was based on the Lotus Elise in an effort—typical of every lean Silicon Valley startup—to leverage existing subsystems wherever possible (even this was a challenge: in the early years, suppliers would not even return their phone calls). The success of the high-priced, low-volume Roadster funded the development of the Model S sedan, which is in turn funding the development of a lower-price, mass-market vehicle. The shock absorbers and airbags are off-the-shelf, but nearly every other component of the Model S is based on processes and technologies developed in-house at Tesla's R&D headquarters in Palo Alto, a short, zero-emission drive from Xerox PARC.

In 2008, Musk personally recruited Franz von Holzhausen, a graduate of Art Center's acclaimed transportation design program and former director of design for Mazda North America, to build a world-class design studio. At the outset, von Holzhausen was the only designer at the Hawthorne studio and was personally responsible for the exterior design of the Model S. Even with his deep history in the auto industry, this represented a challenge of which most designers only dream: "There are very few opportunities in this world to define and launch not just a new model but an entirely new product, and especially an automobile."[36] He now leads a six-person design studio that is responsible for interior and exterior design, as well as units tasked with color matching, clay modeling, digital surfacing, fabrication, design engineering, and product design. Unlike the automotive styling studios that dot the landscape of southern California, von Holzhausen's team in Hawthorne does not engage in futuristic concept studies and works closely with Tesla's R&D divisions in Palo Alto and at its robotic manufacturing plant across the bay in Fremont. A team as compact as this, within a company that is very tightly integrated, is capable of extremely rapid iterations. "In previous jobs at other car companies I'd hand off a design to production and my input ended. Not so at Tesla."[37] Their greatest asset, however, is a CEO who is deeply engaged and fully aligned with their mission; the Tesla design studio is around the corner from Musk's SpaceX venture on Rocket Road, and they meet almost daily.

Precisely because the Model S embodies so many radical innovations, von Holzhausen had to tread a fine line. On the one hand, the exterior design needed to reassure buyers wary of investing in so many untested technologies—a breakthrough vehicle does not have to look "like a science project," and the styling could not be so extreme that a potential buyer could not imagine actually driving one to work. But he also wanted to entice them with the idea that the aesthetics of a zero-emission, all-electric car need not be as timid as the Chevy Volt, the Ford Focus, or the Nissan Leaf. "We had the ability to go wherever we wanted to go," he stated, but in the end, "every millimeter" of the restrained, streamlined silhouette reflects the uncommonly close integration of the Hawthorne design studio with Tesla's mechanical, electrical, aeronautical, and software engineering teams in Silicon Valley, and the business model that sustains them.

The high level of integration of design and engineering achieved by Tesla may have unsettled the Detroit establishment, but it is the norm in Silicon Valley, where even outside the valley's fledgling automotive industry, a common theme is that it is necessary, in the words of industrial designer Fred Bould, to get beneath the skin and "under the hood" of a product. The partnership between Bould Design and Nest Labs, creator of the revolutionary Learning Thermostat, is one more case of how Silicon Valley designers have learned to work with, and not against, their counterparts in engineering, manufacturing, marketing, and management.

Tesla's von Holzhausen told an interviewer that, "We want to be 'an Apple product in a PC world,'" but Nest's Tony Fadell has taken this boast even more literally. Many industry observers were shocked by the announcement that Fadell, who led the development of the beloved iPod and iPhone, had left Apple and turned his attention to "the most unloved products" in the home. Fadell himself has described a typical encounter:

> "So what are you working on lately?" a friend asks over lunch.
>
> "I started a new company. We make thermostats."
>
> They chuckle, take a bite of their salad, "No, seriously. What are you doing?"[38]

Inspired by the iPod's success and informed by iPhone technology, Nest Labs is a textbook case of a company that is using design to breathe new life into products—the nondescript wall thermostat; the despised smoke detector; the clandestine security camera—that most people have, at best, learned to put up with.

Fadell envisioned a simple, palm-sized disk that would enable the purest and most immediate interaction: "They did the heavy lifting," acknowledges Fred Bould. "We came in and helped give it form." Form however, in the age of the digital, the networked, and the micro, is a more complicated matter than it was in 1953 when Henry Dreyfuss created the iconic Honeywell T86 circular thermostat—"The Round"—which sits alongside Nest's isomorphic Learning Thermostat in the Smithsonian's Cooper-Hewitt Design Museum. Six decades ago, at the height of the mechanical age, the industrial designer had the task of wrapping a shell around vacuum tubes, speakers, condensers, and in the case of the T86, a particularly troublesome thermometer. In a digital appliance, in which the key components are more likely to be a dime-sized lithium-ion battery, a flexible OLED display, an array of sensors, and a printed circuit board, form becomes subject to a different and much broader field of determinants—electromechanical and ergonomic, to be sure, but also cognitive, behavioral, and environmental. Bould's elegant, minimalist design met the client's high standards and also those of the design community itself, which has bestowed upon it numerous awards.

The tablets and smartphones and ebooks and roadsters that spill from this cauldron of creativity are evidence of the global impact of companies that have their origins in Silicon Valley. But Nokia, Fujitsu, Philips, and other international firms have also established a presence, and Samsung—the world's largest manufacturer of consumer electronics—has set up centers throughout the Bay Area to conduct user-experience research (in San Jose) and incubate new ventures (in Palo Alto). Behind closed doors in the San Francisco Financial District, Samsung's Design Center America works on new category creators or what SDA director Eliot Park calls "Big Bets": the future of mobile; wearables; smart TV; and machine-to-machine communication popularly known as the Internet of Things.[39]

Samsung established its initial foothold in Silicon Valley in 1994, when it launched a joint design studio with IDEO in Palo Alto. Working in a shared space with their American counterparts, South Korean designers—whose training emphasized industrial styling grafted onto traditional crafts—learned a research-based, innovation-driven, human-centered design methodology. Most important, they learned a new way of thinking at a time when Samsung was evolving from "fast follower" to a position of industry leadership.

Seeking to break out of the provincial environment in which it had been operating, Samsung established a corporate design center in Seoul. To Eliot Park, however, any truly future-oriented program dictated a presence in the Bay Area: Simply put, "We believed that disruptive changes were coming from Silicon Valley more than anywhere else in the world." In contrast to the 1,000 designers in Seoul who work mainly on short-term product offerings, and another 400 researchers studying local market behavior in London, Delhi, Shanghai, and Tokyo, the team in San Francisco—hired from Google, Apple, Microsoft, and eBay—is asking what comes *after* today's products, what emerging technology will create the *next* new market?

Mirroring its highly confidential product development process, Samsung Design America also sponsors open-invitation hackathons to smoke out local talent on topics such as future applications of flexible OLED displays. From Hewlett and Packard to Jobs and Wozniak, the grass-roots, garage-based hacker culture has, in fact, been an integral part of the Silicon Valley from the beginning. Combining the idealism of the Arts and Crafts Movement with the geekiness of the Homebrew Computing Club, the TechShop opened its doors in Menlo Park in 2006, and its mission of making high-end prototyping equipment available to makers, hackers, and do-it-yourselfers quickly spread to San Jose, San Francisco, and across the country. For the price of a $125 membership, citizen-designers gain access to all the technologies of the Industrial Revolution, but also CNC routers, 3-D scanners, laser cutters, and Arduino boards with which to indulge their hobbies, customize their motorcycles before riding to Burning Man, or start a company. Cofounder Jim Newton had already conceived the idea when he parked his tricked-out army truck on the grounds of the first Maker's Faire, which opened in the San Mateo County Fairgrounds and drew a crowd of 13,000 on the first day alone—a number that has since increased by a factor of ten. "I started the TechShop because I needed shop space," he admitted, but this proved to be a seed cast upon fertile ground. With the premise that "innovation is a company's immune system," CEO Mark Hatch estimates that the Tech Shops have generated $10 billion in value on the basis of an initial $26 million investment.[40]

At the other end of the maker's spectrum, Autodesk has opened the Pier 9 Workshop, with a spectacular view of the newly rebuilt San Francisco-Oakland Bay Bridge that its AutoCAD software helped to design. In this state-of-the-art facility employees, their partners, and applicants selected for the Autodesk artist-in-residence program can experiment with an array of state-of-the-art equipment: precision CNC machining tools, 3-D printers, industrial-strength sewing machines, and million-dollar cutters that can slice through steel plate with a jet of water or a beam of light. Lime Lab, a product development consultancy cofounded by Bay Area product design veterans Andre Yousefi and Kurt Dammerman, performs comparable services for external clients. Although the mission of these facilities, in the laconic words of Lime Lab's founders, is simply "to make things," they are in fact redrawing the line between software and hardware, prototype and production, design and manufacture.

But consumer product design is not the only domain to which Bay Area designers have migrated in recent years, as evidenced by sf.citi, San Francisco's nonprofit Citizens Initiative for Technology and Innovation, which throws out sponsored challenges to the design-minded public to solve social problems ranging from the scourge of homelessness to the hazards of driving under the influence of mobile devices. Much as the heroic years of Silicon Valley saw the unlikely marriage of tech culture and counterculture, sf.citi has tapped into an indigenous current of technologically enabled social engagement. Even the lure of six-figure entry-level salaries has not been enough to distract a small but significant number of design activists from a focus on the public interest.

The decisive moment can be specified with surprising precision: In September–October 2000, after a half-decade of preternatural growth, the

Internet bubble abruptly burst and the Silicon Valley design industry, which exists in a symbiotic relationship within the larger Silicon Valley ecosystem, suffered a calamitous shock; the larger consultancies were hit hard, some of the smaller ones disappeared altogether, and a fair number of midlevel designers returned to school to collect a few more degrees and ride out the storm. By the time the dust settled and the wreckage was cleared away, a diverse constellation of forces had emerged, united around the belief that the success of an enterprise should be measured not by corporate profit but by social impact. Suddenly, it seems, designers are claiming authority to address truly wicked problems ranging from malnutrition in sub-Saharan Africa to pediatric obesity in suburban America.[42]

The social agenda can be seen as the latest attempt to take up the challenge posed by William Morris a century ago of "redesigning the world," and inherited by such influential successors as Horst Rittel ("Wicked Problems"), Victor Papanek (*Design for the Real World*) and Valerie Casey (The Designers Accord). The new movement goes beyond advocating safer, cleaner, or more affordable products for the poor; at its most ambitious— some would say its most reckless—it seeks to address the condition of poverty itself. In doing so, it enters a field already crowded with foundations, charities, aid agencies, and governmental and nongovernmental organizations, each with its experts, methods, data sets, and metrics. Carrying the banner of innovation from the corporate to the social sector, designers have once again had to demonstrate that they possess a competence not found elsewhere, and have a critical role to play.

To be sure, many of the established consultancies have contributed time and talent to the public good, and some have forged partnerships that have enabled them to explore issues that fall outside the scope of traditional product development. Under the leadership of ethnographic researcher Jan Chipchase, frog has partnered with the University of California's Institute for Money, Technology, and Financial Inclusion to understand practices around savings and risk in Afghanistan. Fuseproject's Yves Béhar led the design of the widely publicized XO laptop for the nonprofit One Laptop Per Child Foundation. Inspired by its work with Acumen Fund in Kenya and the Centers for Disease Control in the United States, IDEO made its human-centered design methodology available to agencies working at the bottom of social pyramid through the *HCD Toolkit,* which can be freely downloaded from the web.[43] As rewarding as these projects have been, however, it has proven difficult for the consultancies to integrate them into their for-profit model. This has prompted the rise of a cluster of nonprofit design organizations for whom social innovation initiatives are not squeezed in among the projects that pay the bills, but are their sole raison d'être.

Rather than approach development as a problem of technical assistance, volunteerism, or philanthropy, the new nonprofits approach it as a problem of *design*. Like the established firms, they employ industrial and graphic designers, architects and anthropologists, and engineers and economists, and they brainstorm, empathize, and prototype in ways not so different from what one finds in the world of commercial product design. Unlike the typical consultancy, however, they do not present to the client a final deliverable and then set off in search of the next opportunity. The design organizations representative of the "social turn" remain onsite; they document and publish both their successes and failures with disarming transparency; and they have developed rigorous assessment tools that inform future iterations. Several of them use an "open innovation" model and share intellectual property freely over a network of university affiliates, corporate sponsors, and local partners in some of the poorest regions of the earth.

The objective of design organizations in the social sector is to create innovations that are scalable and sustainable—probably the two most hypnotic buzzwords in today's corporate lexicon. In regions where electricity may be sporadic, roads unpaved, and supply chains unreliable, however, these imperatives take on a pressing immediacy. Accordingly, the newest arrivals to Silicon Valley's design culture have experimented with a variety of models intended to sustain themselves, their partners, and their clients.

With its workstations, machine shop, and whiteboards festooned with Post-it notes, D-Rev would look like any of the other lively design studios scattered along San Francisco's emerging "Innovation Corridor" were it not for the scenes of rural Africa adorning the walls and the boxes of artificial knee-joints stacked up in the corners. These are fitting symbols, however, of a company whose mission is to bring well-designed, well-engineered products to people who live on less than $4 per day.

Although it operates as a nonprofit, CEO Krista Donaldson admits that when she accepted the position in 2009, "One of my main goals was to get people away from the nonprofit mentality."[44] Having seen too many pieces of expensive, donated medical equipment sitting unused in open-air rural clinics, well-intentioned casualties of dust, humidity, power surges, missing parts, or untrained personnel, she came to the conclusion that once a product is released, the only way it can be sustained is through normal market mechanisms. D-Rev raises money to support R&D, but as a social enterprise, the products developed in its San Francisco studio will be *sold* to *customers* rather than *donated* to *recipients*.

D-Rev is not an aid organization but a design company with a rigorous methodology, a creative culture, and an evolving portfolio of products. In contrast to the top-down, policy-driven practices of many NGOs, the designers at D-Rev begin with intensive field research into local needs, market conditions, and manufacturing and distribution channels. And although they go through the same ideation and prototyping exercises, unlike the for-profit consultancies that enter and leave the product development process at specified phases, D-Rev controls the entire cycle from identifying needs to assessing results: "If we are asking people to buy our product," says Donaldson, "It had damn well better work and bring value to their lives."

The remark of an Indian pediatrician—"Why is nobody focusing on neonatal jaundice, an easily treated condition that affects millions of newborns every year?"—prompted the latest of D-Rev's products: Brilliance, a phototherapy lamp, is licensed to Chennai-based Phoenix Medical and sells for $400—about 10 percent of the cost of devices found in western hospitals. ReMotion, a polycentric prosthetic knee consisting of five plastic pieces and four standard fasteners, was developed in partnership with the Jaipur Foot Organization and follows the same expanded design methodology. Impact assessment is a critical factor in all development projects, and D-Rev's numbers would be the envy of any nine-person product design company: In the two years since its introduction, over 5,000 amputees have been fitted with ReMotion's Jaipur Knee; nearly twice that number of infants have been treated with the Brilliance phototherapy system.

Having taken good care of the affluent western consumer, the design community is now being asked, in the words of Paul Polak, D-Rev's inspirational co-founder, to "design for the other 90%." Catapult Design, which works out of a shared loft space on a sleazy stretch of Mission Street, prefers to frame the challenge as "designing *with* the other 90%." During her undergraduate studies in Stanford's product design program, CEO Heather Fleming attended a slide presentation by Martin Fisher, founder of the Nairobi-based NGO, ApproTec, and was struck by the similarities between impoverished rural Kenya and the Navajo reservation where she grew up. Driven by the insight that "most of the world is more like the reservation than like San Francisco," in the last days of 2008 Fleming sold her car and used the proceeds to launch Catapult Design.[45] In its first year of operation Catapult earned a whopping $1,000 in fees, but she persisted and the network of clients and partners grew, sustained by a two-year contract with the World Bank on green energy innovation in Indonesia.

Like D-Rev, Catapult is not an aid organization but a design organization. Through workshops, courses, and an evolving program of educational offerings, Catapult shows clients and partners in the international development community how they might use design methodologies to approach their problems differently: people-centered ethnography vs. Washington-based policy analysis; iterative prototyping vs. one-off inventions; creative problem-solving vs. data-driven analytics, and bottom-up empathy vs. top-down expertise. Although Catapult partners with organizations across Asia, Africa, and Latin America, Fleming recognizes that sanitation, mobility, clean water, and public health are issues not exclusive to the Third World, and has struggled to find ways to address poverty and inequality in the United States as well. In 2014 Catapult Design came full circle when Fleming returned to northern Arizona to conduct the first of its learning labs in the heartland of the Navajo nation.

A viable business model—for themselves and for their clients—has been inseparable from the actual offerings of the socially oriented design consultancies. Accordingly, they have experimented with a variety of models that have enabled them to work with the World Bank, USAID, the British Department for International Development, and even wealthy donors such as the Rockefeller and the Bill and Melinda Gates Foundations that cannot reconcile their humanitarian mission with Silicon Valley consulting fees. At IDEO, the response has been to spin off an independent nonprofit to work within the constraints of organizations of this sort. The initiative was conceived during a trip to India in which CEO Tim Brown was accompanied by Acumen founder Jacqueline Novogratz and Acumen Fellow Jocelyn Wyatt: They helped him to see the developing world through the lens of social entrepreneurship, while he continuously peppered them with the designer's "What if . . . ?" and "How might we . . . ?"[46] Wyatt came on board, and since 2011 "dot.org" has adapted IDEO's human-centered design methodology to an array of projects that fall outside of mainstream product design: water and sanitation in Kenya; financial services for low-income communities in Mexico; college access for first generation families in the United States.

As an affiliate of a successful design consultancy, IDEO.org has worked to ensure that traditional product design remains a significant part of its portfolio; its internal staff and resident fellows have worked on low-cost cook stoves, latrines, and solar-powered lighting solutions for the Third World. At the same time, Wyatt and codirector Patrice Martin believe that designers in the social innovation sector do themselves a disservice by celebrating their prototypes and concept studies (and being honored for them in glitzy awards ceremonies) before they can demonstrate that they have had a measurable social impact. Success in this domain is likely to be slow, episodic, and intangible, and a mindful balance of patience and promotion is a condition of survival. Like its peers, IDEO.org chooses its battles carefully, and now turns away far more opportunities than it can accept.

While by no means unique to Silicon Valley, the social turn in design derives in large measure from the Bay Area's left-coast, blue-state tradition of social activism. Partly because they are able to operate within a supportive culture, partly because their location gives them access to experts at Stanford, Berkeley, and the UCSF Medical Center, and partly because Skype can now take the place of airplane tickets to Kenya or the Philippines, the social enterprises have withstood the inflated rents and inflated egos of Silicon Valley. Their determination to remain in the epicenter of innovation has cost them some credibility in both the international aid and the local design communities, but D-Rev's Krista Donaldson has captured the defiant sentiment of most of her fellow social entrepreneurs: "We do what's best for the customer."

Conclusion

In 2007, Valerie Casey suffered what she describes as "a crisis of conscience." Casey, who had held leadership positions at Pentagram, frog, and

IDEO, decided that it was time for designers to break out of the Silicon Valley echo chamber and take responsibility for their larger ethical footprint. Plenty of individual designers and more than a few design firms had set aside some part of their practice to work on issues of sustainability, disability, or social justice, but the challenge of persuading competing firms to come together or to find room in their portfolios for such work seemed overwhelming. In a moment of despair she fired off a late-night email to her friend and confidant, the environmentalist Paul Hawken, who shot back, "Once you see it you can't unsee it."[47]

Shortly thereafter, on a flight between back-to-back client meetings, Casey hammered out ten principles of an environmentally sustainable, ethically responsible design practice. She edited it down to five, which she then circulated to the design community:

1. Publicly declare participation in the Designers Accord.
2. Initiate a dialogue about environmental and social impact and sustainable alternatives with each and every client. Rework client contracts to favor environmentally and socially responsible design and work processes. Provide strategic and material alternatives for sustainable design.
3. Undertake a program to educate your teams about sustainability and sustainable design.
4. Consider your ethical footprint. Understand the impact of your firm, and work to measure, manage, and reduce it on an annual basis.
5. Advance the understanding of environmental and social issues from a design perspective by actively contributing to the communal knowledge base for sustainable design.

Casey then embarked on what she imagined to be a five-year mission to leverage the collective power of the design profession, and it proved wildly successful: By 2012, when the initiative drew to a close, the Designers Accord had broken free from its Bay Area containment and been adopted by 939 design firms, thirty-nine educational institutions, nineteen professional associations, fifty companies, and well over 400,000 individual designers in one hundred countries and on every continent except Antarctica.[48] It has sponsored a worldwide program of workshops, conferences, meet-ups, and conversations formal and informal around shared values and common goals. It has created a platform that enables designers from every discipline to share knowledge and experience. Underlying the Designers Accord is the premise that designers have the power to move the world; they just need a place to stand, and the will to move it in the right direction.

Design came late to Silicon Valley, but it has generated an uninterrupted flow not just of artifacts but of ideas. These, and the people and processes that lie behind them, have had global impact.

CONCLUSION

"Thinging, the thing things."

—Martin Heidegger (1949)

The most far-reaching product of the Silicon Valley design culture is not a mobile device, a medical instrument, or even an app. In fact, it is not a product at all; and like so many other ideas that have come to fruition in the narrow strip of real estate bounded by Highways 101 and 280, it was (in the dreaded phrase of all engineering managers) "not invented here." Design Thinking—the idea that the tools of the designer can be applied to the totality of life—has nonetheless taken root in the ecosystem of Silicon Valley, and like a Tweet or a Like, has spread rapidly across the globe.[1]

The flowering of Design Thinking is a fitting note on which to conclude this history of Silicon Valley design precisely because it captures the inherent difficulty of doing so. In his Compton Lectures of 1968, Herbert Simon famously stated that, "Everyone designs who devises courses of action aimed at changing existing situations into preferred ones." Simon's intention was to open up to scientific inquiry a domain that had been claimed by artisans, craftsmen, and a motley assortment of specialized professional practices. The object of this *nuova scienza* of design followed from Simon's generous definition: In contrast to the natural scientist, whose subject matter is the fixed and immutable universe, the domain of the designer is the "artificial" world of human creation: "The natural sciences are concerned with how things are. Design, on the other hand, is concerned with how things ought to be."[2]

Simon proposed a radical expansion of the perimeter around "design": No longer can it be construed as the practice of fashioning technically efficient functions into aesthetically pleasing forms ("stuffing five pounds of shit into a two-pound box"), but rather a comprehensive approach to the entire field of human experience. As exhilarating as this program might be, it leaves us with an obvious quandary: How shall we define the limits to this new "science of the artificial?" How are we to think of a discipline that encompasses every manner of art and artifice? What common logic might connect an $80,000 electric sedan and an $80 prosthetic knee? The bottom-up populism of the maker's movement and the top-down expertise of contract manufacturing firms? The design of a consumer appliance, a professional service, a pharmaceutical trial, and an educational curriculum? Under the banner of Design Thinking, Silicon Valley has laid claim to the entire field of the ought.

In the antediluvian age when Santa Clara country was still awash in cherry blossoms and Stanford a genteel finishing school, designers in New York and Milan were boldly promoting themselves as masters of an art that could be applied to everything "from lipsticks to locomotives" (the industrial designer Raymond Loewy in 1951) and at scales extending "from a teaspoon to a city" (the architect Ernesto Rogers the following year).[3] In comparison with the ambitious programs of today's designers—income inequality, urban violence, environmental justice, political reform—their bravado seems timid and parochial.

There is no shortage of observers who have concluded that Design Thinking heralds the end of a golden age: The skilled professional has yielded to the "T-shaped" generalist with a limitless appetite and an excess of confidence in the power of design to effect large-scale change.[4] For others, however, it is the disruption that the design profession has been waiting for and the fulfillment of a century-old dream. Designers are being asked to design not only objects, but systems. They are invited into the inner sancta of corporations and NGOs, and are being called upon by the governments of Iceland, Singapore, and Colombia to apply their creative methodologies to whole nations. Designers who have been clamoring for an invitation to the party are now asked to organize it, to orchestrate it, and they not infrequently end up being the guests of honor. Having resigned themselves to being at best a link in a chain, they find themselves functioning as the hub of a wheel.

This returns us, in conclusion, to our starting point: Herbert Simon's provocative, infuriating, inspiring suggestion that the province of design is "how things ought to be." In sixty years the Silicon Valley design profession has moved from a loading dock at the back of a 1950s Hewlett-Packard factory building to the SOMA lofts and Bayfront campuses of some of the world's most powerful companies. It has expanded its field of practice from discrete electromechanical devices to integrated socioeconomic systems, and calved off a host of new disciplines to tackle them. Silicon Valley designers have brought their methods to middle school playgrounds, executive boardrooms, and Navajo reservations. They have watched as their products are launched into space and inserted into the most intimate recesses of personal experience. Their work may be constrained by schedules, budgets, and technology, but these are mere details. The only real constraint is the power of the design imagination.

NOTES

Introduction

1. A sampling of the academic literature would include AnnaLee Saxenian, *Regional Advantage: Culture and Competition in Silicon Valley and Route 128* (Cambridge, MA: Harvard University Press, 1996), pp. 84–88; Martin Kenney, ed., *Understanding Silicon Valley: The Anatomy of an Entrepreneurial Region* (Stanford: Stanford University Press, 2000); Christophe Lécuyer, *Making Silicon Valley: Innovation and the Growth of High Tech, 1930-1970* (Cambridge, MA: MIT Press, 2006).

2. Maria Giudice and Christopher Ireland, *Rise of the DEO* (Pearson: 2014). The design executive officer is the leader of a company, as distinct from the chief design officer, who is an employee. DEOs Tim Brown, Doreen Lorenzo, Yves Béhar, and Valerie Casey have all spoken at Davos; Bill Moggridge and Gadi Amit have both accepted the National Design Award at receptions at the White House. Design leaders are regularly featured at the annual TED conference.

3. Del Coates, in the course of a lively conversation with Ralf Schubert, Chas Grossman, John Gard, and the author (San Jose: August 28, 2013).

4. Some readers may detect here a faint echo of Hayden White's masterwork, *Metahistory: The Historical Imagination in Nineteenth Century Europe* (Baltimore: Johns Hopkins University Press, 1975).

5. Architecture came late to the party for reasons that may have to do with the nature of Silicon Valley itself. Whereas the great architectural monuments of the past tended to be structural expressions of the activities that took place inside—the visible tectonics of democratic Athens, the heavenly vaults of Brunelleschi's Florence, the River Rouge assembly plants designed by the industrious Albert Kahn—it is less obvious how an architect might "express" the activity of writing code. The default solution has been the corporate tilt-up—manufactured offsite and trucked to the (post-) industrial parks that line the freeways, offset by the $30 million

neo-Palladian hilltop villas of their CEOs. But just as the scale of the microchip helped liberate industrial designers from the tyranny of functionalism, so the unfolding requirements of the information economy—and its astounding wealth— have prompted radical new designs for Facebook (Frank Gehry), Apple (Norman Foster), and Google (NBBJ), as well as Samsung, Nvidia, and Stanford. "Information architecture" may yet inspire a genuine "architecture of information."

Chapter 1

1. Comparison is of the 200-series of audio oscillators, HP Electronic Measuring Equipment, catalogs 20-A (1950), p. 6, and 22-A (1955), p. 8, where it is described as "New! Completely Redesigned! Highest Quality Throughout!" (www.hparchive.com, curated by Kenneth Kuhn). "H-P's Raymond Loewy," in *Watt's Current?*, 10, no. 5 (April 1953): 5. *Watt's Current?* was an internal newsletter, "published monthly by and for the employees of Hewlett-Packard Co." Private collection of the late Carl Clement, kindly loaned to the author.

2. John E. Arnold, "Case Study: Arcturus IV," Creative Engineering Laboratory (unpublished, 1953, loaned to the author by Mr. Clement). "The Course Where Students Lose Earthly Shackles," *Life Magazine* (May 16, 1955), pp. 186ff; Suzanne Burrey, "The Question of Creativity," in *Industrial Design* 1, no. 6 (June 1957). We will encounter Arnold again in chapter 5, as founder of the design division in Stanford's School of Engineering).

3. Creative Engineering Seminars (Massachusetts institute of Technology, 1956); unpublished, collection of Carl Clement.

4. "Hew-Pack Designer [Carl Clement] Reports on Recent M.I.T. Creative Engineering Course," *Watt's Current?*, 13, no. 9 (September 1956): 12–13.

5. "H-P Wins WESCON Industrial Design Award, *Watt's Current?*, 17, no. 8 (September 1960): 2.

6. Carl Clement, advertising supplement by Aluminum Company of America, *Fortune* Magazine (December 1962), n.p. Statement of William R. Hewlett, Executive Vice-President, Hewlett-Packard Company, at the Western Electronics Show and Conference (WESCON), Los Angeles (August 34, 1960), *Watt's Current?*, 17, no. 8 (September 1960): 2.

7. In addition to Clement, the members of HP's industrial design group—and, *ipso facto*, nearly the whole of the Santa Clara County design profession—were: Andi Aré, Herb Beaven, Ken Dinwiddie, Dale Gruyé, Allen Inhelder, Tom Lauhon, Don Pahl, and Dick Payne.

8. "At a review, Hewlett asked Clement to comment on the design. Clement, saying nothing, rolled in a cart with a Tektronix 545 on it, produced a dime from his pocket, and demonstrated how the covers could be taken down in ten seconds, providing access to the entire circuitry. Hewlett voted instantly for Clement's proposal." Charles H. House, *The HP Phenomenon: Innovation and Business Transformation* (Stanford: Stanford University Press, 2009), p. 234, from his own interview with Carl Clement. The story is charming, but it should be noted that UL requirements stipulated that for safety reasons, a dedicated tool be needed to open an electronic device.

9. The $250K figure refers to development and tooling costs. Clement to Howard W. Hill, president, Zero Manufacturing Company (June 22, 1970), in which he proposes a generic, off-the-shelf enclosure system suitable for small electronics companies: Clement Papers.

10. H-P's New Cabinet Program—Hit of Show," *Watt's Current?*, 18, no. 4 (April 1961): 2. An internal publication shows a photograph of the 6'5" Packard towering over his designers like a proud parent. House, *The HP Phenomenon.*, pp. 231–35. Mr. House generously shared his own recollections (and his book) with the author in an interview on March 18, 2010.

11. The Art Center School, *General Catalogue*, Department of Industrial Design (1952–1953, 1956–1957); Archives of the Art Center College of Design, Pasadena, courtesy of Robert Dirig, Archivist.

12. The official account of Clement's departure from HP is contained in two documents: "Dear Dave and Bill" (January 1, 1964), and David Packard, "To Whom It May Concern" (January 14, 1964); papers of Carl Clement, which also contain the various award certificates mentioned in this section.

13. "People on the Move," *HP Measure* 1, no. 5 (November 1963): 18. Interview with Allen Inhelder (Portola Valley, August 4, 2010). *Measure,* inspired by the quantitative disposition of Lord Kelvin (1824–1907), succeeded *Watts Current?* as HP's internal publication in July 1963: "I often say that when you can measure what you are speaking about, and express it in numbers, you know something about it; but when you cannot measure it, when you cannot express it in numbers, your knowledge is of a meager and unsatisfactory kind."

14. Wesley E. Woodson and Donald W. Conover, *Human Engineering Guide for Equipment Designers* (Berkeley and Los Angeles, 1954), p. 2–137.

15. [Allen Inhelder,] "Human Factors Case Study of the 608 Signal Generator," collection of Allen Inhelder.

16. "Those Curious, Creative Industrial Designers," *HP Measure* (May 1965). Additional sources of information in this section are interviews with Allen Inhelder (Portola Valley, June 17, 2010), and Roger Wilder (Bethel Island, September 16, 2010).

17. Although Landor's letterhead said "industrial design," he had only one industrial designer on his staff at that time. Landor's proposed logo, a vertically oriented rhomboid enclosing the lower-case letters "hp," was not scalable and could not have been applied to the 3,000 instruments in HP's product line. For ten years Hewlett-Packard fudged the problem by using the Landor logo on its stationery and a redrawn Inhelder design on its products. Needless to say, this fiasco is not mentioned in the official announcement, "A Proud Look for a Proud Name," *HP Measure* (November 1964).

18. Allen Inhelder, "A New Instrument Enclosure with Greater Convenience, Better Accessibility, and High Attenuation of RF Interference," in *Hewlett-Packard Journal* 27, no. 1 (September 1975): 20; online at http://www.hpl.hp.com/hpjournal/pdfs/IssuePDFs/1975-09.pdf.

19. House, *The HP Phenomenon*, pp. 180–81 (http://www.hpmuseum.org/hp35.htm). HP commissioned a study from the Stanford Research Institute that estimated that demand for a pocket-sized calculator would not exceed 1,000 units. Total sales of the HP-35 during its three-year lifespan, 1972–75, exceeded 300,000 units; the "41% profit" figure is an estimate based upon data analyzed by Charles House, kindly shared with the author. Giving credit where credit is due, the *HP Journal* notes that Clarence Studley supervised the overall mechanical design and assembly of the 9100A desktop calculator; styling of the handsome cabinet was done by Roy Ozaki, Don Aupperle, and others in the Industrial Design group, while Harold Rocklitz and Doug Wright handled much of the tooling.

20. Edward J. Liljenwall, "Packaging the Pocket Calculator," *HP Journal* 23, no. 10 (June 1972): 12–13. According to Michael Moritz, the HP calculator was the inspiration for Steve Jobs in commissioning the case for the early Apple computers: Michael Moritz, *The Little Kingdom: The Private Story of Apple Computer* (New York: Morrow, 1984), p. 186.

21. Thomas M. Whitney, France Rodé, and Chung C. Tung, "The 'Powerful Pocketful': An Electronic Calculator Challenges the Slide Rule," *HP Journal* 23, no. 10 (June 1972): 2. "Transcendental" refers to trigonometric, logarithmic, exponential, and other symbolic functions; most calculators at that time could perform only the four basic arithmetic operations. "Reverse Polish Notation" (RPN) is a computer-friendly convention that allows complex expressions to be entered with a minimum of special symbols.

22. Chung C. Tung, "The 'Personal Computer:' A Fully Programmable Pocket Calculator," *Hewlett-Packard Journal* 25, no. 9 (May 1974).

23. Additional sources consulted include David Packard, *The HP Way: How Bill Hewlett and I Built Our* Company (New York: Harper, 1995); House, *The HP Phenomenon*; Michael S. Malone, *Bill and Dave* (New York: Penguin, 2007) and also his engaging book that snagged the title of the present chapter, *The Valley of Heart's Delight: A Silicon Valley Notebook, 1963–2001* (New York: Wiley, 2002).

24. Michael S. Malone, *The Big Score: The Billion Dollar Story of Silicon Valley* (New York: Doubleday 1985), pp. 68, 152 (quoting Noyce). Gordon Moore is quoted in Richard S. Tedlow, *Andy Grove: The Life and Times of an American Business Icon* (New York: Portfolio, 2006), p. 167; also *Intel Annual Report* (1972) (http://www.intel.com/content/www/us/en/history/history-1972-annual-report.html). On the HP-01, see André F. Marion, Edward A. Heinsen, Robert Chin, and Bennie E. Helmso, "Wrist Instrument Opens New Dimension in Personal Information." *HP Journal* 29, no. 4 (December 1977): 2–8.

25. Don Hoefler, "Silicon Valley USA," in *Electronics News* (January 11, 1971).

26. Saxenian, *Regional Advantage*.

27. Between 1954 and 1976 the Pasadena Museum of Art put on eleven shows exhibiting "California Design" from all parts of the state and in all of its aspects— from one-off craft pieces to mass-produced consumer goods to the occasional industrial object. See Eudora Moore, ed., *California Design* (Pasadena Museum of Art, 1953). The southern California "lifestyle" tradition continues in the recent exhibition at the Los Angeles County Museum of Art: *California Design: Living in a Modern Way*, ed. Wendy Kaplan (Cambridge, MA: MIT Press, 2011).

28. Avrom Fleishman, "Design on the West Coast, *Industrial Design* 4, no. 10 (October 1957): 49. Additional information in this section is culled from *Industrial Design at Wescon*, the annual presentation of outstanding electronic products sponsored by the Western Electronic Manufacturers Association, 1958–.

29. Interview with Robert McKim (Santa Cruz, February 22, 2012). Paul Cook, "Design at Raychem, *Design Management Journal* 1, no. 1 (Fall 1989): 14–15. As the company evolved from radiation chemistry to materials science, it stopped relying upon outside contractors and built up an internal design group under the direction of Dennis Siden: "The reason," according to Robert Saldich, Cook's successor, "is that the major part of our design problem is incorporating all of our material science capabilities with the product. And we can't disaggregate the material science from the product design." Cynthia Ingols, "Three Legs of the Stool: An Interview

with Robert J. Saldich, President and CEO, Raychem Corporation," *Design Management Journal* 6, no. 2 (Spring 1995): 14–15. On Friden Calculator, see *Scientific American* (March 1947). Friden, which in 1965 became a division of Singer Sewing Machines, was also the manufacturer of the Flexowriter Automatic Letter Writer; as a console terminal, the "flexo" was one of the earliest and most widely used computer input devices.

30. Budd Steinhilber, *Looking Back*, II:88: unpublished memoir, cited with the kind permission of Mr. Steinhilber.

31. Frank Guyre recalled his years at working on the Agena spacecraft and other projects in conversation with the author (Stanford, November 16, 2011).

32. Bill Dresselhaus, communication with the author (May 30, 2012).

33. "Search at San Jose" (https://archive.org/details/SearchAtSanJose_IBM _RAMAC). The Random Access Method for Accounting and Control (RAMAC) replaced punched cards and magnetic tape with a vertical stack of fifty 24-inch aluminum disks with a whopping storage capacity of five megabytes of data; it nonetheless represents one of the turning points in the history of computing. The control panel of the 305 (electrical engineering), but not the discrete cantilevered door that gives access to it (industrial design), resides in the permanent collection of the Museum of Modern Art. The Michigan consultancy Sundberg-Ferar were the designers of record for the RAMAC. See Hugh B. Johnston, "From Old IBM to New IBM," *Industrial Design* 4, no. 3 (March 1957): 48–57, and also Office of Charles and Ray Eames, *A Computer Perspective: Background to the Computer Age*, 2nd ed. (Cambridge, MA: Harvard University Press, 1990).

34. Thomas J. Watson, Jr., "Good Design Is Good Business," in *The Art of Design Management* (New York: Tiffany, 1975); James F. Ryan, "Why IBM Products Look as They Do: It's by Design," in *Think* (internal publication: May 1973), pp. 45–49. On IBM's Corporate Design Program, see Gordon Bruce, *Eliot Noyes* (New York: Phaidon, 2007), and John Harwood's elegant study, *The Interface: IBM and the Transformation of Corporate Design, 1945-1976* (Minneapolis: University of Minnesota Press, 2011). Eliot Noyes himself narrates an "Industrial Design Progress Report" (December 1957) (http://www-03.ibm.com/ibm/history/ibm100/us/en/icons/gooddesign/).

The Cottle Road campus, and its iconic Building 25 in particular, was the subject of a bitter historic preservation controversy that raged for years. On March 8, 2008, shortly after the matter was decided by the courts in favor of the San Jose Preservation Action Council, the building was destroyed by a predawn fire that has never been explained. It is now a parking lot for a big box home improvement warehouse.

35. Interviews with Donald Moore (Aptos, CA, September 7, 2013) and Edward Lucey (Los Gatos, CA, September 4, 2013). The original San Jose Design Center team consisted of Jack Stringer, John Jagger, Dave Moore, and Dagmar Arnold, a graduate of the Pratt Institute and the first female industrial designer we have encountered in the context of Silicon Valley.

36. "Design in IBM" (internal document, n.a., n.d.), and "The IBM Design Program," from a confidential presentation made by C. C. Hollister (June 1973), graciously provided by Ms. Stacy Castillo, IBM Corporate Archives.

37. Steinhilber, *Looking Back*, II:76. From Los Angeles, Henry Dreyfuss remarked on "how whole-heartedly our eastern clients hailed the establishment of our West Coast office." This was possible only because air mail had made it possible to transfer drawings, sketches, and other details from his New York to his Pasadena office in a mere eighteen hours: *Western Advertising* 49, no. 5 (June 1947): 60.

38. Jay Wilson, interview (Los Gatos, March 15, 2010). Bill Dresselhaus concurs.

39. Friedrich Engel and Peter Hammar, "A Selected History of Magnetic Recording" (http://www.richardhess.com/tape/history/Engel_Hammar--Magnetic_Tape _History.pdf), 2006; Don V. R. Drenner, "The Magnetophon," *Audio Engineering* (October 1947). John Leslie and Ross Snyder, "History of the Early Days of Ampex Corporation," *AES Historical Committee* (October 14, 2010) (http://www.aes.org/ aeshc/docs/company.histories/ampex/leslie_snyder_early-days-of-ampex.pdf). Interview with John Leslie (Portola Valley, September 1, 2010).

40. Myron Stolaroff, in conversation with Ross Snyder, Lone Pine, CA (July 27, 2004). Peter Hammar, "[Harold Lindsay:] In Memoriam," *Journal of the Audio Engineering Society* 30, no. 9 (September 1982): 691–92.

41. Harold Lindsay, "Welcome to New Employees" (March 1976); recording provided to the author by Larry Miller. Lindsay's recollection conveys the spirit that infused the original core group, but it is an exaggeration at best. A substantial literature was already available, albeit mainly in German.

42. Robert ("Robbie") Smits, in conversation with John Leslie, Walt Selsted, Frank Lennert, Ross Snyder, and (remotely) Myron Stolaroff (Portola Valley, CA, December 4, 2001). A recording of this historic gathering was kindly provided to the author by Larry Miller.

43. Harold W. Lindsay, "Precision Magnetic Tape Recorder for High-fidelity Professional Use," *Electrical Manufacturing* (October 1950), pp. 134ff. The Scully disk-cutting lathe was the industry standard for making physical transcription disks in recording studios; the 16-inch vinyl disks wore out quickly and were exceedingly

difficult to edit. Interviews with Larry Miller (San Mateo, California: October 1, 2010, and November 17, 2010), and Peter Hammar (telephone, November 16, 2010).

44. Larry Miller, in conversation with the author (Burlingame, CA, January 13, 2011). This conversation, which included Stanford archivist Henry Lowood, took place in the warehouse in which the remains of the Ampex Museum are stored.

45. This was one of several versions of the company's marketing slogan.

46. The IDSA recognizes Sinel as the first person in the United States to describe himself as an "industrial designer," the term he stamped on his letterhead in 1920.

47. Douglas Tinney, interview (Fremont, September 24, 2010); Jay Wilson to the author (September 4, 2010). Tinney worked at Ampex from 1977 to 1999, and served as head of Graphic Design services. Wilson worked at Ampex from 1973 to 87, and was one of Staley's earliest hires in the industrial design group.

48. Interviews with Darrell Staley (Santa Clara, September 3, 2010) and Jay Wilson (Los Gatos, March 15, 2010). Even today, many of the engineers who still gather for the annual "Old Timers" picnic at Cuesta Park are unaware that an Industrial Design department even existed, or suspect that it was an unnecessary frill foisted upon them by a management cabal bloated with technically illiterate MBAs.

49. Robert Lubar, "Five Little Ampexes and How They Grew," *Fortune Magazine* 61 (April 1960); Richard J. Elkus, *Winner Take All: How Competitiveness Shapes the Fate of Nations* (New York: Basic Books, 2008); as chairman of the board of Ampex, Elkus oversaw a bailout of the sinking firm that kept it afloat for another ten years. Richard S. Rosenbloom, "Ampex Corp. (A)." Harvard Business School Case 658-002. For a more anecdotal but no less insightful commentary, see Malone, *The Big Score*, pp. 62–68.

50. Steinhilber, *Looking Back*, II: 103 [slightly edited].

51. Myron Stolaroff, *Thanatos to Eros, 35 Years of Psychedelic Exploration* (Berlin: VWB, 1994); on Stolaroff's place in Silicon Valley's engineering counterculture, see John Markoff, *What the Dormouse Said: How the Sixties Counterculture Shaped the Computer Industry* (New York: Viking, 2005), chapter 1. Also Theodor Roszak, *From Satori to Silicon Valley* (April 1985) (http://searchworks.stanford.edu/view/323124).

52. Interview with Allen Inhelder (Portola Valley, CA, August 4, 2010); Darrell Staley, IDSA-SF *News* 8 (October 1977).

53. These phrases came up in conversation with Michael Barry and Allen Inhelder, in reference to Ampex and Hewlett-Packard, respectively.

54. Clara Louise Lawrence, "The Valley of the Heart's Delight" (1931):

> "No brush can paint the picture, No pen describe the sight,
> That one finds in April, In the Valley of Heart's Delight."

Chapter 2

1. Noland Vogt, "The Latest from the Organization," *Grapevine* 1, no. 1 (November 1982). In the first issue of GVO's internal newsletter, Vogt reviewed the history of the company and reaffirmed its mission, which was "to provide industrial design and advertising graphics services to industry." *Grapevine* was provided to the author by Steve Portigal; additional information was kindly provided by Ms. Anne Gruyé.

2. Interview with Robert Brunner, Jeff Smith, and Gerard Furbershaw (San Francisco, January 30, 2012).

3. Interviews with Philip Bourgeois (Menlo Park, CA, August 27, 2010, and February 10, 2011) and Mike Wise (Woodside, CA, December 3, 2010). Bourgeois presented the model to Adam Osborne and his entourage at a meeting early in 1983, where it received a standing ovation. Indeed, the excitable Osborne promptly issued a press release announcing the revolutionary new "Executive," which prompted dealers to cancel orders of the Osborne 1—a consequence that has gone down in Silicon Valley lore as the "Osborne Effect." The "ugly duckling" memo is reproduced in Adam Osborne and John Dvorak, *Hypergrowth: The Rise and Fall of the Osborne Computer Corporation* (San Francisco, 1984), pp. 67–9.

4. "Refugees from the human race" was venture capitalist Don Valentine's assessment when first introduced to Jobs and Wozniak: interview with Regis McKenna (Stanford, August 3, 2011). Noland Vogt is quoted in Paul Kunkel, *Apple Design: The Work of the Apple Industrial Design Group* (New York: Graphis, 1997), p. 13. John Gard had a similar experience when Jobs (this time in a three-piece suit) and Wozniak (on a Harley-Davidson) showed up at Inova: interview with the author (Mountain View, CA, March 9, 2010), and Nolan Bushnell declined to invest $50,000 in return for one-third ownership. Jerry Manock, by contrast, had just gone out on his own and was hungry for work, but asked to be paid in advance. Apple is today the world's most valuable corporate property.

5. Interview with Robert Hall and Gary Waymire (Redwood City, CA, February 11, 2011).

6. Kristina Goodrich, "Designs of the Decade," *Design Management Journal* 5, no. 2 (Spring 1994): 47–55. The "Design of the Decade" award recognizes products that

have demonstrably benefitted their clients over time, as measured by percentage share of market increase and other factors.

7. The system, introduced in 1990, is called Metasys, and is regarded by Johnson Controls as a signature product. Information in this section is based on ephemeral literature produced by GVO and its clients in the 1980s and 1990s, in the collection of the author.

8. Jay Wilson, communication with the author (February 24, 2011).

9. Gary Waymire, Michael Barry, and Robert C. Hall, "Materializing Culture," in *Design Management Journal* 6, no. 2 (Spring 1995): 40–45. See also Wasson, "Ethnography in the Field of Design," 37–88.

10. The research branch of GVO was reborn as PointForward of Redwood City, California, led by Gary Waymire, Bob Hall, Michael Barry, and Tom Williams.

11. In 1994 the *Design Management Journal* ran a special issue on the social sciences in design research: vol. 5, no. 1 (winter 1994). RichardsonSmith in Columbus, Ohio, is often cited as one of the first consultancies to offer ethnographic research, and is also reputed to have experienced significant cultural strains.

12. Lucy Suchman, *Plans and Situated Actions: The Problem of Human-Machine Communication* (Cambridge: Cambridge University Press, 1987). Also, Christina Wasson, "Ethnography in the Field of Design," in *Human Organization* 59, no. 4 (2000).

13. "Pacesetter Award Goes to S-P High Power Laser," papers of Carl Clement; "Laser Honor at Wescon Exhibition," *San Francisco Chronicle* (August 24, 1965). As an industrial designer at Spectra Physics, Clement worked in close proximity to the shop staff, which included machinist Paul Jobs, whose high-school age son Steven was just beginning to explore the mysteries of electronics. One of his interns was Jerry Manock, who was to become the first industrial designer at Apple Computer.

14. Clement Laboratories, "Design Brief: Intellectual Augmentation System" (n.d., but presumably June 1972); Carl Clement to William K. English, "Proposal for design of your new Office System" (June 29, 1972): papers of Carl Clement. There is a substantial literature on Xerox PARC, including: Giuliana Lavendel, ed., with the assistance of Carol Leitner and the staff of the Palo Alto Technical Information Center, *A Decade of Research: Xerox Palo Alto Research Center, 1970–1980* (New York: Bowker, 1980); Douglas K. Smith and Robert C. Alexander, *Fumbling the Future: How Xerox Invented, Then Ignored, the First Personal Computer* (New York: William Morrow, 1988), and Michael A. Hiltzig, *Dealers of Lightning: Xerox PARC and the Dawn of the Computer Age* (New York: Harper, 1999).

15. Clement to English, "Proposal for design of your new Office System."

16. The San Francisco demonstration took place on December 9, 1968, and is recognized as one of the turning points in the history of modern computing. The phrase "dealing lightning" is attributed to computer pioneer Chuck Thacker, who witnessed the 1968 presentation and went on to design the essential hardware for the Xerox Alto. Alan Kay felt that he was in the presence of "a biblical prophet." On Engelbart and SRI, see Donald L. Nielson, *A Heritage of Innovation: SRI's First Half Century* (Menlo Park: SRI International, 2004, 2006), W. B. Gibson, *SRI: The Founding Years* (Palo Alto: Publishing Service Center, 1980); Thierry Bardini, *Bootstrapping: Douglas Engelbart, Coevolution, and the Origins of Personal Computing* (Stanford: Stanford University Press, 2000); and Valerie Landau and Eileen Clegg, *The Engelbart Hypothesis: Dialogs with Douglas Engelbart* (Berkeley, 2009). Of particular relevance are the proceedings of a 1986 retrospective collected by Adele Goldberg, ed., *A History of Personal Workstations* (Reading, MA: Addison-Wesley, 1988).

17. Interview with Douglas Engelbart (Atherton, CA, November, 1999). "Stanford and the Silicon Valley: Oral History Interviews," conducted by Judy Adams and Henry Lowood (December 19, 1986–April 1, 1987) W. K. English, D. C. Engelbart, and M. L. Berman, "Display-selection techniques for text manipulation," *IEEE Transactions: Human Factors in Electronics* 8 (March 1967): 5–15. The NLS system has its roots in the concept developed by J. C. R. Licklider of "man-computer symbiosis," which Engelbart reinterpreted as the "coevolution" of humans and technology generally. See J. C. R. Licklider, "Man-Computer Symbiosis," *IRE Transactions on Human Factors in Electronics,* vol. HFE-1 (March 1960): 4–11.

18. In his report to the Air Force Office of Scientific Research, Engelbart emphasized the integrative character of the proposed system, which sought "to help man apply his native sensory, mental, and motor capabilities . . . like most systems its performance can best be improved by considering the whole as a set of interacting components rather than by considering the components in isolation." D. C. Engelbart, "Augmenting Human Intellect: A Conceptual Framework," Summary Report to the Director of Information Services, Air Force Office of Scientific Research. Contract AF49(638)-1024 (October 1962), Introduction.

19. John R. Berry, *Herman Miller: The Purpose of Design* (New York: Rizzoli, 2004), p. 117. Robert Propst's classic treatise, *The Office: A Facility Based on Change*, was published in the same year as Engelbart's demonstration. The AO-II, introduced in 1968, followed the unsuccessful AO-I, designed by George Nelson and introduced four years earlier. See also Robert Propst, "The Action Office" *Human Factors* 8, no.4 (August, 1966): 299–306.

20. Robert Propst, *The Office: A Facility Based on Change* (Zeeland, Michigan: Herman Miller, 1968), p. 23. In 1968, "work station" was not yet a recognized concept.

21. The first Action Office (AO-I) had been designed by George Nelson and released to an unreceptive market in 1964. It was not modular and in fact the panels were glued together with epoxy cement and could not be disassembled. AO-I was widely regarded as an industrial design masterpiece and a commercial failure.

22. Propst, *The Office*, p. 40, for his ideas about the use of computer graphics in facilities planning. Engelbart, like many computer scientists of that era, was enthralled by Christopher Alexander's *Notes on the Synthesis of Form* (Cambridge, MA: Harvard University Press, 1964) and the "Design Methods" movement emanating from U.C. Berkeley. Interview with Jeff Rulifson (Stanford, May 20, 2013).

23. D. C. Engelbart, "Augmenting Human Intellect, pp. 2ff: "Let us consider an augmented architect at work. He sits at a working station that has a visual display screen some three feet on a side; this is his working surface, and is controlled by a computer (his 'clerk') with which he can communicate by means of a small keyboard and various other devices." Provided to the author by Douglas Engelbart, and available in the digital archives of the Doug Engelbart Institute, http://www.dougengelbart.org/pubs/augment-3906.html

24. Jack Kelley, "The Mouse That Roared: A Research Project Documentary" (unpublished, 2007; rev. 2010). Mr. Kelley generously shared this document with me, together with a wealth of insights and information in the course of a lengthy telephone interview (January 14, 2011). The original 100-minute video of this event is part of the Engelbart Collection in Special Collections of Stanford University. It can be viewed online through the Doug Englebart website, http://sloan.stanford.edu/MouseSite/1968Demo.html, especially "clip 12" in which the mouse and handset are clearly visible on the swivel tray. In 1979 Kelley was named director of corporate design of the Herman Miller Company.

25. Wallace B. Riley, "Getting More Mileage from Computers," *Electronics* (January 0, 1969), pp. 117–20.

26. In a strict sense, of course, no innovation is ever wholly "without precedent": In the words of Chuck Thacker, who oversaw the hardware development of the Alto, "We also attached a high value to modeling the capabilities of existing manual media; after all, these have evolved over many hundreds of years. There are good reasons for most of their characteristics, and much has been learned about how to use them effectively. The manual media we chose as models were paper and ink (the display), pointing devices (the mouse and the cursor), and keyboard devices, ranging from typewriters to pianos and organs." Chuck Thacker, et al., *Alto:*

A Personal Computer (August 7, 1979), p. 15 (http://research.microsoft.com/en-us/um/people/blampson/25-Alto/25-Alto.pdf). Also Larry Tesler, "Design of the Intuitive Typewriter" (June 25, 1973), which first introduces the terminology of "Cut/Copy Paste." Papers of Lawrence G. Tesler.

27. "Because the character of the POLOS system is so comprehensive, and because it embraces so many functions, it stands really as a new kind of medium." Nilo Lundgren, "POLOS: PARC On-Line Office System" (Spring 1973). Papers of Stuart Card, PARC. POLOS integrated the functions of writing, typing, dictation, filing, copying, publishing and printing, telephone, mail, and microfiche.

28. The classic papers are J. C. R. Licklider, "Man-Computer Symbiosis," originally published in *IRE Transactions on Human Factors in Electronics,* volume HFE-1, pp. 4–11, March 1960; J. C. R. Licklider and Robert W. Taylor, "The Computer as a Communications Device," originally published in *Science and Technology* (April 1968). They can be found online at: http://memex.org/licklider.pdf. On Licklider, see M. Mitchell Waldrop, *The Dream Machine: J. C. R. Licklider and the Revolution that Made Computing Personal* (New York: Viking, 1996).

29. Butler Lampson to CSL [Computer Science Lab], Palo Alto (December 19, 1972), "Why Alto." This famous internal memorandum, in which Lampson argues for the building of ten to thirty small, relatively inexpensive personal computers, can be found at http://research.microsoft.com/en-us/um/people/blampson/38a-whyalto/webpage.html. The Alto is considered the first workable personal computer, and has been the subject of an immense literature that does not need to be reviewed here. Three of its key designers are recipients of the Turing Award—Butler Lampson (1992), Alan Kay (2003), and Chuck Thacker (2009)—and their numerous presentations and publications are widely available. Thacker and Lampson described their experience at PARC in an illuminating conversation at the Computer History Museum, Mountain View (http://www.youtube.com/watch?v=2H2BPrgxedY&feature=relmfu) (June 4, 2001).

30. SLOT was the first laser printer. Estimates of the number of Altos produced range from 1,000 to 2,000. The lower figure used here is cited by Thacker, McCreight, Lampson, Sproull, and Boggs: "Alto," and may refer to those in use within the Xerox Corporation. See also Roy Levin, "A Field Guide to Alto-Land, or Exploring the Ethernet with Mouse and Keyboard" (rev. April 1979): Xerox Palo Alto Research Center (http://bitsavers.trailing-edge.com/pdf/xerox/alto/memos_1979/A_Field_Guide_to_Alto-Land_Apr79.pdf).

31. Butler Lampson, "Personal Distributed Computing: The Alto and Ethernet Software," in *A History of Personal Workstations,* ed. Adele Goldberg (New York: ACM

Press: 1988), p. 296; see also the companion piece by Chuck Thacker, "Personal Distributed Computing: The Alto and Ethernet Hardware," ibid., pp. 267–89.

32. Interview with John Ellenby (San Francisco, July 27, 2010), and subsequent correspondence. Ellenby organized the Special Programs Group (SPG), in El Segundo, California, a semiautonomous manufacturing unit created to do proof-of-concept work based on Xerox technology including the Alto computers and the Dover, Pimlico, Puffin, and Penguin laser printers: "If Xerox had committed to going forward, SPG was the core of a ready-to-go-to-market company that would have brought the first WYSIWYG truly networked (Ethernet) ball mouse equipped, laser printer supported personal computers to the world." (Ellenby, communication with the author: July 24, 2010). Abbey Silverstone oversaw SPG manufacturing at Xerox El Segundo and Doug Stewart was in charge of SPG engineering and overall operations.

33. Butler W. Lampson, et al., *Alto User's Handbook* (October 1976). Many of the original documents can now be found online: http://research.microsoft.com/en-us/um/people/blampson/15a-AltoHandbook/15a-AltoHandbook.pdf.

34. Tim Mott, interview with the author (Palo Alto, November 22, 2010).

35. George Pake to Paul Niquette, "Response to Gypsy Business Questionnaire" (August 27, 1975): papers of Lawrence G. Tesler. Robert Taylor, associate director of the Computer Science Lab at Xerox PARC, elaborated on this point in a 2010 presentation at the Computer History Museum: "A lab cannot ship products. A lab can ship technology to a group whose business is to ship products" (http://www.youtube.com/user/ComputerHistory#p/search/2/Y0MsrrTo8jY) (May 13, 2010). Interviews with Larry Tesler (Portola Valley, August 14–November 9, 2014) and Robert W. Taylor (Woodside, CA, December 17, 2010). As director of NASA's external research programs and then the Advanced Research Projects Administration's Information Processing Techniques Office (ARPA/IPTO), Taylor provided the initial funding of Engelbart's Augmentation Research Lab.

36. SDD actually had two software centers: conceptual design and prototyping work was led by Charles Irby and done mainly in Palo Alto, while the Southern California branch in El Segundo, led by Eric Harslam, was responsible for implementation. Hardware development was done primarily in Palo Alto. The two centers were connected by a 56-kilobit-per-second Ethernet connection in what amounted to an early realization of Engelbart's vision of electronic collaboration between asynchronous, geographically distributed teams.

37. Budd Steinhilber, *Looking Backward*, vol. 2:99: unpublished memoir, cited with the kind permission of Mr. Steinhilber. The Xerox job went to a graphic designer,

Harry Murphy. Steinhilber continues: "To Harry's credit, he solved that 'document' icon by just turning down one corner of the paper. And for the 'delete' icon? A wastebasket. Brilliant! Harry's icons found their way into Xerox's new STAR System screen display—what we now refer to as the generic 'desktop.'" The desktop metaphor is an aging artifact of the business culture in which and for which the personal computer was developed. It has become a historical curiosity to an emerging generation defined by mobility, multimedia, and multitasking.

38. Charles Irby and Linda Bergsteinsson (ITG) and Thomas Moran, William Newman, and Larry Tesler (PARC), "A Methodology for Interface Design" (January 1977): Xerox internal document, graciously provided to the author by Charles Irby. William L. Bewley, Teresa L. Roberts, David Schroit, and William L. Verplank, "Human Factors Testing in the Design of Xerox's 8010 'Star' Office Workstation," CHI'83 *Proceedings* (December 1983), and David Canfield Smith, Charles Irby, Ralph Kimball, and Bill Verplank, "Designing the Xerox Star User Interface," *Byte*, no. 4 (1982), pp. 242–82.

39. David Liddle, interviewed by a group from the Association for Software Design, in Terry Winograd, ed., *Bringing Design to Software* (New York: Addison-Wesley, 1996), pp. 17–31.

40. Interviews with David Liddle (Menlo Park, CA, February 1, 2011), Charles Irby (Menlo Park, March 24, 2011), and William Verplank (Menlo Park, August 16, 2011, and July 18, 2013). Irby, who led the Information Technology Group and oversaw the design and functionality of the user interface, wrote: "We got our product planning people to identify target office environments. I took the designers out there and had them sit for about a two-day period with these people to understand the tasks that they did . . . . We then came back and put a very large emphasis on the whole notion of a conceptual model—the objects that are dealt with in these tasks and the operations you can apply to those objects when doing the tasks. We had about half of my group doing design prototypes; they were doing software implementations, working right along with the designers on a day-to-day basis . . . . The discipline was applied quite sternly within the design group and I think the payoff was quite large." Charles Irby in Goldberg, *A History of Personal Workstations*, pp. 523–24. See also Jeff Johnson, Teresa L. Roberts, William Verplank, David C. Smith, Charles H. Irby, Marian Beard, and Kevin Mackey, who write, "An important design goal was to make the 'computer' as invisible to users as possible. "The Xerox Star: A Retrospective." *IEEE Computer* (September 1989), pp. 11–29.

41. Larry Tesler to Bert Sutherland, "Hobby and Personal Computers vs OIS" (November 3, 1977): papers of Larry Tesler, cited with permission.

42. In his interview at Microsoft Simonyi told Paul Allen, "It's not that [Xerox] didn't know the answers. That's normal. But they didn't know the questions." Paul Allen, *Idea Man: A Memoir by the Cofounder of Microsoft* (New York: Penguin, 2011), p. 238. Other PARC spinoffs included VLSI Technologies (Douglas Fairbairn) and Aurora Systems, which created the first digital video graphics system for television (Richard Shoup).

43. John Ellenby [et al.], "Proposal for a Capability Investment" (unpublished, internal Xerox report: November 3, 1978). Dr. Ellenby graciously made this historic document available to me and provided additional information in a wide-ranging conversation (San Francisco, March 17, 2011).

44. Alan C. Kay, "Microelectronics and the Personal Computer," *Scientific American* 237 (September 1977): p. 3. Kay predicted that in the coming decade, "both adults and children will be able to have as a personal possession a computer about the size of a large notebook with the power to handle virtually all information-related needs." At the request of the Computer History Museum, Kay created a "meta-mockup"—mockup of the original (lost) mockup, which is on display in the museum's permanent exhibit.

45. "Developing the First Laptop," in Bill Moggridge, *Designing Interactions* (Cambridge, MA: MIT Press, 2007), pp. 10–13 and 169–78. Additional material in this section is based on interviews with John Ellenby (San Francisco, March 17, 2011), Bill Moggridge (Woodside, CA, March 3, 2008), and Mike Nuttall (Portola Valley, CA, March 13, 2011).

46. In his "Wildflower" proposal Ellenby had budgeted for a team of about forty, including hardware and software engineers, a manufacturing base, and flexible administrative support. He did not include industrial design in staffing because he assumed that Xerox would have rejected it on the grounds that "design" meant nothing more than ensuring consistent corporate identity, a task that could be handled internally. Interview with John Ellenby (San Francisco, March 23, 211).

47. John Ellenby, quoted in "The Compass Computer: The Design Challenges Behind the Innovation" in *Innovation: The Journal of the Industrial Designers Society of America* (Winter 1983), pp. 4–8. See also Paul Atkinson, "Man in a Briefcase: The Social Construction of the Laptop Computer and the Emergence of a Typeform," *Journal of Design History* 18, no. 2 (2005), pp. 191–205. Moggridge's team consisted of industrial designer Mike Nuttall and engineer Steve Hobson.

48. Mike Nuttall, the first member of Moggridge's staff to join him in the United States, in conversation with the author, Portola Valley, California (March 11, 2011). In his *Autobiography*, Frank Lloyd Wright claimed that his early experience with the

kindergarten blocks—developed by Friedrich Froebel in the 1830s to help children learn the principles of geometry—had ignited his creative passion: "The maple-wood blocks . . . are in my fingers to this day."

49. My perspective on this episode benefitted greatly from interviews with cofounder David Liddle (Menlo Park, February 1, 2011) and David Rossetti, part of the early engineering team (Milpitas, CA, April 5, 2011. There is probably not a single engineer in the startup culture of Silicon Valley who has not heard—or told—the joke about how God was able to create the universe in only six days: "He had no installed base." Metaphor shared a building complex in Mountain View with another fragile startup, Sun Microsystems. Each bet on the prospects of the other.

50. Kristina Goodrich [Communications Director, Industrial Designers Society of America] to Mike Nuttall (May 15, 1985) and James R. Yurchenco to Steven Holt [Managing Editor, *ID Magazine*] (June 7, 1985); papers of James Yurchenco, graciously provided to the author. Additional information in this section is based on interviews with James Yurchenco (Palo Alto, March 11, 2011) and Mike Nuttall (Portola Valley, CA, March 13, 2011). See also *ID: Magazine of International Design* (July-August, 1985), pp. 90–91 and Hugh Alderssey-Williams, *New American Design: Products and Graphics for a Post-Industrial Age* (New York: Rizzoli, 1988), pp. 171–75 and 176–81.

Chapter 3

1. *Peninsula Times Tribune* (May 11, 1979), in which Marnie Jones is quoted as saying, "There are 127 design offices in Palo Alto, 55 of them downtown." Tepper & Steinhilber Associates, formed in San Francisco in 1964, was among the first to work with the then-new Silicon Valley electronics industry, designing console interfaces, optical disk storage units, video cameras, and a number of innovative medical devices. In 1972 Steinhilber and graphic designer Barry Deutsch formed Steinhilber & Deutsch, a consultancy whose clients included Intel, Atari, Telesensory Systems, GRiD, Convergent, Visicorp, and Electronic Arts. In 1980 they opened a branch office in Mountain View and became Steinhilber, Deutsch, Gard; Papers of Budd Steinhilber: Syracuse University Special Collections, and papers and interviews with John Gard (Mountain View, March 9, 2010,and September 10, 2013).

2. James Ferris, personal communication with the author (April 25, 2011). Material in this section is based on interviews with Bill Moggridge (Woodside, CA: October 3, 2008) and Peter Lowe (Healdsburg, CA: December 15, 2010), and Lowe's commentary in the IDSA-San Francisco Chapter *News* (hereafter *News*) 24, August–September

1979. I am especially grateful to Karin Moggridge and Tim Brown for allowing me unrestricted access to Moggridge's files.

3. Darrell Staley, *News* 8 (October 1977), p. 2.

4. This and the following quotes are from Carroll Gantz, "My 50 Years with the IDSA" (unpublished: 2011), *passim*, graciously shared with the author. Gantz led a movement for internal reform within IDSA and served as President during its most tumultuous years, 1979–82.

5. Marnie Jones to Carroll M. Gantz, president, IDSA (January 28, 1979); papers of Marnie Jones, kindly loaned to the author.

6. Marnie Jones, Secretary and Editor of *NEWS*, to Chapter Officers (January 2, 1978); papers of Marnie Jones.

7. The choice of venue, in this densely networked region, may have been justified by the fact that Ridge Vineyards was founded by three of SRI's most prominent computer scientists: David Bennion, Charles Rosen, and Hewitt Crane. Landor Associates is a large branding and design firm. Jay Wilson reviewed Raymond Loewy (*Centerline*, April 1980). Industrial designer Del Coates commented—critically—on the limited use of the computer as a design tool in the December 1980 issue.

8. Carroll Gantz, president, IDSA (1979–82), personal communication with the author (April 7, 2011). IDSA'S "critics on the left and the right" included, respectively, Victor Papanek, *Design for the Real World: Human Ecology and Social Change* (New York: Pantheon, 1971), and *Fortune Magazine*, "The Decline of Industrial Design" (February 1968).

9. Gantz, "My 50 Years with the IDSA."

10. Memorandum (n.a., n.d., but most likely Marnie Jones in the immediate aftermath of the conference); papers of Marnie Jones. On this theme, see John Markoff, *What the Dormouse Said: How the Sixties Counterculture Shaped the Personal Computer Industry* (New York: Viking, 2005), Fred Turner, *From Counterculture to Cyberculture: Stewart Brand, the Whole Earth Network, and the Rise of Digital Utopianism* (Chicago: University of Chicago Press, 2006), and Theodor Roszak, *From Satori to Silicon Valley* (2000): Stanford University Library Special Collections, "Making the Macintosh," accessible online at http://searchworks.stanford.edu/view/5465486: primary documents.

11. "Conference Motivation," memorandum, Industrial Designers Society of America San Francisco Chapter (n.d., but clearly summer 1978); papers of Marnie Jones.

12. The steering committee consisted of Peter Lowe (conference coordinator), Darrell Staley (administration), Marnie Jones (program), Jim Goldberg (master of ceremonies), Karlina Ott (students), and Dave Anderson and Arden Farey (advisors).

13. *Thrival Manual: The 1978 Annual Meeting of the Industrials Designers Society of America, Asilomar, Monterey, California, September 26–30*, kindly loaned to the author by Peter Lowe, who drove the author of *Unsafe at Any Speed* back to the airport in his 1976 Ford Pinto!

14. Jay Wilson, "Results of Core Group" (September 30, 1978), papers of Marnie Jones; "Stand up for Safety, Nader Urges Designers," *Monterey Peninsula Herald* (September 28, 1978).

15. Material from this section is drawn from the records of the Stanford Design Conference, in the possession of the author (who unwisely attempted to revive it many years later). The distinction between a "design" and a "designed" conference arose in conversation with Richard Saul Wurman (May 29, 2012), who spoke at the Stanford conference in the early 'eighties and went on to found the TED Conferences in 1984 in nearby Monterey.

16. Marnie Jones to Eudorah Moore (April 12, 1979); papers of Marnie Jones. Peter Lowe, "What is the Center for Design?" in *Centerline: The Newspaper for People Concerned with Design in Northern California* (Palo Alto, CA, February 1980). Peter Lowe was the center's executive director; Marnie Jones was the professional interaction coordinator; Philene Bracht served as Public Interaction Coordinator. Eudorah Moore, it should be noted, instigated the annual series of exhibits at the Pasadena Museum of Art, which introduced the concept of "California Design."

17. In the first issue of *Centerline*, Jones estimates that there were 12,000 design professionals working in the Bay Area in 1980, though this included many who were in no way connected to "Silicon Valley" industries (Palo Alto, February 1980), p. 5.

18. Arden Farey, head of design at Ampex until he was stricken with multiple sclerosis, was one of the center's few paid employees. Farey led the Task Force that developed IDSA Code of Ethics, which he presented to universal acclaim at *Thrival*.

19. Marnie Jones to Eudorah Moore (April 12, 1979); papers of Marnie Jones. "New Palo Alto group has designs on better things," *Peninsula Times Tribune* (May 11, 1979). Carroll Gantz, a self-described "staunch conservative" who had viewed the Bay Areans as "hippies" afflicted with "the apparent disrespect of youth," sent them his "highest compliments for a superb publication." [*Centerline* 5/80].

20. "Just for the Look of the Thing," *Design* 368 (August 1979). Other material in this section is based on interviews with Bill Moggridge (Woodside, CA, October 3, 2008,

and ongoing) and Mike Nuttall (Portola Valley, CA, September 9, 2008, March 13, 2011, and ongoing).

21. "Bill Moggridge Associates Industrial Designers," promotional brochure (undated, but 1979), in the author's collection.

22. Bill Moggridge, "The Lessons of Silicon Valley," *Design* 371 (November 1979): 50–52.

23. Bill Moggridge, quoted in "The Compass Computer: The Design Challenges Behind the Innovation" in *Innovation: The Journal of the Industrial Designers Society of America* (winter 1983), pp. 4–8. Reyner Banham, "The Great Gizmo," in *Industrial Design* 12 (September 1965): 48–59; reprinted in *A Critic Writes: Essays by Reyner Banham* (Berkeley: University of California Press, 1996). See also Nigel Whitely, *Reyner Banham: Historian of the Immediate Future* (Cambridge, MA: MIT Press, 2001).

24. "The Computer Peripheral as Open Book," *Design* 384 (December 1980): 48–49.

25. Matt Sanders, cofounder of Convergent Technology, quoted in ibid.

26. Todd Lynch, hardware engineering manager, quoted in "Convergent Technologies, Inc.—WorkSlate," an internal postmortem most likely written by Matthew Sanders, in the possession of the author. Additional perspectives were provided in interviews with Karen Morss Toland, Convergent's director of product marketing (Redwood City, July 29, 2011), and Mike Nuttall (Portola Valley, July 22, 2011).

27. Michel's unseemly boast caught the attention of GRiD CEO John Ellenby, who felt that ID Two's work for such a close competitor represented an unacceptable conflict of interest. By mutual agreement, Nuttall spun off Matrix Design in 1983 to continue his work with Convergent. Matrix and ID Two would reunite in 1991, together with David Kelley Design, to form IDEO.

28. Stephen Wozniak, "Homebrew and How the Apple Came to Be" (http://www.atariarchives.org/deli/homebrew_and_how_the_apple.php).

29. Steve Jobs, quoted in Moritz, *The Little Kingdom*, p. 186.

30. Ron Wayne was the cofounder, along with Jobs and Wozniak, of Apple Computer. This episode is recalled in a presentation by Atari founder Nolan Bushnell in Redmond, Washington (October 20, 2009) (http://www.bizjournals.com/seattle/blog/techflash/2009/10/atari_founder_nolan_bushnell_on_steve_jobs _amazoncom_and_more.html). See also Paul Kunkel, *Apple Design*, p. 13.

31. Telesensory Systems was founded by John Linville, a prominent professor of electrical engineering at Stanford who had invented the Optacon, a device that enabled his blind daughter to read.

32. Jerrold Manock, in conversation with the author (Palo Alto, November 7, 2011), and via telephone from Burlington, VT (May 28, 2011). Additional information about the Apple II can be found in Moritz, *The Little Kingdom*, pp. 187–94, and Kunkel, *Apple Design*, pp. 14–16.

33. Steve Jobs, interview with the author (Cupertino, November 11, 1998).

34. Steve Jobs, interviewed by David Sheff, *Playboy Magazine* (February 1, 1985).

35. James Ferris, personal communication (October 16, 2011). Ferris, it will be recalled, was a partner in Ferris-Lowe in the early 1970s. Tom Suiter, Ferris's successor as head of Creative Services, described Jobs as "the best creative director I've ever been around in my life." (interview with Tom Suiter, Menlo Park, September 15, 2014). For another insider's account, see Regis McKenna, *The Regis Touch* (Reading, MA: Addison-Wesley, 1985), pp. 151–73, and also a special supplement to *Communication Arts* (May/June 1985). This footnote affords us an opportunity to put to rest a misrecollection planted by Andy Herzfeld and propagated by Walter Isaacson and innumerable bloggers: it was Ferris, not Jobs, who advocated the aesthetics of Porsche (whose creative director he became after leaving Apple); Jobs was still driving his decidedly unvoluptuous Mercedes.

36. Clement Mok, *Apple Creative Service* (2013), privately printed portfolio graciously shared with the author, and interview (San Francisco, October 14, 2014). Chiatt-Day served as Apple's external advertising agency. The internal Creative Services group, under the successive leadership of James Ferris, Tom Suiter, Clement Mok, and Hugh Dubberly, handled about 100 projects a year—"We did everything that Chiatt-Day did not." (Tom Suiter, in conversation with the author: Menlo Park, September 15, 2014).

37. Interview with Davis Masten and Christopher Ireland (Atherton, November 30, 2010).

38. Jim Yurchenco, internal IDEO e-mail, announcing his retirement, cited with permission. The "gig" lasted thirty-five years.

39. Dean Hovey, interviewed by Alex Pang (Los Altos, June 25, 2000). This is one of a series of interviews conducted as part of the Stanford University Libraries project, "Making the Macintosh: Technology and Culture in Silicon Valley" (http://searchworks.stanford.edu/view/6559489)

40. The transfer of the mouse, the Ethernet, and the icon-based graphical user interface from Xerox PARC to Apple is part of the lore of Silicon Valley and no two accountings of it quite match up. It is fortunately not the business of this book to add yet another. Information in this section is based on the author's interviews

with Dean Hovey (Palo Alto, May 18, 2011), David Kelley (Mountain View, July 11, 2011), James Yurchenco (Palo Alto, March 11, 2011), and Larry Tesler (Portola Valley, August 14, 2014), as well as the Alex Pang interviews referenced in the preceding note. Among the more credible sources are Michael A. Hiltzig, *Dealers in Lightning: Xerox PARC and the Dawn of the Computer Age* (New York: Harper, 2000), chapter 23; Alex Soojung-Kim Pang, "The Making of the Mouse," *American Heritage of Invention and Technology* 17, no. 3 (Winter 2002): 48–54. For a first-person account, see Larry Tesler, "The Legacy of the Lisa," *MacWorld* (September 1985), his interview in *Byte*, no. 2 (1983), pp. 90–114, and also his presentation at a forum held at the Computer History Museum in Mountain View, October 28, 1997 (http://www.computerhistory.org/collections/catalog/102746675).

41. Jim Sachs, interviewed by Alex Pang (Redwood Shores, March 29, 2000); see n. 27. In one of the more egregious errors that mar Walter Isaacson's hastily published biography, it is claimed that following the PARC visit, "Jobs went to a local industrial design firm, IDEO," to work on a commercially feasible mouse. In fact, IDEO was not founded until 1991, more than ten years after these events had receded into history; it is not, and never has been, an "industrial design firm," a distinction that is fundamental to any serious understanding of the relation between technology and design in Silicon Valley. See Walter Isaacson, *Steve Jobs* (New York: Simon and Schuster, 2011), p. 98.

42. David Kelley, interviewed by Alex Pang (Palo Alto, July 24, 2000); see n. 27. User testing at Hovey-Kelley was rather ad hoc—"You know, you'd use your intuition, and show it to whoever you could find—'What do you think about this one? Okay, now what about this one?'"—and ergonomic evaluation at Apple was performed by "a cast of anonymous secretaries." (Bill Lapson, project manager, "Lore of the Mice," typed ms., July 28, 1982, from the collection of the late Jim Sachs); http://searchworks.stanford.edu/view/6630103. It is instructive to compare this with the process that drove the first generation of innovators at Fairchild Camera and Instruments, the company that spawned nearly the whole of Silicon Valley: "There was no such thing as an instrumentation marketplace in those days. If you wanted something you sat down and started drawing it. Someone would look over your shoulder, make a suggestion, and you'd try it. It was that simple—and that complicated." Murray Siegel, quoted in Michael Malone, *The Big Score*, p. 88.

43. LISA, despite rampant speculations to the contrary, is an acronym for Logically Integrated Stand-alone Assistant. The rationale for the one-, as opposed to two- or three-button mouse was grounded in the conviction that since "the Lisa interface

will be learned by absolute novices . . . its human factors must meet the most strict standards in order to minimize the natural effects of resistance to the introduction of unusual devices into the office." The same principle governed the design of the LISA interface: "As far as possible, the user interface attempts to have only one way to accomplish any action, and any user action has but one effect throughout the system." Larry Tesler and Bill Atkinson, "One Button Mouse" (August 18, 1980), and Bill Atkinson, Jef Raskin, and Larry Tesler, "Eternal [sic!] Specifications for the LISA User Interface" (August 22, 1980); papers of Larry Tesler, cited with permission.

44. This discussion has benefitted from an extraordinary series of first-person narratives created for the author by Bill Dresselhaus, product design leader and design manager for the Lisa (April–June, 2012). Additional material is based on early promotional literature generously supplied to the author by James Ferris, Apple's first creative director. Also Tesler, "The Legacy of the Lisa."

45. Jef Raskin, "Thoughts on Annie: Design Considerations for an Anthropophilic Computer" (May 28–29, 1979): Stanford University Libraries Special Collections (hereafter SUL/SC), Jef Raskin papers, M1147, box 8, folder 13; a selection of archival documents can be found online at http://searchworks.stanford.edu/view/6630103

46. Paul Kunkel, *Apple Design*, pp. 14–16, where Manock is quoted as saying, "Steve [Jobs] was obsessed by the idea that the case appear to be a single piece. He didn't want any visible partlines or screwheads showing." Other members of the early team were Laszlo Zeidek, Steve Balog, Dave Roots, and Ben Pang.

47. Jef Raskin, "The Genesis and History of the Macintosh Project (February 16, 1981): Jef Raskin papers, SUL/SC: M1147, box 8, folder 11. Andy Hertzfeld, *Revolution in the Valley* (Sebastopol, CA: O'Reilly, 2005), pp. 181-83, and associated website: http://www.folklore.org/StoryView.py?project=Macintosh&story=Revolution_in_the_Valley.tx).

48. "Apple Engineering Notebook, Book No. 37, assigned to Jerry Manock" (June 16, 1980); collection of Jerrold C. Manock, graciously provided to the author.

49. Jerry Manock [mgr. Macintosh], Clive Twyman [mgr. DOS], Jim Stewart [mgr. Peripherals], Bill Mackenzie [mgr. Advanced Products Division], and Rob Gemmell [mgr. PCs] to John Scully and Steve Jobs (July 3, 1983), draft letter in which the divisional managers call for tighter coordination of Apple's design functions and executive level support. Papers of Jerrold C. Manock, graciously provided to the author.

50. Jerry Manock, ed., "Product Development: A Designer's Viewpoint," Apple Product Design Guild, (March 17, 1983); papers of Jerrold C. Manock, graciously provided to the author.

51. Keith Cassell, "Proposal for a Corporate Design Center" (October 30, 1981). Papers of Jerold C. Manock: M1880, box 1, folder 3.

52. On Design Semantics, see Reinhart Bütter and Klaus Krippendorff, guest editors, *Design Issues* 5, no. 2 (Spring 1989).

53. Steve Jobs, Design Council Meeting (March 1982), cited in "Product Development: A Designer's Viewpoint." Interview with Rob Gemmell (Portola Valley, May 3, 2011) and Terry Oyama (Palo Alto, July 20, 2011). Jobs had initially dismissed the Macintosh idea, and it riled Raskin to no end that he later came to own it: "It is another running joke that the way to convince Jobs of something is to tell him about it, listen to him reject it, and then wait a week until he comes running to tell you about his latest idea." Jef Raskin to Mike Scott, "Working with Steve Jobs" (February 19, 1981): Jef Raskin papers, SUL/SC: M1147, box 8, folder 5.

54. "Project Snow White," ed. Jerrold C. Manock (Rev. 05, August 12, 1982): collection of Jerrold C. Manock, graciously provided to the author. This descriptive notebook was created to stimulate interest among international design consultants.

55. Stephen Bartlett, personal communication with the author (June 13, 2011). I am grateful to Mr. Bartlett for sharing with me their work and perspectives.

56. In addition to Hartmut Esslinger, the key members of the team were his original partners, Andreas Haug and Georg Spreng, Herbert Pfeifer, Steven Peart (a graduate of RCA in London) and an American, Tony Guido. Esslinger in fact produced a series of preliminary studies in a "Sony," "Americana," and radical line-and-slab vernacular: Hartmut Esslinger, *Keep It Simple: The Early Design Years at Apple* (Sttutgart: Arnoldsche Verlagsanstalt, 2014); prepublication edition kindly made available to the author by Professor Esslinger.

57. Interview with Hartmut Esslinger (Mountain View, April 20, 2011). This interview was conducted by the author for the Computer History Museum and will become part of its Silicon Valley Oral History collection. On the Snow White compettion, see also Paul Kunkel, *Apple Design*, pp. 28–35.

58. The phrase is borrowed from Hans-Georg Gadamer's philosophical classic, *Truth and Method* (London: Sheed and Ward, 1989).

59. Various published figures exist; this one comes directly from Hartmut Esslinger (see n. 25).

Chapter 4

1. The chart was originally created in 1977 by Don C. Hoefler, the journalist who first published the phrase "Silicon Valley," together with Harry Smallwood and James E. Vincler. It has been updated and reprinted by SEMI, the manufacturing trade group of the semiconductor and nanotechnology industry(http://corphist.computerhistory.org/corphist/documents/doc-45ff3e214d9ea.pdf?PHPSESSID=d20fe9a0dbce91cecb8181fa92e4d84e). According to RitaSue Siegel, an authoritative consultant to the design industry, some 5,000 US companies had internal design departments at this time; only about eight consultancies had more than ten people, mostly in the Midwest where they were located near corporate headquarters or manufacturing centers (*Design* [June 1982], pp. 22–27). Whipsaw Design in San Jose, Studio NONOBJECT in Palo Alto, fuseproject, Ammunition, Astro Studios, and New Deal Design in San Francisco are among the more prominent mid-size consultancies whose founders can trace their roots to IDEO, frog, or Lunar; see chapter 6.

2. The proliferation of design disciplines in recent years has led to predictable terminological confusion. For a guide to this alphabetic labyrinth (XD; UX; IxD; HFE; HCI, HCC . . .), see Analia Ibargoyen, Dalila Szostak, and Miroslav Bojic, "The Elephant in the Conference Room: Let's Talk about Experience Terminology," *CHI 2013 Extended Abstracts*, April 27–May 2, 2013.

3. Interview with David Kelley (Computer History Museum, Mountain View, July 11, 2011).

4. A fifth founding partner, Don Taylor, set out on his own a short time later.

5. Beth Sherman, "Silicon Valley Style," *i-D Magazine* 33, no. 3 (May–June 1986): 49–53.

6. Peter Müller, quoted ibid. and in conversation with the author (Woodside, April 19, 2011).

7. Peter Lowe and Peter Müller maintained the partnership until 1991, when Lowe sold his stake in the firm and scaled his interests upward to help found the World Design Foundation; Müller continues to operate Interform as a virtual consultancy. Information in this section is derived from various sources, including interviews with Peter Lowe (Healdsburg, December 15, 2010), Peter Müller (Woodside, April 15, 2011), Jeff Smith and Gerard Furbershaw (Palo Alto, October 21, 2011), Robert Brunner (San Francisco, March 16, 2010), and "Blue Moon," an unpublished memoir by Furbershaw graciously made available to the author.

8. Furbershaw, *Blue Moon*.

9. When it came time to shift from 2-D to 3-D solid modeling software, Lunar switched to Pro/E, a state-of-the-art program developed by Parametric Design. frogdesign, at that time, was using *Euclid*, a CAD package produced by the French company Matra Datavision; David Kelley Design relied on HP's *ME30*; Apple used *Unigraphics*, a high-end CAD system used in the aerospace industry.

10. Robert Howard and his family died in a catastrophic highway accident as these words were being written. His death was mourned across the Silicon Valley design community.

11. "Telepresence for Intra-abdominal and Endoscopic Surgery," Grant Application: Department of Health and Human Services (September 28, 1990), p. 32; papers of Philip S. Green, cited with permission of the author, who graciously consented to an interview (Palo Alto, October 19, 2011).

12. In the interest of terminological accuracy, it should be noted that the Advanced Research Projects Administration (ARPA) had in 1972 become the Defense Advanced Research Projects Administration (DARPA); the Stanford Research Institute separated itself from the university during the Vietnam War era and in 1977 changed its name to SRI International. Finally, although the term has attained widespread currency, strictly speaking, neither the SRI system nor the da Vinci can be called a "robot," which implies an autonomous, programmable apparatus.

13. This was the respectful estimation of lab director Donald Nielson, in conversation with the author (Menlo Park, October 7, 2011); see also Nielson, *A Heritage of Innovation: SRI's First Half-Century* (Menlo Park: SRI International, 2006), pp. 5-1–5-6. Philip S. Green, "Commercialization of SRI International's Telepresence and Minimally Invasive Surgery Technologies: Prospectus for a New Business Venture" (March 30, 1992); papers of Philip S. Green, cited with the permission of the author.

14. Interview with Jeff Salazar, vice president of design, Lunar (Palo Alto, September 23, 2011).

15. "The arc of the story carries us back, beyond a gross mechanical interlude, to the ancient shamanic healer who retreated to a sacred grove and, with minimally invasive gestures and incantations, rid the suffering body of its demons." Barry M. Katz, "The Science of Incision," *Metropolis* 16, no. 3 (October 1996): 53–58. For a more grounded, less cosmic account of the transfer of the telepresence technology from SR to Intuitive, see Nielson, *A Heritage of Innovation*, pp. 5-1–5-6.

16. Information in this section is drawn in part from interviews with Dr. Gary Guthart, CEO, and Salvator Brogna, senior vice president of engineering, Intuitive

Surgical (Sunnyvale: October 21, 2011), who graciously allowed the author to operate the Da Vinci system; Stacey Chang (Palo Alto, October 10, 2011); Ricardo Salinas (San Francisco, November 10, 2011).

17. *Methodology Handbook* (draft), David Kelley Design (March 1991), cited with permission.

18. Bill Moggridge, submission for the Prince Philip Designers Prize, courtesy of the late Bill Moggridge.

19. In the Japanese boardgame *Go*, the term *atari* has approximately the same aggressive connotation as "check" in a game of chess. Nick Montfort and Ian Bogost suggest that, "To make a breakthrough, Bushnell needed to merge his experience as an electrical engineer and as a midway barker." See *Racing the Beam: The Atari Video Computer System* (Cambridge, MA: MIT Press, 2009), p. 7. See also the open-ended documentation to be found on the website of the Atari History Museum (http://www.atarimuseum.com). I am grateful to Nolan Bushnell for setting aside the time to speak with me about Atari (February12, 2015).

20. Henry Lowood, "Video Games in Computer Space: The Complex History of Pong," *IEEE Annals of the History of Computing* 31, no. 3 (July–September 2009): 5–19.

21. *Atari Age* 1, no. 5 (February 1983): 6 (http://www.ign.com/articles/2008/03/11/al-alcorn-interview). Malone, *The Big Score*, p. 353. Atari's revenues during its early years handsomely repaid Bushnell and Dabney's $500 investment:

1974: $11,967,733.
1975: $18,912,846.
1976: $38,952,275.

Papers of Al Alcorn: Stanford Special Collections: M1758, box 1, folder 1/4.

22. When the Atari 5200 SuperSystem was introduced in 1982, the VCS was retroactively renamed "Atari 2600," for its original product number. In contrast to the previous generation of game-dedicated consoles, the 2600 incorporated a complete CPU (a version of the famous MOS Technology 6502 that went into the Apple II). As a platform, it could thus be used to play as many different games as there were cartridges. Industrial design for the 2600 was the work of Douglas Hardy and Fredrick Thompson; connectors for the 2600 were among the first Western electronics components to be manufactured by the Chinese company, Foxconn. [Information in this section was supplemented by interviews with Chas Grossman (Sunnyvale: June 18, 2012).

23. Al Alcorn as told to Steve Bloom, "The incredible, incredible story of Atari— from a $500 lark to a $2 billion business in 10 short years" (cited in Steve Fulton,

"The History of Atari, 1971-1977" (http://students.expression.edu/historyofgames/files/2011/10/Atari_History_GamasutraFeature.pdf).

24. Alan Miller, quoted in Steven L. Kent, *The Ultimate History of Video Games* (New York: Three Rivers Press, 2001), p. 113. Kassar's unguarded remark, which had not been intended for publication, appeared in an interview with *Fortune Magazine.* The *Kulturkampf* between Atari and Warner should have been evident from the first meeting between the incoming and outgoing CEOs: Kassar arrived in a tailored suit, reeking of cologne and an MBA; Bushnell showed up, reeking of something else and wearing a t-shirt that said, "I love to fuck." Tristan Donovan, "The Replay Interviews: Ray Kassar" (http://www.gamasutra.com/view/feature/6364/the_replay_interviews_ray_kassar.php).

25. Scott Cohen, *Zap! The Rise and Fall of Atari* (New York: McGraw-Hill, 1984), pp. 87–93.

26. Warren Robinett, "Adventure as a Video Game," in *The Game Design Reader,* ed. Katie Salen and Eric Zimmerman (Cambridge, MA: MIT Press 2006), p. 692.

27. On the professionalization of industrial design and graphic design, respectively, see Arthur Pulos, *American Design Ethic* (Cambridge, MA: MIT Press, 1983) and *American Design Adventure* (Cambridge, MA: MIT Press, 1988), and Steven Eskilson, *Graphic Design: A New History* (New Haven: Yale University Press 2007), p. 29.

28. Warren Robinett, quoted in Kent, *The Ultimate History of Video Games,* p. 179. Dona Bailey and Ed Logg were the creators of *Centipede* and *Asteroids*; Ed Rotberg, Howard Delman, and Roger Hector between them created a dozen games including the blockbuster, *Battlezone;* Dave Stubben and Dave Theurer were the designers, respectively, of *Football* and *Four-Player Soccer*; Warren Robinett, designed and programmed *Adventure.*

29. Warren Robinett, *Inventing the Adventure Game* (unpublished ms., 1983–84), cited with the kind permission of Mr. Robinett, who answered additional questions in an interview (Palo Alto: April 1, 2012). The "rooms" in *Rocky's Boots* read sequentially to form a tutorial, and for the shapes of the objects ("symbol gizmos") he chose the standard symbols used by electrical engineers in their diagrams of computer circuits.

30. Alan Kay, Microelectronics and the Personal Computer, *Scientific American* 237, no. 3 (September, 1977), pp. 230–244.

31. Atari Business Plan, Papers of Al Alcorn: Stanford Special Collections: M1758, box 1, folder 1/4.

32. "Atari Chief Scientist Composes his Thoughts" in *InfoWorld: The Newsweekly for Microcomputer Users* 4, no. 23 (June 14, 1982): 34–37.

33. Alan Kay, "Computer Software," in *Scientific American* 251, no. 3 (September 1984): 59. Only gradually did a literature emerge that addressed the computer from the point of view of the user, rather than the programmer—in other words, not as a technical problem but a design problem: The early classics include James Martin, *Design of Man—Computer Dialogues* (Englewood Cliffs, NJ: Prentice-Hall, 1973); Harold Smith and Thomas Green, eds., *Human Interaction with Computers* (London: Academic Press, 1980); *The Psychology of Human-Computer Interaction*, the foundational text by Stuart Card, Thomas Moran, and Alan Newell, was published only in 1983 (Hillsdale, NJ: L. Erlbaum Associates, 1983). The Architecture Machine Group, precursor to the MIT Media Lab, was founded in 1967 by Nicholas Negroponte. "ArcMac" was a pioneer in the use of a spatial, rather than text-based metaphor as the basis for a graphical computer interface.

34. As chief scientist, Alan Kay oversaw the research programs at three affiliated labs: the main facility, in Sunnyvale, but also a small lab in Los Angeles and the Cambridge lab, run by Cynthia Solomon, codeveloper, with Seymour Papert and Wally Feurzig, of the LOGO programming language.

35. Interview with Randall Smith (Redwood City, by telephone, December 9, 2011), and Smith, "Computers and the Theory of Relativity: Testing Our Ability to Educate Out Intuition by Simulating Four Dimensional Space-time" (October 10, 1983): Atari Research memo: papers of Kristina Hooper Woolsey, graciously made available to the author. On the Question Machine, which anticipates SIRI and the coming age of ubiquitous information, R[obert] Stein to IE Distribution, "First Question Journal" (February 24, 1983), ibid., and Michael Naimark, "The Question Machine," *Whole Earth Review* 65 (Winter 1989).

36. The key texts include: Vannevar Bush, "As We may Think," *Atlantic Monthly* 176, no. 1 (July 1945): 101–08; J. C. R. Licklider, "Man-Computer Symbiosis." *IRE Transactions on Human Factors in Electronics* (1960), and Licklider and Robert W. Taylor, "The Computer as a Communications Device." *Science and Technology* (April 1968); and Theodore Nelson, "Complex Information Processing: A File Structure for the Complex, the Changing, and the Indeterminate," *Association for Computing Machinery: Proceedings of the 20th National Conference* (New York: ACM, 1965), pp. 84–100.

37. Stephen Weyer, Alan Borning, Dave McDonald, Craig Taylor to Alan Kay, "Encyclopedic Research Plans: Draft" (July 1, 1983); Alan Borning, "The User's View of the Electronic Encyclopedia" (memorandum, July 30, 1982); Weyer et al., "Encyclopedia status and immediate plans" (August 1, 1983); "Intelligent Encyclopedia: A Seminar

with Charles van Doren, 12/20–21, 1982"; papers of Kristina Hooper Woolsey, cited with permission. Kay's remarks were cited in an interview with Robert Stein (telephone, May 30, 2012); see also his contribution to Ian Piumarta and Kimberly Rose, eds., *Points of View: A Tribute to Alan Kay* (Glendale, CA: Viewpoints Research Institute, 2010). The lineage, which may be said to have begun with Ted Nelson's Project Xanadu, continues through Apple HyperCard, to Wikipedia.

38. Kristina Hooper [Woolsey] to [Michael] Naimark et al. (July 24, 1983): papers of Kristina Hooper Woolsey, cited with permission. My understanding of the background to the Atari and Apple labs benefitted from stimulating discussions with Kristina Hooper Woolsey (San Francisco, March 6 and March 20, 2012).

39. Kristina Hooper [Woolsey] to A[tari]R[esearch]Lab]S[unnyvale] (May 31, 1984): papers of Kristina Hooper Woolsey; interviews with Eric Hulteen (Palo Alto, November 7, 2012) and Brenda Laurel (Palo Alto, July 18, 2011). The gory details are narrated by Allucquère Rosanne Stone, *The War of Technology and Desire at the End of the Mechanical Age* (Cambridge, MA: MIT Press, 1995), pp. 147–55, and Also Howard Rheingold, *Virtual Reality* (New York: Summit Books, 1991). The closing of the labs actually happened in two equally brutal stages, in February–March and then in June. Atari had ported the best-selling Pac-Man game to its home system, but vastly overestimated its sales.

40. The dramatization is set in 2010, by which time virtually all of its principal elements had been realized. John Sculley with John A. Byrne, *Odyssey: Pepsi to Apple, A Journey of Adventure, Ideas, and the Future* (New York: Harper, 1987); Hugh Dubberly, "The Making of Knowledge Navigator," in *Sketching User Experience: Getting the Design Right and the Right Design,* ed. William Buxton (Boston: Elsevier, 2007). Interviews with Hugh Dubberly (San Francisco, February 19, 2013), and Laurie Vertelney (Palo Alto, September 21, 2012). Knowledge Navigator was one of a series of futuristic visualizations created by Creative Services to explore the application of computing power to medicine, early childhood education, and other topics.

41. HyperCard (or WildCard, as it was originally named) was developed by a small team under the direction of Steve Atkinson, who had previously created MacDraw and MacPaint, and was released at MacWorld in 1987. Graphic designer Susan Kare created the Mac's visual language of trashcans, suitcases, etc. The term *icon* found its way to Silicon Valley, via computer scientist Jeff Rulifson, from an Ontario highway engineer who was daunted by the requirement of accommodating both English and French in road signage. David Smith of the Stanford Artificial Intelligence Lab used it in his 1975 PhD dissertation, "Pygmalion: A Computer Program to Model and Stimulate Creative Thought" (Basel: Birkhäuser, 1977), and subsequently brought this graphical language to his work on the Xerox STAR.

42. It may bear stating at this point that no attempt is made in what follows to recite the history of Apple, which has been—and will doubtless continue to be—the subject of innumerable books, articles, blogs, websites, tweets, YouTube videos, and more. Nor is it possible to do much more than acknowledge the non-Silicon Valley roots of much of the Silicon Valley design culture: MIT and BBN (Bolt, Beranek, & Newman) in Cambridge; early HCI research by Thomas Moran and others at Carnegie-Mellon University, and pioneering projects just as ARCMAC's Aspen Movie Map (1978) and Ted Nelson's Project Xanadu (conceived in 1960).

43. Charles Kerns, Lab Members' Retrospective (2009), Golden Age of Multimedia: Innovations of the Apple Multimedia Lab, 1987–1992 (http://web.nmc.org/pachy/goldenage/). See also "Visual Almanac: Technical Report" (San Francisco, 1991). This and other technical reports are available at Christina Hooper Woolsey, "The Golden Age of Multimedia: Innovations of the Apple Multimedia Lab, 1987–1992" (http://web.nmc.org/pachy/goldenage/). The principal "product designers" (as they were called) behind the Visual Almanac were Woolsey Hooper, Sueann Ambron, Fabrice Florin, Nancy Hechinger Steve Gano, Robert Mohl, Margo Nanny, Kristee Rosendahl, and Nick West. For an interesting perspective, see Mizuko Ito, *Engineering Play: A Cultural History of Children's Software* (Cambridge, MA: MIT Press, 2012), pp. 92ff.

44. Kristina Hooper Woolsey, "Multimedia Content in Computer Environments," address to UCLA Roundtable in Multimedia (April 1, 1991); papers of Kristina Hooper Woolsey.

45. "Multimedia Lab Projects: From Professional Publications to Casual Multimedia," San Francisco (February 12, 1992). The cosmic allusion—entirely appropriate, in our view—is to Alexander Koyré's classic study of the Scientific Revolution, *From the Closed World to the Infinite Universe* (Baltimore: Johns Hopkins Press, 1957). In 1987 the AIGA held its national conference in San Francisco, which was widely seen in the graphic design community as recognition that the Bay Area was emerging as a significant design hub.

46. *The Visual Almanac: An Interactive Multimedia Kit—Companion* (prerelease version: Apple Computer, 1989), pp. 1–12.

47. Quoted in Janice Maloney, "Apple's Multimedia Lab: A Linear History," in *Digital Media* (September 1992). Also lab member Steve Gano, "Multimedia Technology Is for Casual, Everyday Use," in *Interactive Multimedia: Visions of Multimedia for Developers, Educators, and Information Providers,* ed. Sueann Ambron and Kristina Hooper (Redmond, WA.: Microsoft Press, 1988), p. 255. A companion volume, *Learning with Interactive Multimedia*, was published in 1990.

48. *Human Interface Guidelines: The Apple Desktop Interface*, n.a., but authored by Kristina Hooper Woolsey (Reading, MA: Addison-Wesley, 1987), p. 3. Twenty-five years later one of the author's undergraduate students, reflecting upon the supposedly "real-world" origins of the desktop metaphor, responded, "Whose dumb-ass idea was that?" She and her peers do their work in bed, at Starbucks, and on the train. None of them had ever worked at a desk, or expects to.

49. Of particular relevance is an internal research initiative dubbed Screenplay, sponsored by Mountford, coordinated by Laurie Vertelney, and facilitated by ID Two, intended to explore how the computer interface might evolve over the next ten years. Screenplay: A Summary Report (October 1988); papers of Laurie Vertelney. See also Mountford's conversation with Bill Moggridge in *Designing Interactions*, pp. 553–64.

50. S. Joy Mountford, "A History of the Apple Human Interface Group," *SIGCHI* 30, no. 2 (April 1998). She continued: "This created one of the most amazing legacies of my career and extended the family of interface. ... It was also one of the most personally meaningful and rewarding projects I have championed in my life." Additional information in this section is derived from interviews with S. Joy Mountford (San Carlos, July 11 and August 9, 2012). Mountford would take this program with her when she migrated from Apple to Interval Research. Also Mountford and Bonnie Johnson, "Educational Challenges for the New Interactivity," *Design Management Institute* (summer 1997), and G. B. Salomon, "Designing casual-use Hypertext: The CHI '9 InfoBooth," *Proceedings of CHI '90* (New York: ACM Press, 1990), pp. 451–58.

51. Laurie Vertelney, "Two Disciplines in Search of an Interface," in *The Art of Computer-Human Interface,* ed. Brenda Laurel (Reading, MA: Addison-Wesley, 1990), pp. 45, 55. The title of this collection undoubtedly references the classic work by Stuart Card, Thomas P. Moran and Alan Newell, *The Psychology of Human–Computer Interaction* (Hillsdale, NJ: Laurence Erlbaum, 1983).

52. Bill Moggridge to Laurie McDaniel [Vertelney] (June 30, 1987).

53. Bill Moggridge, submission for the Prince Philip Designers Prize, courtesy of the late Bill Moggridge, and ongoing conversations between Moggridge and the author, c. 2002–2012. Interview with Bill Verplank (Menlo Park, August 16, 2011), and in Moggridge, *Designing Interactions*, pp. 126–33. Of particular relevance to this discussion is Brigitte Jordan and Austin Henderson, "Interaction Analysis: Foundations and Practice, *Journal of the Learning Sciences* 4, no. 1 (1995): 39-103.

54. Bill Moggridge to Laurie McDaniel [Vertelney] (June 30, 1987). The late Niels Diffrient (1928–2013) is the author of *Humanscale 1/2/3* (1974) and subsequent volumes, the standard reference work on physical ergonomics.

55. Between 1976 and 1982, Xerox's share of the global copier market dropped from 82 percentto 41 percent. Gary Jacobson and John Hillkirk, *Xerox: American Samurai* (New York: Macmillan, 1986), pp. 256–60.

56. Interview with Arnold Wasserman (San Francisco, October 18, 2011) and Elizabeth Sanders (telephone, February 8, 2012). The author is painfully cognizant of the *Mad Men* tone of this passage; unfortunately, he must stand by its accuracy. In his defense, it might be noted that it took Xerox's human factors experts one and a half years of fieldwork to figure this out.

57. [John Rheinfrank et al.,], "Design at the Interface: A Strategy for the '80s" (April 14, 1981), papers of Arnold Wasserman, box 4 (temporary classification, pending transfer to the Archives of Carnegie Mellon University); John Rheinfrank, William Hartmann, and Arnold Wasserman, "Design for Usability: Crafting a Strategy for the Design of a New Generation of Xerox Copiers," in *Usability: Turning Technology into Tools,* ed. Paul Adler and Terry Winograd (New York: Oxford University Press, 1992), pp. 15–40. Wasserman was trained as an industrial designer (he had at one time managed Raymond Loewy's Paris office), and did graduate work at the University of Chicago in design history and theory.

58. In addition to the published sources cited, information and perspectives contained in the following section are derived from stimulating conversations with Drs. Austin Henderson (Palo Alto, March 25, 2013), Jeanette Blomberg (Portola Valley, April 6, 2013), and Jeff Rulifson (Stanford, May 20, 2013).

59. Allen Newell to George Pake, "Notes on a Proposal for a Psychological Research Unit" (January 1971; reproduced for distribution to AIP, October, 1974): papers of Stuart Card, who generously made it available to the author together with a full set of "AIP Memos," 1974–83.

60. Card, Moran, and Newell, *The Psychology of Human–Computer Interaction,* chapter 12: "Applying Psychology to Design," and interview with Dr. Card (Stanford, March 29, 2013). In a retrospective on Allen Newell, Card wrote, "While evaluation was important, the real payoff was clearly in design. Design is where the action is. The goal was to get some theory that could actually be used in design practice." "The Human, the Computer, the Task, and Their Interaction." Papers of Stuart Card (PARC. A Xerox Company). For informed perspectives on the larger context, see Jonathan Grudin,"Three Faces of Human–Computer Interaction, *IEEE Annals of the History of Computing* 27, no. 4 (October 2005): 46–62; Liam Bannon, "From Human Factors to Human Actors: The Role of Psychology and Human–Computer Interaction Studies in System Design," *Design at Work,* ed. J. Greenbaum and M. Kyng (Mahwah, NJ: Lawrence Erlbaum, 1991), pp. 25–44; David Meister, *The History of Human*

Factors and Ergonomics (Mahwah, NJ: Lawrence Erlbaum, 1999). Already in 1973 the author of one of the foundational texts observed, "the terminal or console operator, instead of being a peripheral consideration, will become the tail that wags the whole dog.... The computer industry will be forced to become increasingly concerned with the usage of people, rather than with the computer's intestines." Martin, *Design of Man-Computer Dialogues*, pp. 3–4.

61. Austin Henderson, in conversation with the author (Palo Alto, March 25, 2013).

62. Jeff Rulifson et al., "Studies of Office Procedures and Information Flow" (May 1976), and Eleanor Wynn, "The Office Conversation as an Information Medium" (December 1976): papers of Jeff Rulifson, xox 3; Archives of the Computer History Museum, Mountain View, California (not yet processed at the time of this writing). Another source was the American business theorist Theodor Levitt, whose classic essay, "Marketing Myopia," appeared in the *Harvard Business Review* in 1960. Levitt argued that companies that took a myopic view of their industry—"railroads" rather than "transportation," "movies," rather than "entertainment," and by extension, "copy machines" rather than "information systems," were destined for extinction. I was fortunate in being able to discuss these themes in a wide-ranging conversation with Dr. Rulifson (Stanford, May 20, 2013).

63. Lucy Suchman, "Consuming Anthropology," draft essay graciously made available to the author, to be published as chapter 6 in *Interdisciplinarity: Reconfigurations of the Social and Natural Sciences,* ed. A. Barry and G. Born (London: Routledge).

64. Lucy Suchman, "Anthropological Relocations and the Limits of Design," *Anthropology* 40 (October 2011): 1–18, and "Work Practice and Technology," introductory remarks originally made to the final gathering of her group (June 15–17, 1999), published in *Making Work Visible: Ethnographically Grounded Case Studies of Work Practice,* ed. Margaret H. Szymanski and Jack Whalen (Cambridge: Cambridge University Press, 2011).

65. Even the simple task of mounting the video cameras revealed their competing disciplinary biases: should the camera be mounted low, to focus tightly on the control panel (Henderson), or higher up, to capture the larger context (Suchman)? The findings from this study became the basis for John Seely Brown's keynote address to CHI in 1983, "When User Hits Machine." See also Suchman's influential book, *Plans and Situated Actions: The Problem of Human–Machine Communication* (Cambridge: Cambridge University Press, 1987).

66. "1980s Operability/Appearance Design Strategy" (July 1982), papers of Arnold Wasserman, box 2 (temporary classification), and John J. Rheinfrank, William R.

Hartman, and Arnold Wasserman, "Design for Usability: Crafting Strategy for the Design of a New Generation of Xerox Copiers," in Adler and Winograd, *Usability.*

67. Bill Moggridge, submission for the Prince Philip Designers Prize, courtesy of the late Bill Moggridge. The hierarchy of the sciences is of course a trope that extends backward to August Comte, if not to Aristotle.

68. From "Under Which Lyre. A Reactionary Tract for the Times" (1946):

> Thou shalt not sit
> With statisticians nor commit
> A social science.
> W. H. Auden, *Collected Poems*, ed. Edward Mendelson (New York: Random House, 1976), pp. 259–63.

69. Stein's posting of these scenarios elicited the following comment from Alan Kay (April 15, 2012):

> Hi Bob (and visitors):
> People reading this should realize that there was nothing new to be thought up to make these scenarios (they were for Warner execs who were not sophisticated about computers despite having bought Atari).
> The ideas were all drawn (pretty much without exception) from the visions and demonstrations of the ARPA-IPTO research community in the 1960s, ca 1968. Main sources were Licklider, Taylor, Doug Engelbart, Nicholas Negroponte, Ivan Sutherland, Seymour Papert, some of my ideas back then (such as the wireless tablet computer), and many others from our colleagues . . . .
> McLuhan warned us (using books and TV) indirectly about how strongly people were going to try to regain some sense of identity via an electronic global village. The hope by all of us from the 60s was that education—and The Encyclopedia Britannica whom Bob and I tried to get to understand at length what was going to happen—would help to create a sense of the real value here.
> But this didn't happen, and we wound up with a pop culture.
> Best wishes,
> Alan
> http://futureofthebook.org/blog/2012/04/11/these_drawings_date_from _1982/:

Chapter 5

1. Tsutomu ("Tom") Matano, in conversation with the author (San Francisco, April 12, 2005).

2. As with other chapters in this book, the following discussion is intended to be representative rather than comprehensive, and focused in this case more on design pedagogy more than design theory. A singular omission is the "Design Methods" movement represented by, *inter alia*, Horst Rittel and Christopher Alexander at U.C. Berkeley in the 1970s; see also notes 59 and 66. And in the interest of full disclosure, the author wishes to state that he serves as professor of industrial and interaction design at California College of the Arts, and consulting Ppofessor of mechanical engineering at Stanford. He has not yet found his way onto the faculty of San José State, which would turn this academic balancing act into a hat trick.

3. Camillo Olivetti belonged to the class of 1895. "Hewlett and Packard were a couple of my boys. I lent them $600 to get started, and that was the only money they ever had to borrow!" Frederick Terman interviewed by Bill Moggridge, c. 1980; papers of the late Bill Moggridge.

4. Stanford University Archives: SC 165, series IV, box 1, folder 3: Reports to the President. On Terman, see C. Stewart Gillmor, *Fred Terman at Stanford: Building a Discipline, a University, and Silicon Valley* (2004, Stanford University Press). For two histories running decidedly against the grain, see Stuart W. Leslie, *The Cold War and American Science: The Military-Academic Complex at MIT and Stanford* (New York: Columbia University Press, 1993), and Rebecca S. Lowen, *Creating the Cold War University: The Transformation of Stanford* (Berkeley: University of California Press, 1997). The north–south artery, El Camino Real, formerly the Spanish "royal road," forms the boundary between town and gown.

5. Lydik Jacobson, chairman of mechanical engineering, to Terman, for transmission to President Wallace Sterling," Stanford University Archives and Special Collections, SC 165, series IV, box 1: Reports to the President, Folder 3 (1956–57). "Student Shop Program—Stanford University: History, Current Operations Goals" (July 1974), papers of Professor David Beach.

6. Arnold, "Case Study: Arcturus IV." Suzanne Burrey, "The Question of Creativity," in *Industrial Design* 1, no. 6 (June 1957).

7. Soderberg, quoted in Morton H. Hunt, "The Course Where Students Lose Earthly Shackles," *Life Magazine* (May 16, 1955), p. 196. Arnold, who had studied rat psychology at the University of Minnesota, taught himself some basic engineering concepts

while working as a night watchman in an oil plant. After the war he entered a master's program in mechanical engineering at MIT.

8. "Design Division Program Lets Engineering Students Attack 'Human Frontier'," *Stanford Engineering News*, no. 40 (March 1963); in the collection of the author. The Industrial Design Educators Association (IDEA) was formed in 1957 by Joséph Carriero, Arthur Pulos, and James R. Shipley.

9. "Design at Stanford" (n.d.), Papers of James Adams, SC 949, box 13. Additional information in this section is derived from formal interviews and ongoing and frequently informal conversations with Professors James Adams, David Beach Matt Kahn, David Kelley, Larry Leifer, Robert McKim, Bernard Roth, Sheri Sheppard, and the late Rolf Faste.

10. John Arnold, "What Is Creativity?" and "Creative Product Design," notes for the Creative Engineering Seminar (1959), Stanford University, Stanford University Archives and Special Collections, SC 949, box 1: "The ideal situation would be to have, in addition to a few specialists in the various fields, a greater number of men [sic] who have fundamental training in and knowledge of a number of related fields." John Arnold, ibid.

11. Forty years later faculty still refer to the atrium that separates the engineering professors from their "d.school" counterparts as the "demilitarized zone".

12. Interview with Robert McKim (Santa Cruz, February 22, 2012). Previous passages are drawn from McKim's lecture, "Non-Verbal Education and the Environment," delivered at the 1967 Stanford Alumni Conference, and "Designing for the Whole Man" (1959), Department of Special Collections, SC 949, box 13: James L. Adams papers. Having introduced the practice of "need-finding" into the product design curriculum, McKim ultimately became disillusioned with the consumerist trivia that often resulted: "There are a lot of needs that should not be addressed."

13. James L. Adams to John Arnold (25 February, 1960): Department of Special Collections, SC 949, box 13, James L. Adams papers.

14. See, for example, R. F. Butts, *A Cultural History of Western Education* (New York: McGraw-Hill, 1955), p. 570: "Practical-minded persons argued that education was derelict in its duty if it did not give students a practical training for some job in life and for earning a living. Others were equally convinced that the distinctive task of schools and colleges was to give students a well-rounded liberal education that would fit them to lead a full and worthwhile life, leaving specialized training to other agencies." Also H. W. Button and E. F. Provenzo, *History of Education and Culture in America* (Englewood Cliffs, NJ: Prentice Hall, 1989), and Patrick N. Foster,

"Lessons from History: Industrial Arts/Technology Education as a Case," *Journal of Technical and Vocational Education* 13, no. 2 (Spring 1997).

15. Herber Sotzin, "Retrospect and Prospect in Industrial Arts" (1960), San José State University Special Collections and Archives, MSS 2009-12-01, SJSU Industrial Arts Department, series I.

16. Wayne Edward Champion, "Exploration in Curriculum for Applied Arts Design: A Dissertation Submitted to the School of Education of Stanford University in Partial Fulfillment of the Requirements for the Degree of Doctor of Education" (June 1956), p. 25, Stanford University Archives.

17. In at least one respect, however, the demography of design at Stanford and San José State was identical: all of the students were male.

18. Champion, "Exploration in Curriculum for Applied Arts Design," p. 12 (emphasis in the original). The appendices to the dissertation include sample exercises as well as student evaluations. In the following year Talcott Parsons published his translation of Max Weber's *The Protestant Ethic and the Spirit of Capitalism*, which concludes with the famous passage from Goethe: "Specialists without spirit, sensualists without heart; this nullity imagines that it has attained a level of civilization never before achieved." Trans. Talcott Parsons (New York: Scribners, 1958), p. 182.

19. Champion, "Exploration in Curriculum for Applied Arts Design."

20. "SJS First State College to Offer New Program," *Spartan Daily* (n.d., 1960): San José State University Special Collections and Archives, MSS 2009-12-01, SJSU Industrial Arts Department, series II: Industrial Arts Department Scrapbook, 1957–1979; also the following quote.

21. Dr. Kermit Seefeld, chairman of the Industrial Arts Department at the University of California, Santa Barbara: "Seefeld argued these students are only less capable by the standards of academicians." *San José News* (May 7, 1960).

22. "Bachelor of Science Degree in Industrial Design" (1959), papers of Professor Leslie Speer who kindly made this document available to me. Wayne Champion, "We were all Mavericks: A Brief History of the So-called Interdivisional Industrial Design Program at San José State University, about 1957–1984" (privately printed; spelling and punctuation adjusted), and Champion's "Summary of Report to the Canadian Government on Industrial Design Education" (January 1973): papers of Ralf Schubert. Louie Melo, "Industrial Arts Facilities at San José State," *Journal of Industrial Arts and Vocational Education* (March 1961).

23. Wayne Champion, quoted in the "Alcoa Student Design Merit Awards" (1964), SJSU Special Collections and Archives, MSS 2009-12-01, SJSU Industrial Arts

Department, series I, box 1. Champion's own record of professional practice was limited to a two-year stint making construction drawings and illustrating technical reports at United Airlines.

24. Nelson Van Judah, "The Bucky Chronicles," *Centerline,* Palo Alto Center for Design (December 1980), the second of a three-part series. I am indebted to Marnie Jones, first for preserving this invaluable resource, and second for allowing me extended use of it, and also to James Ferris (personal communication,(May 7, 2012).

25. Ralf Schubert to Kathy Cohen (September 22, 1979), papers of Ralf Schubert. See also Jack Crist, *Human Factors and Ergonomics*, where he writes, "There is a strong consensus among design educators that [social science and humanities] courses represent the most vital area for the future development of design education." "Chat with Champion," in *News* 9: San Francisco Chapter, Industrial Designers Society of America (November 1977), p. 2. Champion had some experience in logistics: During his wartime service in the U.S. Navy, he had been assigned the task of assembling the elements of a complete model shop—including five officers, 120 enlisted men, and a quarter of a million dollars worth of equipment—and shipping it to Oahu for the production of topographical and intelligence models. Information in this section is drawn from numerous internal documents, including Wayne Champion, "Memo to the Self Study Committee" (March 16, 1979), and Jack Crist, "Industrial Design Program Self-Evaluation" (n.d., but clearly spring 1979): papers of Ralf Schubert, who guided me through them in a wide-ranging interview (San José, June 14, 2012), and with Kathleen Cohen, then acting chair of the art department (Los Altos, March 2, 2012).

26. Ralf Schubert to Fred Spratt, "Continuing Philosophical Concerns" (May 1, 1984), papers of Ralf Schubert.

27. Arlene N. Ackerlund to Ralf Schubert, "Dean's Recommendation" (spring 1984); Katherine McCoy, president, IDSA, to Gail Fullerton, president, SJSU (May 10 1984), and Fullerton's response (August 1, 1984). The case concerned Ralf Schubert, an industrial designer with twenty years of professional experience who had the bad luck to join the faculty at the precise height of the controversy. Mr. Schubert graciously shared with me his extensive documentation of his case, from which these citations are drawn.

28. The reference is to Aby Warburg's famous lectures on the Schifanoia frescoes in Ferrara (1912), where he denounces the academic *Grenzpolizei* who patrol the frontiers of the disciplines.

29. Frederick Meyer, "Why an Art School: Remembering Dr. Meyer" (Oakland: California College of Arts and Crafts Alumni Society, 1961), p. 8.

30. William Morris, *The Lesser Arts*: "I hold that, when they are so parted, it is ill for the Arts altogether. The lesser arts become trivial, mechanical, unintelligent, incapable of resisting the changes pressed upon them by fashion or dishonesty; while the greater . . . become nothing but dull adjuncts to unmeaning pomp, or ingenious toys for a few rich and idle men."

31. Margaret Penrose Dhaemers, *California College of Arts and Crafts, 1907-1944*; master's thesis, Mills College (1967); Robert W. Edwards, "Out of the Ashes: How Frederick Meyer's Bold Vision was Born," *Glance* 15, no. 1 (winter 2007). Later in life, Meyer explained his decision to locate the college in the East Bay: "My experience with students in San Francisco made me think it was better to hold the school in Berkeley where alcoholic beverages were not on sale." Quoted in *CCAC Review*, Winter 1972/73.

32. "Jo Sinel: Father of American Industrial Design," interviewed by Robert Harper, Librarian, California College of Arts and Crafts (beginning June 4, 1969): Sinel Collection, CCAC. In 1946, the Society of Industrial Designers (of which Sinel was a founding member) recognized nineteen schools and courses in industrial design.

33. Jo Sinel, "Recent Trends in Industrial Design," in Department of Art Education *Bulletin* 8 (1942), Sinel Collection, box 26, S73c.

34. "Dear Student," brochure circulated to prospective students for a course to have begun on September 18, 1939, Sinel Collection, box 31, S381.2; emphasis and ellipsis in original. In an address to a trade group, Sinel had earlier lamented that there is "not one single institution that is equipped to give adequate training in form as applied to the products of industry." Jo Sinel, "Design Impels Consumer Response," *Bulletin of the American Ceramic Society* 13, no. 11 (November 1934), Sinel Collection, California College of the Arts, box 10, S2.21.

35. "Jo Sinel: Father of American Industrial Design," p. 45.

36. Percy Seitlin, "Joseph Sinel: Artist to Industry" (n.d., but around 1930), Sinel Collection, box 10, S2.21.

37. Marilyn Hagberg, "To Design Is to Order: Interview with Wolfgang Lederer in California College of Arts and Crafts *Review* (winter 1971). By the time of this interview, some thirty years later, the Design Division had grown to sixteen full- and part-time faculty teaching about 300 undergraduate design majors and graduate students in graphic, environmental, and industrial design.

38. Wolfgang Lederer, "Bridging Two Worlds in Graphic Design, Education, and Illustration," an oral history conducted in 1988 by Harriet Nathan, Regional Oral History Office, The Bancroft Library, University of California, Berkeley, 1992.

39. Material in this section is drawn from annual catalogs and class schedules, and a vast amount of ephemera on student life. CCA College Archives, Meyer Library, Oakland.

40. In addition to the main regional accrediting organization (the Western Association of Schools and Colleges, or WASC), design programs fall under the purview of the National Association of Schools of Art and Design (NASAD), the National Architecture Accrediting Board (NAAB), the Accreditation Board for Engineering and Technology (ABET), and an alphabet soup of professional affiliates including the American Institute for Graphic Arts (AIGA), the Industrial Design Society of America (IDSA), the American Institute of Architects (AIA), and the American Society of Mechanical Engineers (ASME).

41. David Meckel, interview in *Design: The International Magazine for Designers and Their Clients* (June 1990), p. 77; Barry Katz, "Bigger than the Bauhaus," *Glance*, vol. 15, no.1 (Winter 2007), pp. 32–43. Additional material in this section is drawn from the CCA college archives and from interviews with Sue Ciriclio (San Francisco, October 25, 2012), Michael Vanderbyl (San Francisco, July 17, 2012), and David Meckel (San Francisco, September 24, 2012), who described the acquisition of the building as a turning point: "If we had not acquired that building we would probably have remained a boutique school." John Stein, CCAC's, bare-knuckled CFO, negotiated purchase price down from $9.5 to $3.5 million; one year later this square block of prime real estate was appraised by the city at $45 million.

42. Robert McKim, *Experiences in Visual Thinking* (Monterey, CA: Cole, 1972). The concept of abductive reasoning is derived from the pragmatic philosophy of Charles Sanders Peirce; it may be thought of as the everyday culmination of a sequence that begins with deductive logic, in which conclusions follow necessarily from first principles, and inductive logic, which extrapolates from empirical observations to generalized conclusions that are logically consistent but not certain. Abductive reasoning accepts that one's data will never be complete, and may support multiple, simultaneous, and conflicting interpretations. It is sometimes interpreted as, "Take your best shot."

43. "IMAGINARIUM ONE/Script," draft provided to the author by Gregory Kress and Michael Turri, who as graduate students reconstructed the IMAGINARIUM from contemporary photos and documents many years after it had been dismantled. Although clearly an artifact of the sixties, the domes at San José State and Stanford belong to a rich tradition linking speculative imagination to engineering and technology: see Eugene Ferguson, *Engineering and the Mind's Eye* (Cambridge, MA: MIT Press, 1992).

44. "Medical Passport" uncannily anticipates the current drive toward electronic medical records, arguably the most important trend in the healthcare industry today. Oral History of David M. Kelley, conducted by Barry M. Katz, Computer History Museum, Mountain View, CA, July 11, 2011. Ms. Kristin Burns, longtime manager of the Design Division, kindly provided me with a partial list of Master's thesis projects, 1968–2005. IDSA activist Marnie Jones recalls that she was one of two women to enter the program in her year, and the only one to advance to the second year before she dropped out.

45. Interview with Matt Kahn (Stanford, October 20, 2012). Kahn died in June 2013, on the 50th anniversary of the founding of the Stanford design program.

46. Wendy Ju, W. Lawrence Neeley, Larry Leifer, "Design, Design, and Design: An Overview of Stanford's Center for Design Research," Position Paper for Workshop on Exploring Design as a Research Activity, CHI 2007, San Jose, CA., courtesy of Professor Ju, and T. Carlton and L. Leifer, "Stanford's ME310 Course as an Evolution of Engineering Design," invited paper, courtesy of Professor Leifer. CDR is codirected by Professors Larry Leifer and Mark Cutkosky.

47. James L. Adams, *The Building of an Engineer: Making, Teaching, and Thinking* (Stanford, CA.: privately printed 2011), p. 140.

48. Arlene Okerlund to Ralf Schubert, "Appointment of Floyd Delbert Coates" (August 30, 1983), papers of Ralf Schubert.

49. Interview with Del Coates, San José (July 20, 2012). See also Ivan Sutherland, "Sketchpad, a Man-Machine Graphical Communication System." Doctoral dissertation (MIT, January, 1963), p. 22. Coates's later work is grounded in the theory of semantic differentiation, introduced by Charles E. Osgood, George J. Suci, and Percy H. Tannenbaum in their classic work, *The Measurement of Meaning* (Urbana: University of Illinois Press, 1957). Their framework is applied to design in his book, *Watches Tell More Than Time: Product Design, Information, and the Quest for Elegance* (New York: McGraw-Hill, 2003).

50. Del Coates, selected articles and editorials for *Industrial Design Magazine*, 1980–83, including: "Most Design Shops Expected to Have a CAD System by 1990," (November–December 1980), p. 13, and "Computerized Color Rendering Arrives for the Design Office" (November–December 1981), p. 36. The account of his address to the ISDA in Los Angeles is by Allen Samuels (ibid., p. 8). Coates's philippic on the use of computers in design recalls the conclusion drawn by Joséf Hoffmann and Koloman Moser in response to the relentless advance of industrialism: Love it or hate it, "It would be madness to swim against this current." *Wiener Werkstaette*, "Working Programme" (1905).

51. Interview with Brian Kimura (San Jose, December 5, 2012). Kimura had worked at the San Francisco office of Skidmore Owings and Merrill and for Steelcase, two companies that were deeply involved in the so-called "workspace" movement.

52. "Remarks on the Governance of the School of Art and Design," Karl Toepfer, dean, College of Humanities and the Arts (May 3, 2007), and memorandum of Toepfer and Dean Lisa Vollendorf (July 9, 2013), graciously shared with me by the authors. Robert Milnes, who served as director of the School of Art and Design from 1990 to 2005, noted the natural trajectory of programs to evolve into formal departments, but suggested that "SJSU's case was sadly more one of arrested development, where the programs should have been departments for quite a while, and the School of Art and Design should have been part of a new college, separate from the humanities." Correspondence and telephone interview (December 10–11, 2012).

53. The Arts and Crafts Movement itself hovered in an uncertain void between its founder's competing objectives: "Apart from the desire to produce beautiful things, the leading passion of my life has been and is hatred of modern civilization" (William Morris, "A Rather Long-Winded Sketch of My Very Uneventful Life" (from a letter of 5 September, 1883). The intractability of this dilemma was evident within a decade of Morris's death. In the disillusioned words of his most loyal follower, Charles W. Ashbee, "We have made of a great social movement a narrow and tiresome little aristocracy working with high skill for the very rich" (C. R. Ashbee, "Memoirs," unpublished typescript, 1938, vol. 4, Victoria and Albert Museum Library, p. 201; see. Alan Crawford, *C. R. Ashbee: Architect, Designer, and Romantic Socialist* [*Journal of Design History*. 1, no. 1 [1988]).

54. "It is a paradox of the rapidly changing technological world that the generalist may be more likely to survive and succeed than the specialist, Overspecialized technicians, in design as in any other field, often become prisoners of technology, trapped by obsolescence, while the more flexible generalist continues to enjoy creative latitude." Division of Design information brochure (undated, but 1977–79), California College of Arts and Crafts, CCA College Archives.

55. Michael Vanderbyl, *CCAC News* (September 1989).

56. *CCAC News* (spring 1990). "Product design," in the vernacular of the trade, usually refers to the conception and development of new products; the formal definition of "industrial design," as adopted by the IDSA, is "the professional service of creating and developing concepts and specifications that optimize the function, value and appearance of products and systems for the mutual benefit of both user and manufacturer." See the IDSA website: http://www.idsa.org/what-is-industrial-design. For a historical perspective on the formation of the profession, see Carroll

Gantz, *The Industrialization of Design: A History from the Steam Age to Today* (Jefferson, NC: McFarlane, 2011), chapters 8–10.

57. Steven Skov Holt, "Hypermarketecture," in *rana: integrated strategic design magazine*, no. 2 (Sunnyvale, CA: 1996), p. 34; author's recollection.

58. *CCAC News* 2, no. 5 (n.d., but most likely spring 1995).

59. Jeremy Mende, personal communication (December 11, 2012); Amy Williams, in the context of a collaborative program on wearable technology (summer, 2014).

60. It must once again be emphasized that this discussion is deliberately and necessarily selective. It does not include the Department of Design and Industry at San Francisco State, the numerous graduate and undergraduate design schools at the Academy of Art University (including game design and web design), the College of Environmental Design at University of California at Berkeley, as well as several smaller, specialized schools—Cogswell College, the Rudolf Schaeffer School of Design—which rose and fell during the period under discussion. For a revealing insight into the fortunes and misfortunes of design at the sprawling Berkeley campus of the University of California, see Ira Jacknis, "The Lure of the Exotic: Ethnic Arts and the Design Department at UC Berkeley," *Chronicle of the University of California* (spring 2004).

61. For a sampling of recent literature on Design Thinking, see Tim Brown, with Barry Katz, *Change by Design: How Design Thinking Transforms Organizations and Inspires Innovation* (Harper Collins: New York, 2009); Roger Martin, *The Design of Business: Why Design Thinking Is the Next Competitive Advantage* (Cambridge, MA: Harvard Business School, 2009); Thomas Lockwood, ed., *Design Thinking: Integrating Innovation, Customer Experience, and Brand Value* (Allworth: New York, 2009); Nigel Cross, *Design Thinking: Understanding How Designers Think and Work* (Berg: Oxford, 2011). For continuously updated information on the Hasso Plattner Institute for Design, see the d.school website, http://dschool.stanford.edu.

62. "Program Review: School of Art and Design" (March 2000), p. 8, and "Innovation through Diversity and Education Grant: Product Design and Development to Bridge the Digital Divide" (n.d., but c. 2000–1): papers of Del Coates. "Land-grant" colleges were authorized by the 1862 Morrill Act to focus on the teaching of practical subjects—agriculture, science, and engineering—in order to address the social and technical transformations of industrializing America. My analysis in this section has been informed by interviews and correspondence with Professors Leslie Speer (October 18, 2012), John McClusky (November 19, 2012), Brian Kimura (San José, December 5, 2012), Robert Milnes (December 12, 2012), and Karl Toepfer (July 10, 2013).

63. J. A. English-Lueck, *Cultures@Silicon Valley* (Stanford: Stanford University Press, 2002). The Silicon Valley cultures project was a collaboration overseen by faculty members Charles Darrah, J. A. English-Lueck, and James Freeman, and engaging students from nearly a dozen SJSU anthropology courses.

64. John F. McClusky and Charles N. Darrah, "Leaving the Research to the Experts: Collaborating with Anthropologists to Emphasize Core Competencies in Industrial Design Education," presentation to ICSID (International Council of Societies of Industrial Design), San Francisco, 2007.

65. As the instigator of this plot, the author can state with authority that in no sense did this imply a rejection of the craft tradition: As he has repeatedly insisted, "We did not 'drop the crafts.' We changed the name of the school."

66. Michael Vanderbyl, *CCAC News* (September 1989).

67. *Centerline*: Publication of the Palo Alto Center for Design (June 1980 and July 1980), which reviewed architecture and design programs at Stanford, SJSU, and CCAC, as well as the University of California at Davis, UC Berkeley, Chico State, Academy of Art College, Cogswell College, and the Rudolf Schaeffer School of Design. Burdick might well have added a reference to Sayre's Law, which states that in academic controversies, the passions run so high because the stakes are so low.

Chapter 6

1. Interviews with Soleio Cuervo (San Francisco, September 12, 2013) and Aaron Sittig (San Francisco, October 9, 2013). As is the case with virtually every other project described in this book, the "like" button was a team effort and no clear line can be drawn between concept and execution; Aaron Sittig was design strategy lead and one of Facebook's earliest employees, and Jonathan Pines was principal engineer. Worldwide, the "like" button is clicked about 50,000 times per second, making it one of the most successful products in the history of Silicon Valley, if not the world.

2. Interview with Donald Norman (Palo Alto, December 4, 2012). For a retrospective, see the special issue of ACM/SIGCHI dedicated to the Apple Advanced Technology Group, vol. 30, no. 2 (April 1998).

3. Paul Allen, *Idea Man: A Memoir by the Cofounder of Microsoft* (New York: Penguin, 2011), pp. 275–77. Allen retained Cheskin Research to assist in naming and defining the scope of the new venture. On the basis of a day-long brainstorm he agreed that "Valhalla" was not quite right and changed the name to Interval.

4. Even from the grave Interval remains a compulsively secretive organization. Its archives were transferred to and then reclaimed from Stanford University Library's Department of Special Collections and employees were asked to sign a confidentiality agreement as part of their severance agreement. Fortunately, some refused, others had left the lab before the so-called "gag order" was in place, and given the fact that Interval employed some 170 people at the time of its closure (as well as dozens of partners, contractors, and interns) it is inevitable that some documentary material has leaked out. The author wishes to thank the many Interval alumni who have shared their insights with him.

5. Bonnie Johnson, summary report (July 14, 1992), Papers of Terry Winograd, Stanford University Libraries, SC 1165, box 26.

6. David E. Liddle, "Computing in the 21st Century." Interval Research Offsite, "How Will People Live and Work in the Future?" (February 11–13, 1993), p. 118; p. 122. Cited with the permission of Vulcan Inc.

7. Ibid., p. 122. Jane Fulton Suri, "Scenarios," notes for InterCHI'93 tutorial with Bill Verplank and Bill Moggridge (papers of Arnold Wasserman), "Scenarios help us leap gracefully from the present to the future and from analysis to synthesis . . . . They form the basis for evaluation and decisions which can lead into a more detailed design effort." See also Colin Burns, Eric Dishman, William Verplank, and Bud Lassiter, "Actors, Hairdos and Videotape: Informance Design," CHI'94 (April 1994). ID Two had already begun to formalize its human-centered design methodology through workshops for clients including Apple and Xerox. The workshops ultimately evolved into a distinct service offering known as IDEO U, which the company had the poor judgment to entrust for several years to the author. Only the tireless work of his associate, Nancy Nichols, enabled IDEO U to remain profitable.

8. The "pick-and-shovel" metaphor emerged in an interview with David Liddle (Menlo Park, April 4, 2012). The central place given to design at Interval was announced by David Liddle, Meg Withgott, and Debby Hindus, "An Overview of Interval Research Corporation," CHI Conference Companion (Boston, April 24–28, 1994). The research plan for that year called for them to bring in "captive designers" (Bill Moggridge was the first) and observe them at work. Interval Research Corporation, 1994–95 plan.

9. Interview with David Liddle (Menlo Park, April 4, 2012).

10. Paul Allen to John Markoff, New York Times (November 13, 1996). On the projects referenced in this section, see Richard G. Shoup, "Space, Time, Logic, and Things," Proceedings of the Workshop on Physics and Computation, PhysComp '94 (Dallas,

November 17–20, 1994), pp. 36–43; Michael Naimark, "A 3D Moviemap and a 3D Panorama," *Proceedings of SPIE*, Stereoscopic Displays and Virtual Reality Systems IV (San Jose, February 11–14, 1997); Pierre St. Hilaire, "Holographic Video: The Ultimate Visual Interface?" in *Optics and Photonics News* (August 1997); Brenda Laurel, Rachel Strickland, and Rob Tow, "Placeholder: Landscape and Narrative in Visual Environments," *Computer Graphics* 28, no. 2 (May 1994).

11. Christopher Ireland and Bonnie Johnson, "Exploring the Future in the Present," *Design Management Journal* (Boston, Spring 1995), and interview with Christopher Ireland (Palo Alto, October 10, 2013); also Darrell Rhea, "A New Perspective on Design: Focusing on Customer Experience" (Fall 1992).

12. This is an extremely condensed statement of the thesis of Laurel's influential book, *Computers as Theater* (Reading, MA: Addison-Wesley, 1991).

13. Interview with Brenda Laurel (Los Gatos, September 21, 2013); Brenda Laurel, *Utopian Entrepreneur* (Cambridge, MA: MIT Press, 2001), and the second edition *Computers as Theater* (prepublication draft kindly made available to the author).

14. For a pre- and postmortem, see, respectively, Thomas Bass, "Think Tanked," *Wired* (December, 1999) and Tia O'Brien, "Interval: The Think Tank that Tanked," *SV News* (September 3, 2000).

15. Interview with Terry Winograd who provided the author with an invaluable mental map of the discipline (Stanford, October 30, 2013), and also the papers of Terry Winograd, Stanford University Libraries, SC 1165, esp. boxes 6, 7, 9, and 15). The proceedings of the Pajaro Dunes conference are collected in Winograd, *Bringing Design to Software*. This volume also reproduces Kapor's original "Software Design Manifesto," where the founder of the Lotus Development Corporation argues that software design is as distinct from software engineering as architecture is from construction. Neither is intrinsically superior: the point is rather to bring together "the world of technology and the world of people and human purposes."

16. The literature on Apple is endless and readily available, and tends to default toward a romantic conception of genius that has been otherwise out of fashion for the last 150 years or so. See, for instance, Leander Kahney, *Jony Ive: The Genius behind Apple's Greatest Products,* which was announced as this manuscript was being completed.

17. Interview with Sam Lucente (San Francisco, November 11, 2013); Netscape's Navigator, IBM's Web Explorer, and Microsoft's Internet Explorer were the main combatants in the so-called "Browser Wars" of the 1990s. On Lucente's campaigns at Hewlett-Packard, see Bill Breen, "Streamlining," in *Fast Company* (October 2007).

18. Although the Internet has spawned a cottage industry of quote-hunters, no evidence has yet emerged that Henry Ford ever said this. With apologies to K. M. Elisabeth Murray, biographer of the first editor of the Oxford English Dictionary, it might be said that we remain *Caught in the* [WorldWide] *Web of Words* (New Haven: Yale University Press, 2001).

19. This section has been informed by ongoing discussions with CEO Tim Brown, including one formal interview (Palo Alto, November 5, 2013), as well as cofounders David Kelley, Mike Nuttall, and the late Bill Moggridge; I have also been privileged with unrestricted access to company records. See also Brown, *Change by Design*; Tom Kelley, *The Art of Innovation: Lessons in Creativity from IDEO, America's Leading Design Firm* (New York: Crown, 2001). In the interests of full disclosure, the author wishes to repeat that he is affiliated with IDEO as an external "IDEO Fellow."

20. Tim Brown, "The Future of Industrial Design" (http://artworks.arts.gov/?p=17624), commenting on Bonnie Nichols, National Endowment for the Arts Research Report #50, "Valuing the Art of Industrial Design" (Washington, DC, August 2013). Interview with Tim Brown (Palo Alto, November 5, 2013).

21. Material in this section is based on Interviews with Doreen Lorenzo, President Emerita of frog (Skype, September 26, 2013) and Mark Rolston, Chief Creative Officer Emeritus (San Francisco, September 18, 2013); also Lorenzo, "Designing the Future of Communications," TwilioCon 2012 (http://www.everytalk.tv/talks/2816-TwilioCon-Designing-the-Future-of-Communications), and Rolston, "Design and the Coming Iceberg," DesignMind (September 9, 2013) (http://designmind.frogdesign.com/blog/design-and-the-coming-iceberg.html).

22. Interview with John Edson (San Francisco, September 18, 2013). As this book was going to press Edson announced that Lunar has been acquired by the consulting firm McKinsey. As he noted in an email, "This is definitely the era of design."

23. Lunar's website, http://www.lunar.com

24. Unless otherwise identified, information, insights and perspectives cited in the following paragraphs are drawn from interviews with Yves Béhar, president of fuseproject (San Francisco, September 26, 2013); Dan Harden, president of Whipsaw (San Jose, September 23, 2013); Branko Lukić, president of Studio NONOBJECT (Palo Alto, August 30, 2013); Brett Lovelady, president of Astro Studios (October 2, 2013); Gadi Amit, president of New Deal Design (San Francisco, October 8, 2013); and Robert Brunner, president, Ammunition Group (October 9, 2013). I have also drawn liberally from their speeches, blogposts, articles, and books.

25. The five second-generation firms profiled here represent only the largest, most prominent, and most diversified of the independent consultancies. A complete list—far beyond the scope of this volume—would expand their numbers into the dozens, and the "third generation" into the hundreds.

26. Interview with Michael Gough (San Francisco, April 16, 2002). Additional insights are derived from Gough's splendid internal compilation, *57 Things You Should Know If You Want to Work in XD* (Adobe Systems, 2011).

27. Airbnb, which rocketed from two futons on the floor of a San Francisco apartment to a $13 billion company in six years, was founded by two graduates of RISD's Industrial Design program, Joe Gebbio and Brian Chesky. A textbook case of disruptive innovation, they are designing not just a product but a company.

28. Interview with Astro Teller (Mountain View, December 18, 2013).

29. Douglas Bowman, "Goodbye, Google" (http://stopdesign.com/archive/2009/03/20/goodbye-google.html); Marissa Mayer, quoted in Miguel Helft, "Data, Not Design, Is King in the Age of Google," *New York Times* (May 9, 2009).

30. Interview with Jon Wiley, design lead, Google Search (Mountain View, December 20, 2013), and Wiley, "Whoa! Google Has Designers," UX Week 2011 (http://vimeo.com/29965463). Chris Wiggins, creative director, cigital, "Evolving the Google Design and Experience" (http://googleblog.blogspot.com/2011/06/evolving-google-design-and-experience.html) (June 28, 2011); Matias Duarte, quoted in Dieter Bohn and Ellis Hamburger, "Redesigning Google: How Larry Page Engineered a Beautiful (Revolution" (January 24, 2013) http://www.theverge.com/2013/1/24/3904134/google-redesign-how-larry-page-engineered-beautiful-revolution). "Project Kennedy" and "moonshots" refer to JFK's challenge to NASA of "landing a man on the moon and returning him safely to earth." See also the profiles of Google's design leads in Farhad Manjoo, "How Google Taught Itself Good Design, *Fast Company* (October, 2013).

31. Insights and information contained in this section are derived in part from interviews with Kate Aronowitz (Palo Alto, December 11, 2011), Aaron Sittig (San Francisco, October 9, 2013), Soleio Cuervo (San Francisco, September 12, 2013), and Maria Guidice (Menlo Park, November 8, 2013), as well as presentations made to participants in a Facebook Academic Summit that the author attended on July 30, 2013). See also David Kirkpatrick, *The Facebook Effect: The Inside Story of the Company That Is Connecting the World* (New York: Simon & Schuster, 2010).

32. Zuckerberg's Law, as promulgated at the annual Web 2.0 Summit in San Francisco (November 5–7, 2008), states that, "next year, people will share twice as much

information as they share this year, and next year, they will be sharing twice as much as they did the year before." It has been described as the software counterpart to Moore's Law of the speed of microprocessor.

33. "Thoughts on Being Digital," notebooks of Softbook designer Aleksey Novicov, and interview (Palo Alto, April 4, 2014). The first decision the founders of Softbook Press had to make was whether they were building a computer or a book.

34. Lab126: Readers puzzled by Amazon's military-grade encryption methods might note that "A" is the 1st letter in AmaZon's A-Z pursuit of literary hegemony, and "Z" is the 26th. I am grateful to Gregg Zehr, president of Amazon's Lab126, for an informative interview (Cupertino, November 11, 2013).

35. Principal research themes include connected mobility, alternative energy, and driverless vehicles. Seminar with Sven Beiker, executive director, CARS (January 9, 2013). Waze (https://www.waze.com) is a real-time, crowd-sourced, GPS-based navigation system: Lyft is a peer-to-peer ride-sharing program (https://www.lyft.com); Uber (https://www.uber.com) is a web-based mobile application that summons vehicles for hire.

36. Information and perspectives in this section emerged in conversation with Franz von Holzhausen (telephone, from Hawthorne, California, November 7, 2013), and in person (Mountain View, September 25, 2014).

37. Passages taken from press releases and published interviews with Franz von Holzhausen, chief of design, Tesla Motors (http://www.teslamotors.com/blog/model-s-designing-perfect-endurance-athlete; http://www.thecarconnection.com/news/1042446_franz-von-holzhausen-brings-a-clean-slate-to-tesla-design; http://www.teslamotors.com/it_CH/about/press/releases/franz-von-holzhausen-joins-tesla-motors-chief-designer; http://www.greencardesign.com/site/interviews/interview-franz-von-holzhausen). Author's interview with Dan Adams, manager, Powertrain Assembly (Palo Alto, October 3, 2013).

38. Tony Fadell, "Thermostats? Yes, Thermostats." (blogpost, October 25, 2011) (https://nest.com/blog/2011/10/25/thermostats-yes-thermostats/).

39. Interview with Eliot Park, CEO, Samsung Design America (San Francisco, November 5, 2013), who is the source of the following quotes. Executive Vice President Donghoon Chang kindly arranged for me to visit the Corporate Design Center in Seoul.

40. Interviews Jim Newton (San Jose, February 11, 2015) and Mark Hatch (San Francisco, August 29, 2014). Make Magazine (http://makezine.com), whose editorial

offices are located across the Golden Gate Bridge in Sebastopol, sponsored the first Makers Faire on October 22–23, 2006 (http://makerfaire.com). The first TechShop opened in Menlo Park in the following year (http://www.techshop.ws). BioCurious, in Sunnyvale, has extended the maker-hacker culture to biotechnology and the life sciences generally. See Mark Hatch, *The Maker Movement Manifesto* (New York: McGraw-Hill, 2014), and Chris Anderson, *Makers: The New Industrial Revolution* (New York: Crown, 2012). Skeptics who are suspicious of the amateurish quality of many of these productions should recall that the word *amateur* derives from the Latin *amare*, "to love." In fields ranging from writing to sex to design, professionals do for money what amateurs do out of love.

41. PCH ("Pacific Coast Highway") Lime Lab was founded by Andre Yousefi and Kurt Dammerman.

42. It is an inspiring moment, but not without its contradictions. See, for instance, Bruce Nussbaum's provocation, "Is Humanitarian Design the New Imperialism?" *Fast Company* (July 7, 2010). For a sampling of the controversy engendered by this article, see the running commentary in the online *Design Observer* (http://designobserver.com/feature/humanitarian-design-vs-design-imperialism-debate-summary/14498/). In truth, not a single one of the supposed imperialists Nussbaum exposes operates independently of local "field partners" in the countries and communities where they are active. See also the ongoing review of public interest design by John Cary and his associates: http://www.impactdesignhub.org/resources/glossary//.

43. Jan Chipchase, Mark Rolston, Cara Silver and Joshua Blumenstock, "In the Hands of God: A Study of Risk and Savings in Afghanistan" (frog with the Institute for Money, Technology, and Financial Inclusion, University of California at Irvine, 2013); http://one.laptop.org; IDEO's Human Centered Design Toolkit can be freely downloaded (http://www.hcdconnect.org).

44. Interview with Krista Donaldson, CEO, D-Rev (San Francisco, November 1, 2013); http://d-rev.org /. D-Rev Annual Report-2012 and D-Rev Annual Report-2011. See also Paul Polak, *Out of Poverty: What Works when Traditional Approaches Fail* (San Francisco: Berrett-Koehler, 2008).

45. Interview with Heather Fleming, CEO, Catapult Design (San Francisco: October 28, 2013) (https://catapultdesign.org/). As the premises of the Appropriate Technology movement have been called into question by Polak and others, ApproTec has changed its name to KickStart; see Paul Polak, "The Death of Appropriate Technology, I, II" (September 10 and 17, 2010) (http://www.paulpolak.com/the-death-of-appropriate-technology-2/).

46. Interview with Jocelyn Wyatt [and Patrice Martin], codirectors, IDEO.org: San Francisco (October 28, 2013); https://www.ideo.org/. *Year One* (IDEO.org: San Francisco, 2012). Disclosure: the author is a fellow at IDEO.

47. Interview with Valerie Casey (Palo Alto: November 4, 2013). See also Alan Chochinov, "The Designers Accord: A Conversation with Valerie Casey" (http://www.core77.com/blog/featured_items/the_designers_accord_a_conversation_with_valerie_casey_9401.asp).

48. "The Designers Accord: In Review, 2007–2012" (http://www.designersaccord.org). John Maeda, design partner at Kleiner Perkins Caufield & Byers, chairs the eBay Design Advisory Council:

> Technology has matured. We don't buy things because they have better technology; we buy them because they're better designed. People in technology generally don't understand what design is. I think there's an opportunity and responsibility for designers to play a larger role in economic development and leadership. I call it moving from lowercase *design* to capital D *Design* to dollar sign *De$ign*. It's going to be important for design to take a larger role in the technology economy.

Interviewed by Tina Essmaker. The Great Discontent (https://thegreatdiscontent .com/interview/john-maeda).

Conclusion

1. The genealogy of "Design Thinking" has become an academic cottage industry. Its origins lie arguably in the Ulm Model developed by Horst Rittel and his colleagues at the *Hochschule für Gestaltung* and imported by Rittel to the Design Methods Group at the University of California at Berkeley in the early 1960s. Canonical texts include Horst Rittel and Melvin Webber, "Dilemmas in a General Theory of Planning, *Policy Sciences* 4 (1973): 155–69; Alexander, *Notes on the Synthesis of Form,* and *A Pattern Language: Towns, Buildings, Construction* (Oxford: Oxford University Press, 1977); John Chris Jones, *Design Methods: Seeds of Human Futures* (New York: Wiley, 1970); and Peter Rowe, *Design Thinking* (Cambridge, MA: MIT Press, 1987).

2. Herbert Simon, *The Sciences of the Artificial* (Cambridge, MA: MIT Press, 1969), pp. 55–59.

3. Raymond Loewy, *Never Leave Well Enough Alone: The Personal Record of an Industrial Designer from Lipsticks to Locomotives* (New York: Simon & Schuster, 1951). Ernesto

Nathan Rogers issued his call for architects to take responsibility for everything *dal cucchiaio alla città* in 1952.

4. See, for instance, the blogs of Gadi Amit, who dismisses Design Thinking as a confused marketing slogan conceived by consultancies in need of a new offering (*Fast Company*: November 28, 2009), and Donald Norman, for whom it is a benign but "useful myth." (*Core 77*, June 25, 2010).

INDEX